Presidents from
Taylor through Grant,
1849–1877

PRESIDENTS FROM TAYLOR THROUGH GRANT, 1849–1877

Debating the Issues in Pro and Con Primary Documents

JEFFREY W. COKER

The President's Position: Debating the Issues
Mark Byrnes, Series Editor

GREENWOOD PRESS
Westport, Connecticut • London

Library of Congress Cataloging-in-Publication Data

Presidents from Taylor through Grant, 1849–1877 : debating the issues in pro and con primary documents / [compiled] by Jeffrey W. Coker.
    p.   cm.—(The president's position : debating the issues)
    Includes bibliographical references and index.
    ISBN 0–313–31551–5 (alk. paper)
    1. Presidents—United States—History—19th century—Sources. 2. United States—
Politics and government—1849–1877—Sources. I. Coker, Jeffrey W. II. President's
position.
    E176.1.P9227 2002
    973′.09′9—dc21   2001054705

973·6

British Library Cataloguing in Publication Data is available.

Library of Congress Catalog Card Number: 2001054705
ISBN: 0–313–31551–5

First published in 2002

Greenwood Press, 88 Post Road West, Westport, CT 06881
An imprint of Greenwood Publishing Group, Inc.
www.greenwood.com

Printed in the United States of America

The paper used in this book complies with the
Permanent Paper Standard issued by the National
Information Standards Organization (Z39.48–1984).

10 9 8 7 6 5 4 3 2 1

CONTENTS

SERIES FOREWORD

When he was running for president in 1932, Franklin D. Roosevelt declared that America needed "bold, persistent experimentation" in its public policy. "It is common sense to take a method and try it," FDR said. "If it fails, admit it frankly and try another. But above all, try something." At President Roosevelt's instigation, the nation did indeed take a number of steps to combat the Great Depression. In the process, the president emerged as the clear leader of American public policy. Most scholars see FDR's administration as the birth of the "modern presidency," in which the president dominates both domestic and foreign policy.

Even before FDR, however, presidents played a vital role in the making of public policy. Policy changes advocated by the presidents—often great changes—have always influenced the course of events, and have always sparked debate from the presidents' opponents. The outcomes of this process have had tremendous effects on the lives of Americans. The President's Position: Debating the Issues examines the stands the presidents have taken on the major political, social, and economic issues of their times as well as the stands taken by their opponents. The series combines description and analysis of those issues with excerpts from primary documents that illustrate the position of the presidents and their opponents. The result is an informative, accessible, and comprehensive look at the crucial connection between presidents and policy. These volumes will assist students doing historical research, preparing for debates, or fulfilling critical thinking assignments. The general reader interested in American history and politics will also find the series interesting and helpful.

Several important themes about the president's role in policy making emerge from the series. First, and perhaps most important, is how greatly the president's involvement in policy has expanded over the years. This has happened because the range of areas in which the national government acts has grown dramatically and because modern presidents—unlike most of their predecessors—see taking the lead in policy making as part of their job. Second, certain issues have confronted most presidents over history; tax and tariff policy, for example, was important for both George Washington and Bill Clinton, and for most of the presidents in between. Third, the emergence of the United States as a world power around the beginning of the twentieth century made foreign policy issues more numerous and more pressing. Finally, in the American system, presidents cannot form policy through decrees; they must persuade members of Congress, other politicians, and the general public to follow their lead. This key fact makes the policy debates between presidents and their opponents vitally important.

This series comprises nine volumes, organized chronologically, each of which covers the presidents who governed during that particular time period. Volume one looks at the presidents from George Washington through James Monroe; volume two, John Quincy Adams through James K. Polk; volume three, Zachary Taylor through Ulysses Grant; volume four, Rutherford B. Hayes through William McKinley; volume five, Theodore Roosevelt through Calvin Coolidge; volume six, Herbert Hoover through Harry Truman; volume seven, Dwight Eisenhower through Lyndon Johnson; volume eight, Richard Nixon through Jimmy Carter; and volume nine, Ronald Reagan through Bill Clinton. Each president from Washington through Clinton is covered, although the number of issues discussed under each president varies according to how long they served in office and how actively they pursued policy goals. Volumes six through nine—which cover the modern presidency—examine three presidencies each, while the earlier volumes include between five and seven presidencies each.

Every volume begins with a general introduction to the period it covers, providing an overview of the presidents who served and the issues they confronted. The section on each president opens with a detailed overview of the president's position on the relevant issues he confronted and the initiatives he took, and closes with a list of recommended readings. Up to fifteen issues are covered per presidency. The discussion of each issue features an introduction, the positions taken by the president and his opponents, how the issue was resolved, and the long-term effects of the issue. This is followed by excerpts from two primary documents, one representing the president's position and the other representing his opponents' position. Also included in each volume is a timeline of significant events of the era and a bibliography of sources for students and others interested in further research.

As the most prominent individual in American politics, the president receives enormous attention from the media and the public. The statements, actions, travels, and even the personal lives of presidents are constantly scrutinized. Yet it is the presidents' work on public policy that most directly affects American citizens—a fact that is sometimes overlooked. This series is presented, in part, as a reminder of the importance of the president's position.

Mark Byrnes

TIMELINE

1848

January	Gold discovered in California
February	Treaty of Guadalupe Hidalgo ends Mexican War
August	Free Soil Party nominates Martin Van Buren for president
November	Zachary Taylor elected president

1850

March	Narciso Lopez launches expedition to liberate Cuba
July	Zachary Taylor dies; Millard Fillmore sworn in as president
September	California admitted into Union as free state
September	Congress passes Compromise of 1850

1852

March	Harriet Beecher Stowe publishes *Uncle Tom's Cabin*
November	Franklin Pierce elected president

1854

February	Gadsden Purchase adds territory to the Southwest
May	Pierce signs Kansas-Nebraska Act
July	Republican Party founded
October	Ostend Manifesto released

1856

May	Sack of Lawrence, Kansas, by proslavery mob

May	John Brown's massacre at Pottawatomie Creek, Kansas
May	Preston Brooks attacks Charles Sumner on Senate floor
November	James Buchanan elected president

1857

March	Supreme Court issues decision on *Dred Scott* case
August	Lecompton Constitution rejected by Kansas voters

1858

August	Lincoln-Douglas debates begin in Illinois Senate race

1859

October	John Brown leads raid on arsenal at Harper's Ferry, Virginia

1860

November	Abraham Lincoln elected president
December	South Carolina secedes from Union

1861

April	Fall of Fort Sumter
April	Lincoln suspends writ of *Habeas Corpus* in border states

1862

July	Congress authorizes enlistment of African American troops
July	Lincoln signs Homestead Act

1863

January	Lincoln issues Emancipation Proclamation
January	Lincoln approves military draft
July	U.S. Army defeats Confederates at Gettysburg
July	Vicksburg falls to Union forces

1864

March	Congress passes Wade-Davis Reconstruction Bill
March	Lincoln names Ulysses S. Grant Supreme Commander of Union Armies
November	Lincoln reelected

1865

March	Freedmen's Bureau established
April	General Robert E. Lee surrenders at Appomattox Court House, Virginia
April	John Wilkes Booth assassinates Lincoln
December	Thirteenth Amendment ratified

1866

April	Andrew Johnson vetoes Civil Rights Bill

June	Congress passes Fourteenth Amendment
September	Ku Klux Klan founded in Tennessee
1867	
March	Congress passes first Military Reconstruction Act
March	Congress passes Tenure of Office Act
March	Secretary of State William H. Seward negotiates Alaska purchase
1868	
March	Andrew Johnson's impeachment trial begins
July	Fourteenth Amendment ratified
November	Ulysses S. Grant elected president
1869	
May	Transcontinental Railroad completed
1870	
March	Fifteenth Amendment ratified
1871	
April	Grant signs Ku Klux Klan Act
1872	
March	Congress begins investigation of Credit Mobilier scandal
August	Liberal Republicans nominate Horace Greely for president
November	Grant reelected
1873	
September	Panic of 1873 begins
1874	
April	Grant vetoes Greenback Bill
November	Democrats win control of House of Representatives
1875	
March	Grant signs Civil Rights Act
May	Whiskey Ring uncovered
1877	
February	Compromise of 1877 ends Military Reconstruction

INTRODUCTION

The years 1848–1877 were among the most pivotal in the nation's history. Over the course of three decades, the United States endured a catastrophic civil war, abolished slavery, expanded westward and added eight states to the Union, witnessed the beginnings of industrialization, and experienced significant change in the fabric of society and culture. In politics, the era saw the demise of one national party and the birth of another. The country also faced difficult questions of state sovereignty and federal responsibility, answered ultimately by secession and war. In short, it was a time of growth, consolidation, tragedy, and triumph for a dynamic and youthful nation.

Above all, these years were marked by overwhelming growth, regardless of how that term may be considered. The population of the United States was a modest 5 million in 1800; by 1850 it had more than quadrupled, and by 1877 had doubled again to reach over 45 million citizens. Much of the increase was in cities. New York City, the nation's most populous city, boasted 60,000 residents in 1800; fifty years later it reached over half a million. Cities that in 1800 were little more than frontier outposts, such as Cincinnati, St. Louis, and Chicago, emerged as major population and commercial centers as Americans pushed westward. While the nation would report a majority of citizens living in rural areas until the historic 1920 census, rapid urbanization in the first half of the nineteenth century heralded significant change in many aspects of American life.

By mid-century, the ethnic composition of America was in flux; much growth was a result of immigration. As late as 1840 most new arrivals were British and Protestant, but the following decade brought massive change. Famine and political upheaval in Ireland and Germany resulted in a tidal wave of Catholic immigration that transformed parts of the country. In the Eastern cities, particularly New York, impoverished Irish Catholics poured into neighborhoods and immediately met with hostility. Violence, and at times rioting, became commonplace as Protestants felt threatened by those guided by "Popery." These new immigrants also had a significant impact on politics, as urban Catholic workers became an important political bloc. Moreover, many Protestants who feared these changes reacted by forming an anti-Catholic political party, the"Know-Nothings."

Population growth was complemented by economic prosperity. During the first half of the nineteenth century, the gross national product, the total amount of wealth produced in a given year, doubled every fifteen years. Between 1800 and 1850, average household income increased by over 100 percent. While there had been severe setbacks, such as the financial panics of 1819 and 1837, these proved temporary as the economy gathered strength throughout the antebellum, or pre–Civil War, era. Even the Civil War proved only a minor hurdle in this regard. By 1870, prosperity had returned at even faster rates. Per capita wealth (the average amount of wealth per individual in a given year) between 1850 and 1880 almost doubled, despite the destruction wrought by the war and continued population growth. These years gave Americans good reason to believe in progress.

The nature of the economy was also in transition. Agriculture and limited manufactures by artisans had been the economic base of the country since the eighteenth century, but the beginnings of industrialization foreshadowed great changes to come. As early as the 1830s, some manufacturing was moving from individual craftsmanship to managed production. The textile industry, which had introduced the factory system in England, was copied in the Northeast. Industrialization generated a new class of laborers who worked in the factories as unskilled or semiskilled wage workers. Segments of cities were developing into working-class neighborhoods, as more prosperous residents began to move away from urban centers.

Most of these changes were occurring in the Northeast. The South remained steadfastly agricultural throughout the antebellum era. Cotton indeed had become "King" by 1860. While some areas continued to produce tobacco, indigo, or sugar, cash-crop cotton farming spread across the Deep South in the early nineteenth century. Almost half a million acres of land were devoted to cotton cultivation by 1850. During the twenty years before the Civil War, cotton exports increased twentyfold, to over $300 million annually. As a result, fortunes were made. The planter class, which only amounted to about three or four thousand out of a population of 9 million, owned the vast majority of this sector's wealth.

The economic growth of the young nation was rivaled only by the staggering territorial gains of the antebellum era. The Louisiana Purchase of 1803, which increased the size of the United States by one-third, assured Americans that expansion across the continent was inevitable. By the

1840s, this confidence had mushroomed to the pervasive sentiment that the nation's "manifest destiny" was to expand its boundaries to the Pacific Coast. During the James Polk administration, such attitudes developed into policy, as Democrats championed territorial acquisition.

The first wave of expansion brought Texas and Oregon into the Union. Texas had declared independence from Mexico a decade earlier when in 1845 expansionists in Congress finally achieved the votes to approve annexation. Leaders within the Republic of Texas, with few exceptions, enthusiastically supported the action as the Lone Star State was admitted in December of that year. Mexicans viewed annexation as the culmination of a ten-year effort by Americans to seize control of the area by hook or by crook. Ill feelings between the two nations over Texas preceded greater hostilities to come. During Polk's presidency, the United States also settled a longstanding dispute over the boundary of Oregon, which opened up that area for settlement. These impressive gains in the West, however, paled in comparison to the areas acquired from the Mexican War.

The war, lasting only seventeen months, was a time when expansionist sentiments reached a fevered pitch. There had been costs. More than 12,000 Americans died, the vast majority from disease. The gains, however, were overwhelming. The Treaty of Guadalupe Hidalgo, signed on February 2, 1848, increased the size of the United States in dramatic fashion yet again. The Mexican Cession included all of New Mexico and California and put to rest disputes over the region of southern Texas. The United States agreed to pay Mexico $15 million, a small price for 500,000 square miles of territory. With the exception of the Gadsden purchase of 1853, the war had finalized America's conquest of North America. Understandably, the war also generated a great wave of national pride.

An irony of this rousing patriotism was that these same actions served as the basis for bitter political conflicts that led to sectionalism. Politics in the antebellum era was focused primarily on the nation's rapid growth. In the 1830s, a stable two-party system emerged in the wake of Andrew Jackson's rise to prominence in the Democratic Party. Jackson, a man of immense fame based on his exploits during the War of 1812, presented himself as champion of the "common man" and enjoyed support across the board. Part of his success may be attributed to the elimination of property requirements for voting in many states in the 1820s. Now Jackson, who had revolutionized politics by stressing a lack of refinement and education, built a political empire that dominated politics until the Civil War.

The Democrats were a party of more than symbolism, however. Reflecting the strength of its southern base, the party maintained a states' right orientation throughout the antebellum era. Democrats also tended to support low tariffs. Both positions were tested during the Jackson administration, when South Carolinians protested the so-called Tariff of Abominations, passed in 1828, that placed high duties on several exports, including cotton, tobacco, and indigo. Attempts by the South Carolina state legislature to nullify the tariff led to a showdown between the administration and those who championed the sovereignty of states. In the end, under the threat of military action and with the aid of a compromise tariff, South Carolina backed down. For the moment, Democrats who talked of states' rights placed Union ahead of section.

The Jacksonians' opposition soon coalesced into the Whig party. Whigs were less unified in their programs and ideology, but all were strongly opposed to Jackson and his followers. The party faced the same challenge as the Democrats—to maintain party unity in the face of various regional interests. Generally, the Whigs promoted Kentucky Senator Henry Clay's "American System," a nationalist economic strategy that advocated internal improvements funded by revenue tariffs. Whigs were strong in the Northeast, but also had followers in the West and the South. For two decades, both national parties sought majorities by appealing to their varied constituencies, a task that required them to skirt divisive issues where compromise could not be reached.

The issue that lay beyond the scope of compromise was slavery. Slavery's emergence as the central issue of the 1850s began two decades earlier with a surge in the number of "abolitionists," who combined evangelical Christianity with romantic idealism to seek a more humane and just society. In 1831 in Boston, William Lloyd Garrison launched the *Liberator*, a newspaper that promoted abolitionism and had a great impact on the intellectuals of New England. Some abolitionists believed that Southerners had a right to determine the status of slavery in their own states but with time would come to see the institution's inhumanity. Others claimed that the United States government had a responsibility to end slavery immediately. Both wings of the movement agreed that slavery should never be allowed to expand into new areas.

Until westward expansion occurred in the 1840s, debates over slavery tended to be philosophical. For most people, abolitionism meant radicalism. Congressional debates over the annexation of Texas, however, foreshadowed the intense disagreements that would soon become common. Northern Whigs complained that Southerners, particularly Democrats, were most concerned with adding another slave state to the Union, upsetting the balance of free and slave states achieved by the Missouri Compromise. Congressional opposition blocked the move for years; Texas achieved statehood only through adept political maneuvering by Democrats and strong support from the Polk administration.

War with Mexico raised the stakes considerably. Whigs in the North found it difficult to oppose the war publicly, particularly in its early stages. By 1848, a heated battle was brewing between a small but vocal bloc of Northern congressmen and Southern expansionists. The trigger was the bold action of a freshman congressman from Pennsylvania, David Wilmot, who in August 1846 proposed that slavery be prohibited in any territory obtained as a result of the war. In a well-designed speech, Wilmot declared his support for the war and for westward expansion but added that freedom-loving Americans also should oppose the expansion of slavery anywhere. The House of Representatives passed the Wilmot Proviso on two occasions, but it failed to clear the Senate floor. Nevertheless, the concept came up again and again during debates over slavery in the West.

The significance of the Wilmot Proviso was that congressmen now were forced to face the issue directly. Over the next few years, a number of positions emerged regarding slavery in the Mexican Cession that won the support of particular voters. In opposition to Wilmot, John C. Calhoun of South Carolina asserted that Southerners who owned slaves were protected by the Fifth Amendment to the Constitution, which protected personal property, in any federally controlled territory. As a result, Congress did not possess the authority to ban slavery in any of the western territories. This concept, articulated in the Calhoun Resolutions issued in 1847, became a common argument made by Southerners throughout the 1850s.

Politicians with national aspirations had an incentive to find a moderate position on such a turbulent issue. Senator Lewis Cass of Michigan, a seasoned Democrat, fashioned a strategy that he believed would keep him out of the fray by proposing that citizens within territories should determine the status of slavery themselves. "Popular sovereignty," or squatter sovereignty, soon found other supporters, most notably a young and fiery congressman from Illinois named Stephen A. Douglas. Popular sovereignty had much to recommend it. First, one could relate the concept to self-determination and democracy. Perhaps more importantly, popular sovereignty removed the issue from Washington and placed it in the territories themselves. As the debates over slavery intensified, Douglas's views became more attractive to perceptive politicians.

Considering the range of views on the matter of slavery in the West, conflict was inevitable. Zachary Taylor's presidency was consumed with the problem. In 1849, Americans poured into northern California searching for gold. Theoretical discussions about slavery and statehood quickly became concrete. In the previous year, abolitionists, some Whigs, and even a few Democrats had formed a new political party devoted to "Free Soil" in the West. In January 1850, these groups in Congress waged battle with Southerners over California statehood. Much was at stake. Not only would a new state disrupt the balance of free and slave states in Congress; it also would establish a precedent for statehood in other areas of the Mexican Cession. The debates were historic. Giants of antebellum politics, including Henry Clay, Daniel Webster of Massachusetts, Stephen Douglas, John C. Calhoun, Jefferson Davis, and Thomas Hart Benton brought their tremendous rhetorical talents to bear on the matter. For a time, the controversy became heated to the point that even the Union itself seemed threatened. Calhoun, at the twilight of an epic career, spoke of disunion if the issue were not resolved in the South's favor.

Yet disunion would not occur at that moment. Congress forged agreements that appeased both sections. The celebrations that erupted in the wake of the Compromise of 1850 hid the fact that the measures did little to solve problems in the long run. In fact, they may have made them worse. California had been admitted as a free state, an act that Southerners later would use repeatedly to illustrate their propensity for cooperation and even sacrifice. Antislavery Northerners came to hate the Fugitive Slave Law that cracked down on those who aided escaped slaves who made it out of the South. In short, both sections were sure that the other had benefited more from the Compromise of 1850. Leaders in both sections became less amenable to cooperation and negotiation in later years.

In 1854, the same questions that had brought the nation to the brink in 1850 reemerged. The Kansas and Nebraska regions, an enormous area that stretched from the Mason-Dixon Line northward to the Canadian border, had yet to organize territorial governments. The result of this round of fighting would not be compromise. Douglas emerged as a force in the Senate when he introduced a bill that would allow the region to achieve territorial status. Timing was crucial. Railroad owners in his home state of Illinois envisioned a transcontinental railroad that would run through their state and onward to the Pacific coast. The Gadsden Purchase of 1853, which brought into the Union land in the extreme Southwest, made the prospect of a southern route more likely. Douglas knew that a northern route depended on the speedy organization of Kansas and Nebraska.

The problem, Douglas knew, was that bickering over slavery would result in delay, as it had in California. To push a bill through Congress, he revived the concept of popular sovereignty. His legislation provided that the residents of the territories would determine the status of slavery themselves. The measure appealed to Southerners. Kansas and Nebraska were north of the 36° 30′ line that had separated free and slave areas of the Louisiana Purchase since 1820. Popular sovereignty meant repeal of the measure. Southerners would be permitted to enter any territory with their slaves until a particular legislature voted to ban slavery. Douglas found sufficient support in the West and South to get his measure through Congress. President Franklin Pierce, a Democrat, signed the bill into law.

Douglas believed that popular sovereignty would quell debate over slavery; in fact, the opposite occurred. Northerners reacted to the Kansas-Nebraska Act with outrage, to the point that the Whig Party, long in decline, disintegrated. Moderate Northerners had no truck with Southerners who owned slaves in the South; now, however, slavery might be opened up in new areas of the North. Antislavery, or "Conscience," Whigs, disgusted with the Southern wing of the party for its refusal to condemn the act, bolted from the party. A smaller number of Northern Democrats did the same. These groups combined with abolitionists and independent Free Soilers to found the Republican Party in 1854. The Democrats were now the only truly national party. As such, they saw an opportunity to dominate Washington if they could hold the two sections of the party together. For a short time, they did, but the Republicans attracted more and more supporters in the late 1850s as events polarized the nation. In 1860, the Democratic Party also split into factions.

Those events of the late 1850s began in Kansas, where violence broke out between proslavery and antislavery groups. A strong majority of Kansas residents opposed slavery, yet the better organized proslavery citizens managed to form a legislature and create a constitution that guaranteed slavery. Soon a rival government emerged and produced its own constitution. In Washington, debate raged and even moved to violence when Senator Preston S. Brooks of South Carolina attacked antislavery Senator Charles Sumner with a cane on the floor of the Senate after arguments over slavery moved from the political to the personal. Reporters wrote stories about "Bleeding Kansas" in Eastern newspapers, whipping Americans in both sections into a frenzy. Yet the Democratic Party held together, in 1856 nominating James Buchanan as president, a Northerner with strong Southern sympathies. The election was a harbinger of future events. Buchanan won the election, but the outcome was much closer than most had expected. The Republican party nominee John C. Frémont swept the Northern states and indicated the potential power of that more populous region.

The downward spiral toward political crisis continued throughout Buchanan's embattled administration. Events in Kansas continued to spark hostility, particularly when Buchanan supported the proslavery constitution created at Lecompton. In the end, the voters of Kansas rejected slavery and Buchanan's support in the North declined even further. The 1857 *Dred Scott* case, in which the Supreme Court declared as unconstitutional congressional attempts to block slavery from territories, further outraged Northerners. In 1859, the erratic abolitionist John Brown, already infamous for his 1856 murder of proslavery citizens at Pottawatomie Creek in Kansas, led a group of men on an attack of a federal arsenal at Harpers Ferry, Virginia, with the intent of inciting a slave uprising. Brown, martyred in the North and vilified in the South, was captured and executed, but his actions further polarized the nation. As the nation approached the 1860 election, crisis loomed.

That crisis came with the election of Republican Abraham Lincoln in the fall of 1860. In retrospect, his victory seems unsurprising. The Democratic Party's disintegration was finalized that summer, when during its convention the Southern wing broke away and nominated Vice President John C. Breckenridge of Kentucky for the presidency. Stephen Douglas received the nomination of the remainder of the party. Lincoln, the lawyer and congressman from Illinois, was a perfect selection. As a moderate, he did not alienate voters in the West, who opposed abolitionism, yet offered antislavery proponents a candidate who spoke publicly about the evils of slavery and vowed to block its expansion into new areas. Southerners warned that the election of a Northerner, by a Northern party, would result in secession. In the weeks following the election, leaders in those states made good on their promise. On December 20, 1860, a convention in South Carolina issued as Ordinance of Secession. By February 1, 1861, six other states had followed suit. In April, what heretofore had been a political crisis became a military struggle.

The Civil War was costly in every way imaginable. Over 600,000 Americans died; nearly every family in the nation was touched by the war. The South was devastated. Cities were reduced to ruins, chaos ensued in some areas, and the economy lay in a shambles. Farming lands were rendered useless. In many areas of the South, twenty years or more would pass before crop cultivation returned to prewar levels. The U.S. government spent unprecedented sums of money during the war, averaging $2 million a day. In both regions, inflation drove up prices and threatened an economic catastrophe. Yet clearly the war was more damaging to the South. Northern manufactures actually increased as wartime demand propelled the Industrial Revolution.

In the wake of General Robert E. Lee's surrender at Appomattox Court House, Americans examined their war-torn nation and searched for meaning behind the war. Some changes were recognizable instantly. Others would become apparent only after years of hindsight. Clearly, the war put to rest the most immediate problem of slavery. Lincoln's wartime Emancipation Proclamation abolished slavery in those states in rebellion. After the war, the Thirteenth Amendment ended slavery in the United States altogether. The war, and the Reconstruction era afterward, also clarified questions of federalism. While states retained sovereignty on some matters, the Fourteenth Amendment guaranteed that states did not have the authority to deny individuals basic rights of due process guaranteed by the Constitution.

These Reconstruction matters were not resolved without controversy. The war brought an end to fighting, but white Southerners retained their attitudes about race, politics, and society. In the North, debate raged as to the process by which Southern states would be readmitted to the Union. There were moderates, such as President Andrew Johnson, who envisioned a plan that would restore the nation without fundamental change. Johnson and the moderates believed that white Southerners who had supported secession, with the exception of high-ranking Confederate officials, should participate in new state governments. In his first year in office, he began a process by which the Southern states would be returned to the Union quickly and with the least amount of upheaval possible.

More extreme Republicans, dubbed the Radicals, feared that Johnson's plans for Reconstruction would result in a lost cause for the North if secessionists were allowed back into power with little change. Part of the dispute centered on the status of the Southern states. Lincoln had maintained that secession was an illegal act from the outset that never had been recognized by the United States government. They had, in effect, never formally left the Union. Johnson agreed, also claiming that a small group of Southern leaders was most responsible for the war. Average Southerners participated as loyal citizens of their states. Most, he believed, would return to the Union peacefully. Radicals claimed that secession transformed the Southern states. By breaking their ties with the nation, they had committed "state suicide" and now were considered conquered territory. Reconstruction, Radicals argued, required lengthy occupation of the South to ensure fundamental political and social change.

Johnson pointed out that his plan required states to ratify the Thirteenth Amendment, but radicals argued that this alone would not protect freedmen. Circumstances supported their claims. In some states, the new Southern legislatures began to pass laws that placed restrictions on the freedom of former slaves, the so-called "Black Codes." In some instances, the laws prevented blacks from owning land and required those in debt to work off their debts by laboring in the fields of planters. Radicals such as Thaddeus Stevens and Charles Sumner claimed that within a few years Southern planters would restore the slave system by another name.

The result was a fierce battle between the president and the increasingly Radical-led Congress. Johnson, instead of seeking compromise, became intransigent—a decision that only pushed more legislators to the Radical fold. By the end of 1866, Congress had taken the initiative and launched a stricter program of Reconstruction that included military occupation of the South until certain requirements were met regarding the status of freedmen. These included passage of the Fourteenth Amendment and the Fifteenth Amendment, which guaranteed the right of citizens to vote regardless of race, color, or previous condition of servitude. The Radicals also strengthened the Freedmen's Bureau, a government agency charged with providing educational and financial assistance to former slaves. Johnson opposed these changes at every stage. His impeachment trial and near removal from office was the culmination of a bitter contest between the executive branch and the Congress.

Reconstruction continued through the administration of Ulysses S. Grant, yet by the early 1870s the Radicals had lost their momentum. All over the South, Republicans lost their majorities, and in 1874 Democrats took over control of the House of Representatives. Democratic "Redeemers" came to power partly by disenfranchisement of blacks through intimidation. Roguish groups such as the Ku Klux Klan, founded in Tennessee in 1866, used threats and violence to keep blacks from the polls. Southern legislatures also passed measures, such as poll taxes and literacy requirements for voting, as a means of excluding freedmen from civic involvement. By the late 1870s, the number of blacks participating in elections had plummeted.

Voters also turned against the Republican Party in reaction to the wave of scandals that marked the Grant years. The administration faced continual allegations of fraud and misuse of power from the outset that at times implicated individuals close to the president. One incident involved a group of officials, including Grant's close friend and personal secretary Orville Babcock, who skimmed funds from taxes collected on whiskey. Another, in which even the vice president was charged, was a complex case of payments by a construction company made to legislators in the form of stocks in order to receive favorable action on railroad development legislation. The Credit Mobilier scandal, as it came to be known, perhaps was the most egregious example of government corruption of the entire century. Democrats used these allegations to their advantage by portraying all Republicans as complicit in "Grantism."

To make matters worse, a severe financial panic, followed by a six-year depression also generated unrest and hostility toward those in power. The Panic of 1873 focused attention on the economic health of the country as unemployment rose and bankruptcies rocked the financial districts of the major cities. Soon the crisis filtered down to working people, who began to feel the brunt of the depression in decreased wages and higher prices. Discontent found its way into politics. Farmers and laborers, weary of increasing prices, protested high tariffs championed by industrialists; they also advocated increasing the money supply as opposed to the "hard money" position taken by bankers and financiers. As the decade came to a close, economic matters had replaced Reconstruction as the most important issues for voters.

Not surprisingly, these trends aided the Democratic Party. In 1874, Republicans lost control of the House of Representatives for the first time since the Civil War. The Democratic leadership then launched an intense campaign to expose the administration as corrupt and inept. In the 1876 presidential election, Democrat Samuel J. Tilden of New York won the popular vote and tied Republican Rutherford B. Hayes in the electoral college. The election then went to the House of Representatives, where an Electoral Commission bickered for weeks over the outcome. In the end, Hayes won the election, but only after the Republican Party agreed to withdraw the final federal troops from Louisiana and South Carolina. Reconstruction had breathed its last gasp.

The presidents who faced the many challenges of this era were a varied group. Significantly, the period began and ended with war heroes as presidents. Zachary Taylor was swept into office after his successes in the Mexican War. Americans in the North regarded Grant as the savior of the Union. Taylor and Fillmore were the last Whigs to serve in the White House. Franklin Pierce and James Buchanan, both Democrats, found themselves in the almost impossible situation of striking sectional balance during a time of increasing hostility. Both were Northerners who tended to side with Southerners on issues regarding slavery. Abraham Lincoln, the first Republican president, displayed a firm resolve to maintain the Union and offered a firm hand at a necessary point in the nation's history. Andrew Johnson inherited many unresolved problems from Lincoln but did not inherit his diplomacy and political adroitness. Ulysses S. Grant provided symbolic leadership for the nation, but lacked the skills to guide the country through such a difficult era.

The issues presented here offer a glimpse into the leadership abilities of these presidents and the challenges confronting the young nation. The documents reveal that these administrations faced diverse challenges—domestic and foreign, economic and political, social and cultural. The issues selected for each presidency were those most pressing for the nation at the time. As such, they received a great deal of attention both in the press and in the halls of Congress. Documents have been selected that best illustrate the positions of both the presidents and their opponents. The vast majority of each president's views are culled from speeches or official documents. His opposition most often came from congressional speeches or newspaper and magazine articles.

The volume is arranged chronologically and thematically. Each section begins with a biographical sketch of the president. For each issue, an introduction offers the reader historical context, followed first by the president's position on the issue—most often in his own words—followed by an opposing viewpoint. These documents allow the reader to analyze and evaluate these debates by engaging the historical characters directly. For students who wish to learn more about these administrations and the issues of their day, a list of recommended readings is included at the end of each chapter. The ways in which the presidents handled the crises of their times are of immense value in understanding America, past and present.

1

ZACHARY TAYLOR AND MILLARD FILLMORE

(1849–1850) and (1850–1853)

INTRODUCTION

On a cold, dreary day in early March 1849, a throng of supporters huddled outside the Capitol in Washington, D.C., to witness the swearing in of America's twelfth president. For the newly elected commander-in-chief, General Zachary Taylor, the inauguration brought to a close a harrowing journey from his home in Louisiana that included a painful injury when a trunk fell on him in Indiana, a bad cold that hounded him as his steamer crept up the icy Ohio River, and endless celebrations at every stop along the way. As the weary and weathered fifty-four-year-old general looked out onto the crowd through a bracing wind, he had to wonder if he was ready for such responsibility.

Others asked the same question. His predecessor, James K. Polk of Tennessee, had scoffed, when hearing of Taylor's election, that "Old Rough and Ready" was wholly unqualified to serve as president of the United States. Although Taylor's distinguished military record placed him alongside former presidents George Washington, Andrew Jackson, and William Henry Harrison, there was widespread concern that the nation, during such a critical time, required a more experienced leader. Even within his own party many believed that the man at his side, Vice President-elect Millard Fillmore of New York, actually was the better candidate. But Taylor, who had been nominated by the Whig Party the previous summer by virtue of his popularity, would lead the country in these divided times.

Divided times they were. On one hand, the United States was enjoying an extraordinary period of economic growth that roused patriotism and national confidence. Evidence of prosperity was everywhere. Coal and iron production soared in the 1840s and provided labor for a rapidly growing population. Railroad lines began to link cities together for travel and trade. Telegraphs had ushered in a communications revolution. Agricultural production continued to increase, especially "king cotton" in the South. Americans, with good reason, saw themselves as citizens of a thriving, forward-looking nation where opportunity abounded.

This air of confidence was bolstered by the startling territorial gains made in the West. The Polk administration had overseen the acquisition of the Oregon Territory in the Northwest and the annexation of Texas as the nation's sixteenth state. All the while, the slogan of "Manifest Destiny" assured Americans that Providence guided expansion. In 1846, the United States plunged into war with Mexico, resulting in another wave of patriotism. On the heels of victory, which resulted in the addition to the nation of the gargantuan Mexican Cession (California, Arizona, and New Mexico), a romantic view of nationhood seemed to be emerging that downplayed identification with individual states or regions. On the surface, the 1840s were an age of growth and confidence.

Yet a great irony of the age was that expansion, while generating national pride, also contributed to sectional disputes that threatened the cohesion of the country and its nationally based political parties. As early as 1836, signs of division over westward expansion materialized as Northern Congressmen blocked the annexation of Texas following its successful war of independence with Mexico. The source of controversy was slavery. If Texas were admitted to the Union as a slave state, the balance in Congress would be tipped to favor Southern interests. Democrats in the North crossed party lines to join with Northern Whigs to oppose annexation; Polk, in 1845, had fulfilled a campaign promise by garnering enough votes to admit the Lone Star State into the Union. The battle over Texas was heated, and most understood that the acquisition of new territory would generate similar political debate.

These divisions were exacerbated as abolitionism grew from a small political phenomenon to a viable national movement. Much of the movement's success may be attributed to the talent and energy of its leaders. Reformers thundered from pulpits and meeting halls; among them were the editor William Lloyd Garrison, the theologian Theodore Parker, the minister Theodore Dwight Weld, and former slave Frederick Douglass. Religious revivalism, which had flourished in the 1830s during the Second Great Awakening, gave Northern evangelicals opportunities to spread the message of the immorality of slavery. At the same time, Southern reaction only served to strengthen abolitionism. Beginning in the late 1830s, a number of Southern states enacted bans on public speeches that championed abolition. In some cases, the mails were regulated to prevent the dissemination of abolitionist literature. In 1836, Southern leaders in the U.S. Congress managed to pass a "Gag Rule" that forbade any discussion of slavery in the legislature. Abolitionists argued, with some justification, that Southerners sought to undermine basic principles of democracy to protect slavery; their actions served to strengthen Northern concerns about the political power of the South.

Until 1846, Congress operated on the assumption that the volatile issue of slavery should be avoided whenever possible. The Mexican War, however, made silence impossible. For Southerners, the new territories of the Southwest naturally would become slaveholding areas. Northerners, especially those who had questioned the war, saw the Mexican Cession as a means by which Southerners could come to dominate the United States Congress. In this atmosphere of suspicion and concern, David Wilmot, a Democratic congressman from Pennsylvania brought the government to the brink of crisis.

In August 1846, Wilmot proposed that slavery be banned from all new territories acquired as a result of the Mexican War. Many Whigs and Democrats in the North supported the measure. Southerners screamed that the "Wilmot Proviso" violated the Missouri Compromise of 1820, which had established a precedent that territories below the 36° 30' line would allow slavery. The Wilmot Proviso failed to gain enough votes to pass, but antislavery legislators insisted on reintroducing the measure. If anything, the debate exposed the sectional nature of the slavery issue. For the next two years, politicians with presidential aspirations found themselves in the midst of congressional polarization. Democrats narrowly held both houses, the incumbent Polk was a Democrat, and the primary task of the party was to seek a candidate and a platform that could hold its two hostile wings together. If this could be achieved, the Democrats would easily maintain control of the White House. As the Wilmot Proviso languished on the floor of Congress, the Democratic Party met in Baltimore in the summer of 1848 to nominate a candidate to succeed Polk.

Hopes for a unified Democratic convention were soon dashed. Slavery in the Mexican Cession may have been the most pressing political issue but it was also considered too volatile to address directly. Senator Lewis Cass of Michigan, a moderate on most issues, understood this and adopted the politically astute position of "popular sovereignty" for the West. Cass proposed that territorial governments should decide the issue of slavery themselves, without input from Washington. Popular sovereignty had several advantages. For one, it was cloaked in the language of self-determination. More important, it was a way for politicians to avoid taking a position on slavery that could alienate an entire region of the country. Several leading Democrats believed Cass's plan offered the greatest possibility for overcoming division. He won the nomination over Secretary of State James Buchanan, a Pennsylvania Democrat who supported the Missouri Compromise as the most effective means of determining slavery in the West. Once the nomination was secured for Cass, the party then went out of its way to say almost nothing about the slavery issue in its platform. Clearly, the Democrats believed that the best way to deal with slavery was to avoid the issue.

Avoidance of the issue, however, only made things worse. Antislavery Democrats were stunned by the party's lack of support for the Missouri Compromise, which at least prohibited slavery in territories north of the Mason-Dixon Line. Popular sovereignty, in their view, was a means to open the question back up again. They pushed for a strong statement against slavery in the party's platform, but Southern leaders blocked these attempts. Feeling isolated, a group of New York Democrats left the convention in protest and began planning for a new party convention, which was held in Buffalo, New York, several weeks later. These "Free Soilers," led by former president Martin Van Buren, issued an invitation to all antislavery Whigs and independent abolitionists to join their cause. The result was a Free Soil ticket, with the Democrat Van Buren balanced by Boston patrician and antislavery Whig, Charles Francis Adams, as his running mate. While the Free Soil Party threatened to cut into the support of both parties, Van Buren would likely attract more Democrats, thus weakening that party's chances for victory.

Even Southerners grew restless with the Democrats' vague posturings on slavery. Senator John C. Calhoun, a longtime leader of the proslavery wing of the party, had reached the conclusion that the Missouri Compromise line that separated free and slave territories and the concept of popular sovereignty both were unfair and unconstitutional. Calhoun and a small group of Southern Democrats argued that the new territories of the Mexican Cession, not yet organized as sovereign states, were the shared property of all Americans. As such, Southerners had every right to carry their property, even slaves, into these areas, whether north or south of the 36° 30' line. Calhoun believed that popular sovereignty gave Northerners an avenue to block the interests of slaveholders in the West; he also wanted the Democratic Party to issue a statement as part of its platform that slavery would be protected both where it already existed and in new territories. When party leaders refused, Calhoun and others threatened to leave the convention. In the end, the Democrats had their national candidate and had avoided making strong statements, pro or con, about slavery; in the process, however, the party was badly divided.

When the Whigs began their nominating convention in New York, party leaders saw a great opportunity to win back the White House. The 1840 election, which had provided the Whigs with their first president in William Henry Harrison, taught them the lesson that popularity was as crucial as issues in national campaigns. Harrison had run on his military record; in the wake of the Mexican War, Whigs saw an opportunity to repeat the performance. There were a number of possibilities. Zachary Taylor, the hero of Monterrey widely known as "Old Rough and Ready," and the venerable

Winfield Scott, "Old Fuss and Feathers," who had a distinguished military career that included a leadership role during the War of 1812, were both possibilities. Whigs were encouraged when Taylor would not rule out a run at the presidency, even though he was not a Whig and had never participated in politics. The roadblock to Taylor's candidacy was the party's long-time standard-bearer, Senator Henry Clay of Kentucky. He was a national figure of great repute, had served his country honorably as a congressman for several decades, and had garnered respect from both parties. The problem with Clay, as most Whigs knew all too well, was that he had failed to win the presidency in several prior campaigns. Clay had loyal support, but many feared that Clay's nomination would result in a lost opportunity.

When Zachary Taylor's name was first mentioned as a potential candidate, most Americans knew of his exploits during the Mexican War but did not know much else about him. Despite his rough appearance and unpolished demeanor, Taylor's lineage was that of an American aristocrat. Arriving in Virginia in the seventeenth century, the Taylors became one of the more prominent and well connected families in the colonies. Among his relatives were the famous Lees, including Light Horse Harry Lee, Richard Lee, and a promising nephew of Zachary Taylor, Robert E. Lee. Taylor's father was a planter who moved the family to Kentucky after the Revolutionary War. Zachary, the third of eight sons, grew up on a successful plantation surrounded by loving parents and dutiful servants; the Taylors owned thirty-seven slaves by 1810, and Zachary Taylor was a slaveholder his entire life. He fully planned to follow in his father's and grandfather's footsteps by becoming a successful plantation owner.

As was typical of young men of his station, Taylor joined the military and served under General William Henry Harrison during the War of 1812. He married Margaret Mackall Smith, daughter of a wealthy planter, and after the war remained in military service for several years. During these years, his landholdings grew. He used profits from the sale of land his father had bequeathed him to buy farmland in Tennessee and Louisiana. His plantation in Louisiana, north of Baton Rouge, became his permanent home. He soon returned to military service, as a commander stationed in forts in the Old Northwest. By the late 1830s, Taylor had compiled a distinguished military record that included service in the Black Hawk and Seminole Wars. His financial gains were also considerable. By 1848, Taylor owned several plantations and 145 slaves. In 1846, when hostilities with Mexico began, he was commander of the Second Military Department, based in Ft. Smith, Arkansas. The war would catapult Taylor to national fame and ultimately into the presidency.

While some Americans, especially in the Northeast, opposed the war, few found fault with General Taylor's leadership. With the help of favorable newspaper reports, he gained a reputation for bravery and sound command. After skirmishes with Mexican troops under General Antonio

Lopez de Santa Anna, Taylor commanded forces in successful battles at Palo Alto and Resaca de la Palma. President Polk had little choice but to promote Taylor to Major General and place the entire United States military force in Mexico under his command. Soon after, Taylor led the charge at Monterrey, a fierce battle that dashed any hopes of a Mexican victory. Taylor's troops marched into Mexico City as Santa Anna's army collapsed.

Polk and Taylor always maintained a rather cool relationship, but in the final stages of the war they became heated rivals. The Democratic president had to be concerned with Taylor's close relationship with the Whigs. Those fears were validated when, during the final weeks of the war, leading Whigs such as Georgia Senator Alexander Stephens and Illinois Congressman Abraham Lincoln formed a Taylor-for-President club to rally support for the General. Taylor became convinced that Polk, in an attempt to damage Taylor's public image, had undermined and endangered his command by failing to send adequate reinforcements before the Battle of Monterrey; soon Taylor began to criticize the administration openly. Polk believed that by doing so Taylor was using his position as a military commander to polish his political image. Both, to some degree, were probably correct. Nevertheless, by the summer of 1848, with the war over and the campaign season about to begin, Taylor had become a leading candidate for the Whig Party nomination.

Taylor's war record was his greatest asset, but other factors attracted the attention of the Whigs. For one, he had never held office and seemed altogether uninterested in politics. Given the fractious nature of politics of the period, this was seen as a positive attribute. Taylor had few strong enemies in either party and had little stake in the narrow positions that had emerged on slavery and other divisive issues. He declared from the outset that he would only run as a "national candidate" who would represent the interests of all Americans, regardless of party affiliation. In fact, Taylor would have preferred to run for president as an independent candidate; Whigs convinced him that in order to have a chance of winning, he had to join a party. Some opponents claimed that Taylor's seeming political neutrality was calculated. Regardless, he successfully cultivated an image of rising above the combative nature of party politics.

Yet there remained the question of Taylor's actual views. Here was another asset, for Taylor was one of a very few who might be palatable to both Northern and Southern Whigs. Southerners and slavery advocates might be more receptive to moderate views on slavery if they were voiced by a Southern slaveholder. In fact, Taylor's primary political challenge was to placate Northern Whigs. Some had already left the party and joined Van Buren's Free Soilers, so Taylor had to strike a balance to keep the party together. He did so by clearly opposing the extension of slavery in the new territories gained from Mexico (at least when he spoke to Northern audiences) but declaring that Southerners had every right to own slaves. Taylor's message was one of Union; if Democrats, with some validity, charged that Taylor told Northern voters one thing and Southerners another, they glossed over the fact that Democrats tried unsuccessfully to do the same.

The Whigs, however, left nothing to chance and for balance nominated a Northerner for vice president. Millard Fillmore might have been Zachary Taylor's opposite in almost every way. Taylor was a rough-hewn and rustic aristocrat; Fillmore was a polished and refined son of a pauper. Fillmore's father was a tenant farmer who settled in upstate New York in 1799. Millard was born the following year and grew up on a rented farm in Cayuga County. By all accounts, Fillmore's childhood was one of hard work and little time for amusement, but his parents were anything but cruel. Millard's father was committed to seeing his son enjoy a better life and sent him away to serve as an apprentice for a cloth finisher and later to work in a textile mill. Such tough love paid off, for the young Fillmore had an opportunity to meet people he otherwise might never have encountered.

One such person was Walter Wood, a Quaker judge who saw a great deal of promise in the hard-working young man. Wood encouraged Fillmore to educate himself, which he did by borrowing books from friends, and he apprenticed as a law clerk under Wood's supervision. During these years, he met Abigail Powers, daughter of a minister who also recognized Fillmore's talents and eventually became his wife. With Wood's guidance and Abigail's support, Fillmore was accepted to the New York state bar at the age of twenty-four; he and Abigail soon moved to Buffalo, New York, a booming city on Lake Erie where he began his career. Within a few years Fillmore had built up a reputable and successful practice.

Fillmore also became active in local civic affairs and soon entered politics. Among his notable achievements in Buffalo were funding and participating in the Lyceum, where public lectures and discussions on academic topics took place, helping to found the Buffalo High School Association, and participating in efforts to improve city facilities such as bridges, dams, and roads. Such a high level of civic responsibility made Fillmore a natural candidate for political office. Coming of age in the so-called "Era of Good Feelings," when a single political party, the Republicans, held national sway, Fillmore sided with the National Republican wing of the party, led by Henry Clay. Clay's American System, which called for national support for internal improvements, such as canal and road construction, protective tariffs for emergent industry, and a centralized national system of finance, made sense to someone living in a rapidly growing commercial center. As the Democratic Republicans melded into the Democratic Party, led almost singularly by Andrew Jackson, Fillmore and others gravitated toward the groups that eventually became the Whig Party. First a state representative under the National Republican banner, Fillmore fought the dominant Jacksonians in New York and in 1836 was elected to the United States Congress as a Whig.

In 1842, Fillmore left Congress but did not leave the political arena. He was a virulent critic of Polk's expansionist policies. Fillmore opposed both the annexation of Texas and the Mexican War on the assumption that Southerners were using expansion to increase the size and political power of the slavocracy. Fillmore was no abolitionist; he refused to speak out against slavery in the South, which would mean political suicide for any politician with national aspirations. In 1847 he was elected state comptroller for New York, a powerful economic position, and attended the Whig Party national convention in the summer of 1848. Although Fillmore and his close associates were somewhat surprised by his nomination as the vice presidential candidate, he was a perfect choice to balance the Whig ticket. Urbane, articulate, tall, handsome, and always impeccably dressed, Fillmore provided sophistication and, for many, a degree of reputation to offset Taylor's crude manner. Few realized the irony of their respective campaign roles, given their true backgrounds.

The election of 1848 was a close one. The Free Soilers divided the Democratic Party in New York, and with its son Fillmore on the ticket, the crucial Empire State went to the Whigs. The electoral outcome was divided by region; Taylor carried eight free states and seven slave states while Cass won seven slave states and eight free. The nation seemed to be speeding toward a crisis, but in 1848 both parties had managed to hold together. Also problematic for Taylor and Fillmore was that both houses of Congress now were controlled, albeit by slim margins, by the Democrats. Although the Whigs were right to celebrate their victory, there was great concern that sectional hostility might disrupt the country. Taylor and Fillmore were viewed with suspicion on both sides; Northerners of both parties were leery of a Southern slaveholder in office while Southerners were left wondering about Fillmore's dogged opposition to the Mexican War, Texas statehood, and slavery in the territories.

Hence, as Taylor stood before his supporters in the bitter cold that day in March, he understood that it would take every ounce of political acumen to survive in the polarized climate of Washington. Slavery in the territories, without doubt, was the most pressing matter that Congress would take up in its next session. The Wilmot Proviso remained the option championed by many Northerners, while Southerners claimed that any such legislation might mean secession. There were other slavery-related issues. Southern politicians for years had complained about the lack of legal support for the recapture of escaped slaves. Northern state legislatures and courts, they claimed, had passed laws making it difficult—and in some cases impossible—to retrieve escapees. An influential group of Southerners wanted a new federal law that would forbid anyone from aiding and abetting runaways. Northerners howled that those Southerners who tended to support "states' rights" suddenly wanted the national government to force sovereign states to change their laws. The issue of fugitive slaves sparked a heated controversy that would cry out for resolution during the Taylor and Fillmore administrations.

The sudden population explosion in California as a result of the Gold Rush in 1849 was an unanticipated complication to an already difficult problem. In 1848, President Polk, in what clearly was an effort to encourage settlement, had helped to create a national craze by mentioning publicly that unknown quantities of gold lay buried in California for those who had the resolve to find it. The response was overwhelming. In 1849, about 80,000 prospectors poured into the territory, and small settlements such as San Francisco were transformed into cities in a matter of months. Soon the population had reached the size necessary for statehood and applied for admission, as a free state. Naturally, the issue of slavery became central to the debate. Most Southerners had no expectations that California would become a slave state, but the issue quickly became a bargaining chip in the debate over other issues.

Also part of the dispute was the increasing outrage among some Northerners over the existence of slavery in Washington, D.C. Abolitionists had targeted the eradication of slavery in the capital since the early 1840s; as the debates over slavery in the West polarized, increasing numbers of Northern voters began to support efforts to ban slavery in the District of Columbia. The fact that slavery was a common scene there, abolitionists argued, was an international embarrassment and a mockery of American ideals of liberty. Southerners responded that slaveholders had every right to transport their property, including slaves, into Washington. A bill to abolish slavery, or at least the trade of slaves, in the capital would soon be introduced in Congress.

While slavery dominated politics during the Taylor and Fillmore administrations, there were other challenges. Foreign affairs received a great deal of attention from both men. At midcentury, the United States was only starting to come to terms with its own power. Relations with foreign states, especially the European powers of England and Spain, became of great concern. One area of controversy was Central America, where American investors had begun to travel and dreamed of a canal that would link the two great oceans. The British, who had influence and economic interests in the region, were committed to being an active player in the construction of any trans-Isthmian canal. Voices of protest against British expansionism in Central America grew loud during these years, with some even calling for war. Taylor and Fillmore would face the predicament of ensuring American strength in the Western Hemisphere while seeking to avoid war with England.

The Caribbean was also a place of controversy. As Americans grew more confident of their national strength, many expansionists began to consider the acquisition of Cuba. This key possession of the slowly decaying Spanish empire became the target of many who believed that the United States was destined to take control of the island from its European colonizers. Taylor and Fillmore were both wholly unsupportive of any military action against Spain. Yet a significant number of expansionists, especially in the South, were tantalized by the prospect of revolution in Cuba and sought to aid efforts to overthrow the Spanish government there. The administration had to find a way to deal with those who would disrupt Spanish-American relations while attempting to respect the right of private citizens to become involved in foreign developments.

Taylor, understanding the challenges he faced, chose words carefully during his inauguration. Above all, he sought to strike a chord of national unity. For the most part, he stressed the authority of Congress to resolve the issues at hand and resolved to follow the Constitution is all matters. Such a tepid speech no doubt was necessary given the nature of politics in 1849; however, Taylor's words were not mere calculation. He truly believed that the presidency should be not a vehicle for political change, but rather a guardian of the Constitution and an office that bowed to the will of the legislature on most matters. During the first year of his administration, Taylor consistently applied this conservative rhetoric to the political controversies of the era. Critics, then and now, attacked Taylor for inaction and lack of leadership.

An evaluation of Taylor's leadership has proven difficult given the brevity of his service. He died rather suddenly, in July 1850, in the days following a July 4 celebration in Washington. Taylor had been exhausted and depressed in the difficult weeks leading up to the Fourth. Southerners sought to combine California statehood with a compromise that would extend the size of Texas into eastern New Mexico and guarantee a new fugitive slave law. Taylor's position, with which most Northern Whigs agreed, was that California statehood, and all other issues, should be decided on their own merits and not as part of a bargain between sections. When Florida Senator Henry S. Foote and others sponsored an "omnibus bill" that brought all these measures together for a single vote, Taylor spoke against it and even contemplated the dismissal of some of his cabinet who agreed with the omnibus compromise. Accusations from Southern Democrats that Taylor had betrayed his region and had come under the sway of Northern interests became commonplace during the summer. Southerners were also beginning to talk of secession if California were admitted as a free state without compromise measures as part of the bill. Washington newspapers began to wonder if the Union would hold together in such difficult times.

Vice President Fillmore, however, would be the man to determine the outcome of the crisis. During the day-long celebrations on the Fourth of July, Taylor had responded to the intense heat by consuming large quantities of cherries and ice-cold milk. Later in the day he complained of stomach pain, which grew steadily worse throughout the evening and into the next morning. Doctors diagnosed "cholera morbus," and prescribed large doses of a mercury compound and opium to relieve the pain. After a couple of days of improvement, the president's health declined again. On Tuesday, July 9, following more mercury and forced bleeding, Zachary Taylor died. The funeral, held in Washington, was a splendorous but solemn affair. Among others, Henry Clay, Lewis Cass, and Missouri Senator Thomas Hart Benton—all three passionate political enemies—served as pallbearers. For a short time, regional differences were put aside to honor the deceased president.

Presidents Taylor and Fillmore deserve credit for their leadership during a period of crisis. Fillmore continued the policy of promoting the resolution of these major issues separately; in the end, this policy was adopted as support for the omnibus bill languished. Congress approved, and Fillmore passed into law, a bill establishing statehood for California, a bill that settled boundary disputes between Texas and New Mexico, a new fugitive slave law, and a ban on the trading of slaves in Washington, D.C. Each of the bills met with regional opposition, but each did indeed pass, and the country celebrated the resolution of a crisis that had threatened the Union. No one knew then that the sectional crisis was only delayed for a decade. For the remaining years of his term in office, Fillmore served ably.

By 1852, however, Fillmore had made clear that he had no intention to run for the presidency. The decision was personal, not political. The past four years had been difficult, to say the least, and Fillmore was satisfied with his achievements. The decision proved to be a politically astute one, however. The Whig Party was badly divided. Northern Whigs, at least, could understand Taylor's support of such outrages as the Fugitive Slave Law—he was, after all, a Southern slaveholder. Fillmore's support, however, was characterized by Northern Whigs as a ploy to maintain southern backing at the expense of morality. During the last two years of his presidency, Fillmore endured vituperative attacks from the Northern wing of his own party. In 1852, the Whigs managed to nominate another hero of the Mexican War, General Winfield Scott. However, the party's divisions were too great to overcome. Scott lost the election to the Democrat candidate Franklin Pierce; the Whig Party would dissolve before the next presidential election.

SLAVERY IN NEWLY ACQUIRED TERRITORIES

The status of slavery in the Western territories acquired as a result of the Mexican War was the most pressing issue facing the Taylor and Fillmore administrations. Many Northerners believed that regardless of conditions in the South, slavery should not be allowed into California and the Southwest on political and moral grounds. From an economic standpoint, there was little reason for Southerners to support the extension of slavery into areas where slave labor was little in demand. However, as debate polarized in the 1840s, many Southern politicians took the view that territories were the shared property of all Americans, and that the right of citizens to carry personal property, including slaves, could not be abridged by the government.

In 1846, David Wilmot, a Democrat from Pennsylvania, further heightened the tension by proposing that slavery be excluded from all newly acquired territories, even those below the 36° 30' line established in the 1820 Missouri Compromise. Naturally, the Wilmot Proviso sparked a heated debate that continued on into Taylor's presidency. Members of Congress on both sides understood the importance of the issue. These territories eventually would apply for statehood, when their populations reached the required amount, which meant that the balance in Congress between slave states and free states would be altered.

The process of determining the status of slavery in these territories was quite murky. States, of course, had the sovereignty to accept or exclude slavery as each saw fit. Territories, though, were not states, and multiple interpretations existed as to what this meant. President Taylor did everything he could to maintain a centrist position on the issue. He and Fillmore both tended to support the position of "popular sovereignty," first championed by Democrats Lewis Cass and Stephen A. Douglas. The inhabitants of these territories, the argument ran, had the right to determine their own laws, even though these areas had yet to achieve statehood. By placing the burden of the decision on the territories themselves, political leaders in Washington could avoid taking a strong stand on such a divisive issue. Furthermore, popular sovereignty resonated well with those who believed in local decision making.

The gold rush brought these arguments to a head, as the population of California surged and qualified the territory for statehood. Hence an argument that had been somewhat theoretical became, in 1849, suddenly very real. Northerners howled at the prospect of California being admitted as a slave state. There were virtually no slaves in California, and much of the area lay north of the Missouri Compromise line. Taylor, who was little trusted by Northerners because of his slaveholding background, wanted most of all to appease the Northern wing of his party without alienating his Southern support. This was not an easy task, and Taylor usually chose to avoid speaking out on the issue for fear of angering one side or the other.

When Taylor did speak, he did so cautiously, as in the following speech to the Senate in January 1850. The president understood that the issue was clear with regard to states; the controversy was about the rights of territories to make decisions about slavery. For that reason, Taylor's strategy was to focus on immediate statehood for California and to look toward eventual statehood for other territories of the Mexican Cession. Above all, he sought to avoid conflict that threatened that Union, and in the speech he attacks those who offered "extreme" positions that fueled division—a set of re-marks aimed mostly at Northerners who supported the Wilmot Proviso.

Taylor's position was challenged on both sides by members of congress and newspaper editors who were less concerned with regional balance. Many Northerners rejected the notion that Congress did not have the right to intervene in the territories. In the passage below, taken from an 1849 speech in the House of Representatives, James Wilson of New Hampshire takes the position that the federal government has every right to block slav-ery in these areas. Wilson echoed abolitionists who argued that slavery was not only immoral, but that it also was a plague that corroded all aspects of humanity. He explains to his audience that extending slavery into new re-gions of the West would be identical to the actions of the British King George III, who refused requests by some colonists to abolish slavery prior to the American Revolution. Wilson also warns his fellow congressmen that those who would be responsible for expanding slavery into new areas would answer to history as well.

The issue of slavery in the new territories eventually became one part of the Compromise of 1850. California was admitted to the Union as a free state, while the status of slavery in the territories of New Mexico and Ari-zona would be left open for the time being. Whigs and Democrats cele-brated, but the issue was far from resolved. Southerners continued to argue that territories were constitutionally bound to allow slaveholders into these regions. Northerners argued that such a practice would violate the spirit of the Missouri Compromise by abolishing the North-South line sep-arating free and slave areas. While the immediate crisis abated after 1850, the issue created much enmity that festered and ultimately exploded into Southern secession a decade later.

ZACHARY TAYLOR, ON SLAVERY IN THE WESTERN TERRITORIES (WASHINGTON, DC, JANUARY 23, 1850)

I did not hesitate to express to the people of those Territories my desire that each Territory should, if prepared to comply with the requisitions of the Constitution of the United States, form a plan of a State constitution and submit the same to Congress with a prayer for admission into the Union as a State, but I did not anticipate, suggest, or authorize the establishment of any such government without the assent of Congress, nor did I authorize any Government agent or officer to interfere with or exercise any influence or control over the election of delegates or over any convention in making or modifying their domestic institutions or any of the provisions of their proposed constitution. On the contrary, the instructions given by my orders were that in all measures of domestic policy adopted by the people of Cali-fornia must originate solely with themselves; that while the Executive of the United States was desirous to protect them in the formation of any government republican in its character, to be at the proper time submitted to Congress, yet it was to be distinctly understood that the plan of such a government must at the same time be the result of their own deliberate choice and originate with themselves, without the interference of the Executive.

In advising an early application by the people of these Territories for admission as States I was actuated principally by an earnest desire to afford to the wisdom and patriotism of Congress the opportunity of avoiding occasions of bitter and angry dissensions among the people of the United States.

Under the Constitution every State has the right of establishing and from time to time altering its municipal laws and domestic institutions independently of every other State and of the General Government, subject only to the prohibitions and guaranties expressly set forth in the Constitution of the United States. The subjects thus left exclusively to the respective States were not designed or expected to become topics of national agitation. Still, as under the Constitution Congress has the power to make all needful rules and regulations respecting the Territories of the United States, every acquisition of territory has led to the discussions on the question whether the system of involuntary servitude which prevails in many of the States should or should not be prohibited in that territory. The periods of excitement from this cause which have heretofore occurred have been safely passed, but during the interval, or whatever length, which may elapse before the admission of the Territories ceded by Mexico as States it appears probable that similar excitement will prevail to an undue extent.

Under these circumstances I thought, and still think, that it was my duty to endeavor to put it in the power of Congress, by the admission of California and New Mexico as States, to remove all occasion for the unnecessary agitation of the public mind.

Should Congress, when California shall present herself for incorporation into the Union, annex a condition to her admission as State affecting her domestic institutions contrary to the wishes of her people, and even compel her temporarily to comply with it, yet the State could change her constitution at any time after admission when to her it should seem expedient. Any attempt to deny to the people of the State the right of self-government in a matter which peculiarly affects themselves will infallibly be regarded by them as an invasion of their rights, and, upon the principles laid down in our Declaration of Independence, they will certainly be sustained by the great mass of the American people. To assert that they are a conquered people and must as a State submit to the will of their conquerors in this regard will meet with no cordial response among American freemen. Great numbers of them are native citizens of the United States, not inferior to the rest of our country men in intelligence and patriotism, and no language of menace to restrain them in the exercise of an undoubted right, substantially guaranteed to them by the treaty of cession itself, shall ever be uttered by me or encouraged and sustained by persons acting under my authority. It is to be expected that in the residue of the territory ceded to us by Mexico the people residing there will at the time of their incorporation in the Union as a State settle all questions of domestic policy to suit themselves.

A Compilation of the Messages and Papers of the Presidents, vol. 6, James D. Richardson, ed. (New York: Bureau of National Literature, Inc., 1897), 2566–2568.

REPRESENTATIVE JAMES WILSON (W-NH), SPEECH OPPOSING SLAVERY IN THE WEST (WASHINGTON, DC, FEBRUARY 16, 1849)

I come now to the consideration of the general question of the power and duty of Congress in regard to the subject of slavery in the territories. That Congress has the power to legislate for the territories, I cannot admit of a reasonable doubt. I look upon it now as merely a question of expediency, whether Congress will or not legislate upon that subject. I do not stop to argue about its Constitutionality. The time for argument on that question has long since gone by. That power had been exercised by Congress; had been recognized and acted upon ever since the adoption of the Constitution. If Congress can do anything for the territories, it can make laws in relation to the subject of slavery, to have effect within the territories, as well as anything else. Slavery cannot exist anywhere except by positive law, it being a derogation of natural right. Now, sir, I regard slavery as a blighting, withering curse upon every country with which it is infested. It passes over a country like a prairie fire; it burns up every green thing on the face of the earth, and, not content with that, it penetrates into the soil itself, and burns out its very power of productiveness. You cannot, Mr. Chairman, look out from one of the windows of this Capitol, in any direction, and let your eye traverse the surrounding country, without seeing convincing evidence of this truth. The earth itself, the dilapidated buildings and ruined fences, become vocal in attestation of it. You cannot walk through the public market place of this city without seeing full and convincing proof of it. The dumb beasts, yea, even the yokes and gears and implements of husbandry on the slave plantations all around us, speak out and bear unconflicting testimony of the blighting effects of slavery. Is this institution, then, with such characteristics and attendant evil, to be sent into the territories over which Congress has jurisdiction, by the exercise of law-making power? Or, in other words, shall it be permitted to go and spread itself over those territories to curse and ruin them, when Congress has the power to prevent it?

The American Colonies passed laws to restrain the slave trade here before the Revolution, and asked the royal approval of those laws, which the British King, influenced by the base and sordid motives if his English subjects, withheld. The colonists, seventy-five years ago, were loud in their condemnation of the King for withholding his approval. Shall we, the members of an American Congress, in a free republican government, in this age of Christian light and Christian philanthropy, shall we send an institution to curse and crush the people of our territories, of which our fathers justly complained of their governors for sending upon them three-fourths of a century gone by? . . .

I hold that Congress is bound to take care of the territories, and so execute the trust as will best promote the permanent interest of those who may hereafter be entitled to the beneficial use. As a member of this Congress, I feel that I sustain a part of that responsibility, and it is my desire to acquit myself worthily in meeting it. I desire to acquit myself that my own conscience will not upbraid me, and that, when I shall pass away, no reproach shall fall upon me, or my children after me, for my acts here upon this momentous question. I have, sir, an only son, now a little fellow, whom some of this committee may have seen here. Think you, that when I am gone, and he shall grow up to manhood, and shall come forward to act his part among the citizens of the country, I will leave it to be cast in this teeth, as a reproach, that his father voted to send slavery into those territories? No; oh, no! I look reverently up to the Father of us all, and fervently implore Him to spare that child that reproach. May God forbid it!

The North are not disposed to trespass or interfere with the rights of the South. Where slavery exists within the States, and recognized by the Constitution of the United States, the northern people claim no right to interfere with it by any action of this Government. The people ask no action by Congress on the subject of slavery within the States. But gentlemen need not ask me my vote to extend the institution of slavery one single inch beyond its present boundaries. Did I say *an inch*, Mr. Chairman? Aye, I would not extend it one-sixteenth-thousandth part of a hair's breadth. I would not extend it, because it would be doing an irretrievable wrong to my fellow man; because it would be doing irreparable wrong to those territories for which we are now to legislate; because it would be doing violence to nature and to nature's God; and because it would a wicked and wanton betrayal of the trust confided to me by the free, intelligent constituency which had done me the honor to send me here.

Congressional *Globe*, 30th Congress, 2nd Session, February 16, 1849, 195.

THE FUGITIVE SLAVE ACT

Disputes over slavery in the West spilled over into other issues relating to the "peculiar institution." Southerners for years had complained that Northern states violated federal law, the Fugitive Slave Act of 1793, which required the return of escaped slaves to their masters. There were various ways that state governments and local law enforcement could circumvent the law. One method was so-called personal-liberty laws that guaranteed a trial by jury for escaped slaves before being returned to the alleged slave-holder. Another set of laws, enacted by a some Northern states, prohibited state officials from participating in either the capture or imprisonment of escaped slaves. Northerners claimed that these laws did not change the law regarding fugitive slaves but only regulated the activities of local officials.

Southerners, of course, claimed that personal-liberty laws were a means of skirting federal law and began to call for new, more stringent legislation. In 1850, as slavery in the new territories, California statehood, and other issues were being deliberated, Southerners brought forth a new fugitive slave proposal. To begin, escaped slaves brought into custody were to be brought before a federally appointed commission, rather than a state or local court, to rule on cases. This commission also would have the authority to summon any citizen to aid in an investigation. Additionally, law enforcement officials who failed to enforce the law would be subject to a $1,000 fine; any citizen found to be harboring an escaped slave could be fined up to $1,000, face up to six months imprisonment, and pay civil damages to the slaveholder. No jury trials would hear any case concerning escaped slaves.

The Fugitive Slave Act of 1850 passed as part of the Compromise but clearly was not achieved in the spirit of cooperation. A significant number of Northern legislators abstained from the vote; those who did vote over-whelmingly opposed it. However, near-unanimous support among Southerners in both parties pushed the bill through. President Taylor's position was consistent with his approach to other issues—he would sign the bill if Congress passed it. Personally, Taylor agreed with the sentiment of the law and supported any legislation that would contribute to Compromise on other issues.

Predictably, abolitionists were outraged. Northern newspapers railed that the legislation was proof that Southerners dominated the legislature. Public literary figures, including Ralph Waldo Emerson, James Russell Lowell, James Greenleaf Whittier, and Henry Wadsworth Longfellow, published condemnations. Even a few Southerners, including Senator Cassius M. Clay of Kentucky, the son of a slaveholder, criticized the law for its severity. In the passage that follows, the renowned theologian and abolitionist Theodore Parker offers his critique of the law by writing an open letter to President Fillmore. Parker makes reference to the natural rights of individuals as voiced in the Declaration of Independence and offers examples of escaped slaves he has known to personalize the potential damage done to fugitive slaves. As did many abolitionists, Parker invoked religion to point up the immorality of slavery and the Fugitive Slave Law.

Southerners naturally applauded the bill as an indication that Congress supported the enforcement of longstanding federal law. Senator Henry S. Foote, a Democrat from Alabama, speaks to Congress on the necessity of the law. Foote bases his argument on law and justice—justice for slaveholders who had a constitutional right to their property.

The Fugitive Slave Law of 1850, hailed as part of the Union's salvation, created even more division between the sections than before. Public protest in the North at times resulted in mobs. In Boston, a large group turned out to free a Virginia slave, Anthony Burns, who was to be returned to his master. Federal troops were deployed to protect officials as they transported Burns to a ship. The scene was repeated in Pennsylvania, where President Fillmore was forced to send in military support to protect a jail that held an arrested slave. If anything, the law brought more Northerners into the abolitionist fold, many of whom had been unconcerned with the issue before then.

Northern states also continued to challenge the Fugitive Slave Act in their legislatures. Some passed new laws in the 1850s, which attempted to nullify the law by prohibiting state officials from enforcing it. South Carolina, in its proclamation of secession in 1860, made reference to Northern states that continued to ignore federal law. The Fugitive Slave Laws—both the 1793 and 1850 versions—were repealed in 1864.

SENATOR HENRY S. FOOTE (D-AL), SPEECH IN SUPPORT OF THE FUGITIVE SLAVE ACT (WASHINGTON, DC, AUGUST 21, 1850)

Mr. President, I have no intention of entering largely into this discussion. The State which I have the honor in part to represent on this floor, is not so specially interested in this matter as are those slave States which border on the free States of the Union. I have been willing, more than willing to defer to the judgement of gentlemen representing those border States here. I have been inclined to give my aid and support to any which might originate with them, which they supposed would prove more efficient for the attainment of the object that I trust we all desire to see accomplished.

. . . My view of the matter can be very briefly expressed. It is this: In accordance with the argument of the honorable Senator from North Carolina, there is an absolute obligation upon the Federal Government to see that fugitives from justice and fugitives from labor are restored to the States from which they fled. Nobody will undertake to dispute that that obligation is absolute. Those who framed the Federal Constitution believed doubtless, as I certainly believe, that the Federal Government, with the power bestowed upon it by the Constitution, would be able to carry into effect this particular clause. They believed that they had supplied the Government with adequate means for the enforcement of this provision of the Constitution. I am satisfied they were not mistaken upon that point. This Government is sufficiently potent to secure justice to the slaveholders of the South in connection with this subject. Yet I think that experience so far has demonstrated that no law that can be devised that does not contain some such provision as this will prove efficient. I entertain the confident opinion—and I do not see who can doubt the correctness of that opinion who heard the developments made yesterday by the Senator from Maryland [Mr. Pratt] connected with the history of his own State—that no law which we ever will devise will prove efficient unless it contains some such provision as this. I feel satisfied that if this amendment shall be adopted, and it shall become a part of this law, in the enactment of which I trust we shall shortly participate, it will be efficient for that purpose. I think none can doubt that it will prove efficient if duly enforced. If the Government shall neglect to perform its duty in this matter, shall neglect to pay obedience to the absolute obligation imposed on it by the Constitution, is it not just, it is not right and proper, that those who suffer by its criminal inaction of this subject should be recompensed by the Government? Not on account of having simply lost property in the ordinary way, but on account of having suffered by the mischievous nonaction of this Government, because of its failure to perform its duty under the Constitution.

These being my views, I cannot hesitate to vote for this amendment. I do not see the least ground upon which to rest a shadow of an argument against the constitutionality of the proposition. In my judgement it is gross neglect on the part of Government not to devise proper means for attaining this important object. So far as nonaction on this subject can be denounced as unconstitutional, I shall be prepared to denounce it as unconstitutional and repugnant to the spirit and provisions of the Constitution.

Congressional *Globe*, Appendix, 31st Congress, 1st Session, August 21, 1850, 1601.

THEODORE PARKER, LETTER TO MILLARD FILLMORE REGARDING THE FUGITIVE SLAVE ACT (BOSTON, MA, NOVEMBER 21, 1850)

To President Fillmore
Nov. 21.

Honored Sir,—This letter is one which requires only time to read. I cannot expect you to reply to it. I am myself a clergy-man in this city; not one of those, unfortunately, who are much respected, but, on the contrary, I have an ill name and am one of the most odious men in this State. No man out of the political arena is so much hated in Massachusetts as myself. I think this hatred is chargeable only to certain opinions which I entertain relative to theology and to morals. Still, I think I have never been accused of wanting reverence for God, or love for man, or disregard to truth and to justice. I say all this by way of preface, for I need not suppose you know anything of me.

I have a large religious society in this town, composed of "all sorts and conditions of men," fugitive slaves who do not legally own the nails on their fingers and cannot read the Lord's Prayer; and also men and women of wealth and fine cultivation. I wish to inform you of the difficulty in which we (the church and myself) are placed by the new Fugitive Slave Law. There are several fugitive slaves in the society; they have committed no wrong; they have the same "unalienable right to life, liberty, and the pursuit of happiness" that you have, they naturally look to me for advice in their affliction. They are strangers, and ask me to take them in; hungry, and beg me to deed them; thirsty, and would have me give them drink; they are naked, and look to me for clothing; sick, and wish me to visit them. Yes: they are ready to perish, and ask their life at my hands. Even the letter of the most Jewish of the Gospels makes Christ say, "Inasmuch as ye have not done it unto one of the least of these, ye have not done it unto me!" They come to me as their Christian minister, and ask me to do to them only what Christianity evidently requires.

But *your* law will punish me with a fine of 1000 dollars and imprisonment for six months if I take in one of these strangers, feed and clothe these naked and hungry children of want; nay, if I visit them when they are sick, come unto when they are in prison, or help them, "directly or indirectly," when they are ready to perish! Suppose I should refuse to do for them what Christianity demands. I will not say what I should think of myself, but what would you say. You would say that I was a *scoundrel*, that I was *really* an infidel (my theological brethren call me so), that I deserved a gaol for six years! You would say right. But if I do as you must know that I ought, then your law strips me of my property, tears me from my wife, and shuts me in a gaol. Perhaps I do not value the obligations of religion so much as my opponents of another faith; but I must say I would rather lie all my life in a gaol, and starve there, than refuse to protect one of these parishioners of mine. Do not call me a fanatic; I am a cool and sober man, *but I must reverence that laws of God, come of that what will come. I must be true to my religion.*

I send you a little sermon of mine; you will find the story of a fugitive slave whom I have known. He is now in Quebec, in the service of one of the most eminent citizens of that city. He is a descendent of one of our revolutionary generals, and members of my society aided him in his flight; others concealed him, helped him to freedom. Can *you* think they did wrong? Can you think of the Declaration of Independence—of its self-evident truths; can you think of Christianity, and then blame these men? The Hungarians found much natural sympathy all over the United States, though some men in Boston took sides with Austria; the nation is ready to receive Kossuth; but what is Austrian tyranny to slavery in America? The Sultan of Turkey has the thanks of all the liberal governments of Europe for hiding the outcasts of Hungary, and can you blame us for starting "Joseph" and helping him to Canada? I know it is not possible.

William Craft and Ellen were parishioners of mine; they have been at my house. I married them a fortnight ago this day; after the ceremony I put a Bible and then a sword into William's hands, and told him the use of each. When the slave-hunters were here, suppose I had helped the man to escape out of their hands: suppose I had taken the woman to my house, and sheltered her there till the storm had passed by? Should *you* think I did a thing worthy of fine or imprisonment? If I took all *peaceful* measures to thwart the kidnappers (legal kidnappers) of their prey, would that be a thing for punishment? You cannot think that I am to stand by and see my own church carried off to slavery and do nothing to hinder such a wrong.

There hangs beside me in my library, as I write, the gun my grandfather fought with at the battle of Lexington—he was a captain on that occasion—and also the musket he captured from a British soldier on that the day, the first taken in the war for Independence. If I would not peril my property, my liberty, nay, my life, to keep my own parishioners out of slavery, then I would throw away these trophies, and should think I was the son of some coward, and not a brave man's child. There are many who think as I do: many that say it—most of the men I preach to are of this way of thinking. (Yet one these bailed Hughes, the slave-hunter from Georgia, out of prison!)

There is a minister who preaches to the richest church in Boston. He is a New Hampshire man, and writes as any New Hampshire politician; but even he says "he would conceal a fugitive, of course." Not five of the eighty Protestant ministers of Boston would refuse. I only write to you to remind you of the difficulties in our way; if need is, we will suffer any penalties you may put upon us, BUT WE MUST KEEP THE LAW OF GOD.

The Life and Correspondences of Theodore Parker, vol. 2, John Weiss, ed. (New York: D. Appleton and Co., 1864), pp. 100–103.

SLAVERY AND THE SLAVE TRADE IN WASHINGTON, DC

The growing conflict over slavery fueled a growing fire of antislavery sentiment in the northern United States. Abolitionists argued that while little might be done to end slavery in the Southern states, the fact that slavery was still present in Washington, DC was a moral outrage and an international embarrassment. Northern congressional leaders proposed a ban on slavery in the capital but never had support to pass such a measure. Southerners argued that the property rights of slaveholders had to be respected in the capital. In fact, some Southern congressmen owned slaves themselves and argued that such a law would prevent them from entering the District of Columbia while Congress was in session.

Antislavery activists recognized that an end to slavery in Washington would fail to pass the legislature, so they turned to the slave trade, which also was present in the area. This proposal had better possibilities. The United States government had prohibited the overseas trade of slaves in

1808, and a ban on the trade of slaves in the capital would in no way affect Southerners who owned slaves. Given the growing intensity of the debate, Southerners tended to oppose the measure as yet another step in the Northern effort to abolish slavery. In the following speech, Representative Horace Mann of Massachusetts appeals to lawmakers to consider the moral and international ramifications of continuing to allow the slave trade to exist in Washington. He portrays the United States as a shameful nation that has maintained and sanctioned slavery, even while nations throughout the world have recognized the evils of the institution. Mann describes slaveholding states as the contemporary version of those areas of Africa that had carried out a slave trade in past centuries and claims that even these areas, unlike the United States, have become enlightened to the injustices of slavery. Mann also points out that Liberia, an area of West Africa recolonized by former American slaves, has outlawed slavery and thus is more progressive than the United States itself.

Senator Jefferson Davis of Mississippi, who later became president of the Confederacy during the Civil War, responds with a legal explanation as to why the United States government could not ban the slave trade in the District of Columbia. Despite what abolitionists argue, slaves were privately held property that could be transported anywhere in the United States, particularly to the nation's capital. By appealing to the sanctity of property rights, Davis argues that those who oppose a ban on slavery in the District of Columbia are seeking to take away one of the fundamental guarantees of the Constitution. Interestingly, both Mann and Davis promote the concept of freedom. For Mann, the principle of political freedom requires the abolition of slavery. Davis maintains that Southerners have the freedom to transport property as guaranteed by the Constitution. The debate serves as a microcosm of the broad debate over slavery.

President Taylor, as he often did on slavery issues, tried to remain neutral. Both he and Vice President Fillmore were anxious to see any progress on several issues that gripped Congress; if a ban on slavery were to pass, Taylor was prepared to sign it into law. Fillmore, seen by Southerners as potentially less friendly to the cause of slaveholders, agreed that if both sections could agree on a bill he would not block it. For both men, the bill served as an important bargaining chip to be used to smooth over differences on the most pressing matters—those regarding the western territories.

The issue became another part of the Compromise of 1850, which addressed the status of slavery in the new state of California, but hardly was passed in a spirit of compromise. In the Senate, Northerners voted unanimously for the measure, which was enough to pass the legislation by a very narrow margin in the face of overwhelming opposition by Southerners. Those who opposed the measure echoed Davis in asserting that the law was an affront to the freedom of slaveholders and further convinced Southern politicians that as long as the Northern states held a majority in Congress, there existed a threat to slavery.

REPRESENTATIVE HORACE MANN (W-MA), SPEECH OPPOSING SLAVERY (WASHINGTON, DC, FEBRUARY 23, 1850)

I frankly avow, at the outset, that the bill provides for one part only of an evil whose remedy, as it seems to me, is not only the object of a reasonable desire, but of a rightful and legal demand. The bill proposes the abolition, not of slavery, but only of the slave trade in the District of Columbia. My argument will go to show, that within the limits of this District, slavery ought not to exist in fact, and does not exist in law.

During the last fifty years, and especially during the last half of these fifty years, the world has made great advances in the principles of liberty. Human rights have been recognized, and their practical enjoyment, to some extent, secured. There is not a Government in Europe, even the most iron and despotical of them all, that has not participated in the ameliorations which characterize the present age. A noble catalogue of rights has been wrested by the British Commons from the British nobility. France and Italy have been revolutionized. Even the Pope of Rome, whose power seemed as eternal as the hills on which he was seated, has sunk under the shock. Prussia, and all the Germanic Powers, with the exception of Austria, have been half revolutionized; and even the icy despotisms of Austria and Russia are forced to relent under those central fires of liberty which burn forever in the human heart, as the central fires of the earth burn forever at its core. Great Britain has abolished African slavery throughout all her realms. France has declared that any one who shall voluntarily become the owner of a slave, or shall voluntarily continue to be the owner of a slave cast upon him by bequest or inheritance, shall cease to be a citizen of France. Denmark has abolished slavery wherever it existed in her possessions. The Bey of Tunis, acting under the light of the Mohammedan religion, has abolished it. The priests of Persia declare the sentiment to have come by tradition from Mohammad himself, "that the worst of men is the seller of men." Not only all civilized nations, but the half-civilized, the semi-civilized, the semi-barbarous, are acting under the guidance of the clearer light and the higher motives of our day. But there is one conspicuous exception; there is one Government which closes its eyes to this increasing light; which resists the persuasion of these ennobling motives; which, on the grand subject of human liberty and human rights, is stationary and even retrograde, while the whole world around is advancing; sleeps while all others are awaking; loves its darkness while all others are aspiring and ascending to a purer and brighter sky. This Government, too, is the one which is the most boastful and vainglorious of its freedom; and, if the humiliating truth must be spoken, this Government is our own. In regard to slavery in this District, where we possess the power of exclusive legislation, we stand where we stood fifty years ago. Not a single ameliorating law has been passed. In practice, we are where we were back then; in spirit, there are proofs that we have gone backward.

There are now on the surface of the globe two conspicuous places—places which are attracting the gaze of the whole civilized world—where men and women are brought from great distances to be sold, and whence they are carried to great distances to suffer the heaviest wrongs that human nature can bear. One of these places is the coast of Africa, which is among the most pagan and benighted regions of the earth; the other is the District of Columbia, the capital and seat of Government of the United States.

But, still more degrading than this, there is another contrast which we present to the whole civilized world. The very slaves upon whom we have trodden have risen above us, and their moral superiority makes our conduct ignominious. Not Europeans only, not only Arabians and Turks, are emerging from the inhumanity and the enormities of the slave traffic; but even our own slaves, transplanted to the land of their fathers, are raising barriers against the spread of the execrable commerce. On the shores of Africa, a republic is springing up, whose inhabitants were transplanted from this Egypt of bondage. And now, look at the government which these slaves have established, and contrast it with our own. They discard the institution of slavery, while we cherish it. A far greater proportion of their children than of the white children of the slave States of this Union are at school. In the metropolis of their nation, their flag does not protect the slave traffic, nor wave over the slave mart. Would to God that every opposite of this were not true in our own. Their laws punish the merchandise of human beings; our laws sanction and encourage it. They have erected, and are erecting, fortifications and military posts along the shores of the Atlantic, for seven hundred miles, to prevent pirates from invading the domain of their neighbors, and kidnapping people who, to them, are foreign nations. We open market-places here, at the centre of the nation, where, from seven hundred miles of coast, the sellers may come to sell, and where buyers may come to buy, and whence slaves are carried almost as far from their birthplace as Africa is from America. The Governor of Liberia has lately made a voyage to England and France, and entered into treaties of amity and commerce with them; and he has obtained naval forces from them. To abolish this traffic in human beings. At the same time, we are affording guarantees to the same traffic. Virginia and Maryland are to the slave trade what the interior of Africa once was. The Potomac and the Chesapeake are the American Niger and Bight of Benin; while this District is the great Government barracoon, whence the coffles are driven across the country to Alabama, or Texas, as slave ships once bore their dreadful cargoes of agony and woe across the Atlantic. The very race, then, which was first stolen, brought to this country, despoiled of all the rights which God has given them, kept in bondage for generations, but at last, after redeeming themselves, or being restored to their natural liberty in some other way, have crossed the ocean, established a government for themselves, and are now setting us an example which should cause our cheeks to blister with shame.

Congressional *Globe*, 30th Congress, 2nd Session, Appendix, February 23, 1850, 318–319.

SENATOR JEFFERSON DAVIS (D-MS), SPEECH SUPPORTING SLAVERY (WASHINGTON, DC, MARCH 23, 1850)

I find little controversy between those who have spoken on this bill, except as to the punishment which should be visited upon him who introduced his slave property into the District of Columbia. It is assumed to be an offence, and it is treated as though the only question were whether the individual who introduces a slave into the District shall be fined, or whether the slave shall be manumitted. The power to do this is not referred to any particular grant of the Constitution, but it is attempted to draw if from the fact that like power has been exercised by a State, which, being sovereign in its own territory, may have for public purposes refused, under certain conditions, to allow slaves to be introduced within its own borders. Yet what State ever legislatively refused to allow a Citizen of the United States to pass through its borders with a slave? And that is the nature of the prohibition presented here. No one expects that slaves are to be brought in the District for sale and residence here, and the whole argument directs itself to the traders who may bring slaves here, and keep them in depot with the intention of sending them elsewhere. It is then the right of transit over the District against which this bill is directed, and this is one step further than any State even in the exercise of its sovereign power, has gone. But is it to be inferred that because a sovereign State may exercise certain powers, that Congress possesses the same? The States, as sovereigns, possess all powers which they have not delegated; the Federal Government as a trustee has only those which have been granted to it. Are powers to be usurped? Are all the limitations of the Constitutions to be forgotten? And are we in fact now a consolidated Government, to be controlled by a will of a majority? The Constitution confers on Congress the power to exercise exclusive legislation over the District, within which it might meet for purposes truly and clearly connected with a seat of Government. It was not to confer on Congress the absolute or unlimited power of legislation, but to prevent any one else from legislating in a District ceded for use as the seat of Government. Therefore it must have been that exclusive power was granted. But to this exclusive power there are two limitations: first, the restrictions of the Constitution; and secondly, the intent, the motive, the purposes for which the grant was made. I deny that Congress has the power to pass any law in relation to the District of Columbia, except so far as that law may be connected with object of the grant; and if there be a reasonable doubt as to the constitutional power, the necessity should be immediate and absolute, such as involved the purpose of the grant, which would warrant its exercise.

But if the proposition which is now before us, and which is to prohibit any citizen of the United States from bringing a slave into the District, with a view thereafter of taking him into another State of the Union, be within the power of Congress, it is not derived from such necessity as I have described. If it be drawn from the power of exclusive legislation in the District, why may not we adopt a like provision in relation to every arsenal, custom-house, fort, and dock-yard? The same section of the Constitution which gives to Congress exclusive legislation over the District of Columbia gives it over the forts, arsenals, custom-houses, and dock-yards. Then if a citizen of Georgia, wishing to go to Mississippi with a slave, which he should subsequently sell, passed through a dock-yard of the United States, his slave would be emancipated by general legislation. To this extent would the power here asserted reach, whenever it should please the majority to exercise it.

This, sir, is a species of property recognized by the Constitution of the United States, and the same instrument guarantees to every citizen of the United States the right, unobstructed, to pass with every species of property through any portion of the United States. A sovereign State may forbid the introduction of certain species of property within its limits, there to remain, whether for sale or use. But I do not believe a State has the right to prevent a citizen of the United States from exercising the right of transit with any property which he may legally hold; this is one of the results of our free-trade Constitution. If, then, no State has the right to obstruct or abolish, even on her own domain, that privilege, how can it be supposed that it was intended to confer such power upon their agent? Yet we have before us a proposition to deprive citizens of the United States of the right of transit over territory surrendered to the Government of the United States solely for the purposes of a seat of Government.

Congressional *Globe*, 31st Congress, 1st Session, March 23, 1850, 1641.

AMERICANS AND REVOLUTION IN CUBA

Expansionists who championed an aggressive foreign policy in Central America held a great interest in the island of Cuba and for years entertained the idea of freeing it from Spanish control and acquiring it for the United States. President Polk, in fact, had approached the Spanish crown about purchasing the colony. Such efforts were in vain; the Spanish government, ever mindful of its gradually diminishing empire, viewed Cuba as vital for its strategic interests. Their message was clear: Spain had no plans to give up Cuba.

Nevertheless, expansionists refused to give up on an American-held Cuba. Southern newspaper editors wrote columns describing the harsh treatment of native Cubans by the Spanish colonial government and fueled rumors that a revolution to overthrow the government was seething under the surface of Cuban society. These dramatic stories were strengthened when a group of Cuban exiles in New York began raising funds for an expedition against the Spanish. For many Americans, the time to expel the Spanish from Cuba was close at hand.

The administration's position was unequivocal. Taylor and Fillmore claimed that the United States and Spain had longstanding agreements of cooperation and neutrality dating back to the years following the War of 1812. Neither man had plans to support efforts to challenge Spanish rule on the island, especially at a time when relations with England were strained and domestic issues were so inflamed. Democrats in the South complained that Taylor and Fillmore were ignoring the plight of the oppressed Cubans and cared little that a European power had a colonial possession so close to our own borders.

Criticism of the administration soon erupted into outrage. The incident began when a former Cuban official, Narciso Lopez, escaped from the island and landed in New Orleans. Lopez told a frenzied public about the atrocities in Cuba and explained that a revolution was imminent. Soon Lopez was organizing his own expedition to Cuba and received money from newspapers and other backers. Lopez gained the support of a few U.S. military officers in New Orleans; soon he was collecting volunteers to participate in an invasion of Cuba. Expansionists called on the administration to support his efforts.

When Taylor not only made clear his opposition to such filibusters but also declared that private citizens who engaged in such activities were to be prosecuted, Southerners invoked the concept of individual rights to oppose the policy. Expansionists argued that regardless of the American government's position on Cuba, individuals had every right to participate in expeditions, whether through monetary support or active engagement. Taylor, along with Secretary of State John M. Clayton, held that only the United States government had the authority to engage in international affairs. David Yulee, a Democrat from Florida, argues in the following speech that private citizens have the right to participate in foreign expeditions if they so choose. Yulee also makes a creative argument that once the rebels had landed, Cuba, technically, was engaged in civil war. The United States, he claims, had violated its policy of neutrality in dealing with foreign civil wars by actively working to thwart the rebellion.

President Fillmore spoke out harshly against any efforts to overthrow the Spanish in Cuba. In his second annual message, he opened by addressing the question of Cuban independence from Spanish rule. First, he describes the anti-Spanish efforts as exaggerated in importance. Additionally, Fillmore takes pains to describe the mission to Cuba as illegal and without sanction by United States authorities. He leaves little doubt that the administration's policy would continue to be one of cooperation with Spain. This cooperation might include aid in putting down any future rebellions that have ties to Americans. Fillmore states that private citizens should not have the ability to place the entire nation at peril by fomenting war with another country. For Fillmore, the issue was one of nationalism. Democracy, in his view, did not mean that individuals could intervene in foreign affairs that might affect the country as a whole.

In the short run, the administration won the argument. Lopez launched an expedition that went very badly. Only one of three ships that left New Orleans, in the spring of 1850, eventually made it to Cuba. The would-be liberators were easily defeated; Lopez was executed and many of his men were imprisoned in Spain. Although considered lawbreakers by the administration, they were heroes in Louisiana. Fillmore, sensing public sentiment, negotiated for the return of those American citizens who were captured during the expedition.

In the long run, the expansionists managed to get their war with Spain over Cuba, but that conflict took place forty-eight years later. With the growing sectional conflict over slavery and the eventual outbreak of the Civil War, thoughts of conquest in Cuba faded from the scene for decades.

MILLARD FILLMORE, SENATE SPEECH ON THE CUBAN EXPEDITION (WASHINGTON, DC, DECEMBER 2, 1851)

Since the close of the last Congress certain Cubans and other foreigners resident in the United States, who were more or less concerned in the previous invasion of Cuba, instead of being discouraged by its failure have again abused the hospitality of this country by making it the scene of the equipment of another military expedition against that possession of Her Catholic Majesty, in which they were countenanced, aided, and joined by citizens of the United States. On receiving intelligence that such designs were entertained, I lost no time in issuing such instructions to the proper officers of the United States as seemed to be called for the occasion. By the proclamation a copy of which is herewith submitted I also warned those who might be in danger of being inveigled into this scheme of its unlawful character and of the penalties which they would incur. . . .

Before the expedition set out, and probably before it was organized, a slight insurrectionary movement, which appeared to have been soon suppressed, had taken place in the eastern quarter of Cuba. The importance of this movement was, unfortunately, so much exaggerated in the accounts of it published in this country that these adventurers seem to have been led to believe that the Creole population of the island not only desired to throw off the authority of the mother country, but had resolved upon that step and had begun a well-concerted enterprise for effecting it. The persons engaged in the expedition were generally young and ill informed. The steamer in which they embarked left New Orleans stealthily and without a clearance. After touching at Key West, she proceeded to the coast of Cuba, and on the night between the 11th and 12th of August landed the persons on board at Playtas, within about 20 leagues of Havana. . . .

According to the record of the examination, the prisoners all admitted to offenses charged against them, of being hostile invaders of the island. At the time of their trial and execution the main body of the invaders was still in the field making war upon the Spanish authorities and Spanish subjects. After the lapse of some days, being overcome by the Spanish troops, they dispersed on the 24th of August. Lopez, their leader, was captured some days after, and executed on the 1st of September. Many of his remaining followers were killed or died of hunger, and the rest were made prisoners. Of these none appear to have been tried or executed. Several of them were pardoned upon application of their friends and others, and the rest, about 160 in number, were sent to Spain. Of the final disposition made of these we have no official information.

Such is the melancholy result of this illegal and ill-fated expedition. Thus thoughtless young men have been induced by false and fraudulent representations to violate the law of their country through rash and unfounded expectations of assisting to accomplish political revolutions in other states, and have lost their lives in the undertaking. . . .

Although these offenders against the laws have forfeited the protection of their country, yet the Government may, so far as consistent with its obligations to other countries and its fixed purpose to maintain and enforce the laws, entertain sympathy for their unoffending families and friends, as well as a feeling of compassion for themselves. Accordingly, no proper effort has been spared and none will be spared to procure the release of such citizens of the United States engaged in this awful enterprise as are now in confinement in Spain; but it is to be hoped that such interposition with the Government of that country may not be considered as affording any ground of expectation that the Government of the United States will hereafter feel itself under any obligation or duty to intercede for the liberation or pardon of such persons as are flagrant offenders against the law of nations and the laws of the United States. These laws must be executed. If we desire to maintain our respectability among the nations of the earth, it behooves us to follow as far as may be the violation of those acts within condign punishment.

No individuals have a right to hazard the peace of a country or to violate its laws upon vague notions of altering or reforming governments in other states. This principle is not only reasonable in itself and in accordance with public law, but is ingrafted into the codes of other nations as well as our own. But while such are the sentiments of this Government, it may be added that every independent nation must be presumed to be able to defend its possession against unauthorized individuals banded together to attack them. The Government of the United States at all times since its establishment has abstained and has sought to restrain all citizens of the country from entering into controversies between other powers, and to observe all the duties of neutrality. . . .

All must see that difficulties may arise in carrying the laws referred to into execution in a country now having 3,000 to 4,000 miles of sea coast, with an infinite number of ports and harbors and small inlets, from some of which unlawful expeditions may suddenly set forth, without the knowledge of Government, against the possessions of foreign states.

"Friendly relations with all, but entangling alliances with none," has long been a maxim with us. Our true mission is not to propagate our opinions or impose upon other countries our form of government by artifice or force, but to teach by example and show by our success, moderation, and justice the blessings of self-government and the advantages of free institutions. Let every people choose for itself and make and alter its political institutions to suit it own condition and convenience.

A Compilation of the Messages and Papers of the Presidents, vol. 6, James D. Richardson, ed. (New York: Bureau of National Literature, Inc., 1897), pp. 2649–2653.

SENATOR DAVID YULEE (D-FL), IN SUPPORT OF AMERICAN EXPEDITIONS IN CUBA (WASHINGTON, DC, MAY 21, 1850)

. . . [M]y objection in moving this resolution is partly to call the attention of the Senate to what seems to be to be a very serious usurpation of power on the part of the Executive . . . To understand the character of this movement on the part of the Executive, it will be necessary to refer to the announcement made yesterday simultaneously in two of the papers in this city, which are regarded as organs of the Administration and the official exponents of its current transactions. We are informed that a squadron has been ordered—where? Not to any part of the United States to prevent the "carrying on," according to the meaning of the law, an alleged military expedition against a friendly foreign power; but where? "To *the island of Cuba*," a foreign dominion, beyond our jurisdiction; not to operate upon the high seas, but upon the coast of Cuba, and within the waters and jurisdiction of that island. To do what there? First to prevent the landing of any force, or the carrying out of any enterprise organized in the United States. This is bad enough, but with further instructions—and it is to this aspect of the case I desire especially to invoke attention—with this further remarkable instruction, in the language of the editorial of the Intelligencer: "In the event of a landing having been effected, to prevent the landing of ANY RE-INFORCEMENT OR ANY ARMS OR PROVISIONS under the American flag, intended for such expedition or enterprise."

Without intending to occupy much of the time of the Senate, I desire to present for its consideration one or two principles which seem to me applicable to the circumstances, if they exist as stated in the Intelligencer. In the first place, I consider these instructions to be violative of the personal civil rights of emigration and expatriation. I consider them also a violation of the express right guaranteed to every citizen of the United States by the Constitution of the country, not to be deprived of life, liberty, and property *without due process of law*. It will be understood that in this case no warrant has been issued, no information filed, and there has been no process of law within the contemplation of the Constitution; and yet a squadron has been ordered to the coast of Cuba to arrest persons and to seize property under the American flag, at the discretion of the commander of the squadron! . . . [H]ere we find the Executive of the country employing the fleet of the United States and sending it to foreign parts to arrest American citizens, and to hinder them in their liberty and violate the sanctity of their property, without any legal information and without any due process.

I come to the next, and, as it seems to me, a material ground. The instructions direct that if a landing had been effected, the fleet should be employed to prevent the arrival and landing of reinforcement and supplies of arms and provisions. I contend that this is an outrage on the freedom of commerce, and an outrage upon the Constitution and policy of the country. What is the established national law in regard to civil wars? It is, that whenever a civil war shall rage in a foreign country, each of the parties are to be regarded and treated as belligerent powers. I say now that the moment a landing was effected, as contemplated by these instructions, and the flag of revolution was raised on the island, there are two parties arrayed in hostile interest, and that a war is in being. Belligerent powers are there, and it belongs to the freedom of commerce, and is a neutral right—a right of every citizen in this country—to hire or sell vessels, and send them there with provision and arms for either party able and willing to pay for them. Yet here we find a direction given that, after the anticipated landing is effected and the revolutionary flag may have been raised, and there are two belligerent powers acting on the island in contest for its government, our fleet is to be employed to prevent the landing of reinforcements, arms, and supplies for *one* of the parties.

I contend that this is not only a violation of the rightful freedom of commerce, but is also in violation of the rules of neutrality, as recognized by all nations, and as enforced by this Government from the commencement of its history to the present time. . . . I wish it, therefore, to be understood, and I so declare distinctly, that, according to my apprehension of the law, if the flag of revolution is once raised on the island of Cuba, from that moment it is the right of every American citizen to hire his vessel, or to sell it, to the revolutionary party, equally as to the other party, and to send under the American flag provisions and arms, and whatever else the revolutionary party may require and can pay for. And, further, that every person who chooses to emigrate to the island, and to take part in either side, has the full right to do so, provided he chooses to incur the hazards of the contest. . . . I do not make it a ground of attack now against the Government, but I must say, with regret, that it has seemed to me the sympathies of the Government have of late appeared to lean rather to the side of despotism than to liberal progress.

Congressional *Globe*, 31st Congress, 1st Session, Part II, May 21, 1850, 1032–1033.

CANAL RIGHTS IN CENTRAL AMERICA: THE CLAYTON-BULWER TREATY

The role of the United States in world affairs had been an open question in the decades following independence. While Americans were more focused on domestic concerns than the international scene in the early years of the republic, presidents since Washington continually faced the challenges of a young and relatively weak country in an aggressive world. Although relations with the British and other European powers normalized somewhat following the War of 1812, Europe remained a potential threat to the United States. England maintained its North American presence in Canada, and her designs on the Pacific Northwest could threaten American plans for expansion there. The upheavals of the Napoleonic Wars had, among other things, disrupted Spain's rule in the Western Hemisphere and encouraged independence movements in Latin America. Rumors that Spain might seek a reconquest of its former colonial holdings sparked concern. With these fears in mind, in 1823, President James Monroe proclaimed in a message to Congress that the Americas were off limits to any future European expansion—a policy that came to be called the Monroe Doctrine.

While Monroe's words attracted little attention in 1823, over time they became a cornerstone of American foreign policy in Latin America. By the 1850s, the region, especially Central America, had become one of considerable importance. Americans had long recognized the possibilities of constructing a ship canal across the narrow strip of land that separated the oceans. For decades, shippers had been using Nicaragua and the Isthmus of Panama as a place to transport cargo over land to avoid sailing around South America, a voyage that took months. In the 1840s, American entrepreneurs began to travel to the region to consider investments in a canal, which, if successful, could result in enormous profits. For the United States government, the strategic benefits of a Central American canal were obvious. Naval vessels could be transported from coast to coast, allowing for stronger defense of the West and increased commerce with the Far East.

The political future of Central America therefore became vital to American and European interests. The British had a colonial presence there in British Honduras and were equally intrigued by the notion of a transisthmian canal. The volatile republics of the region, which had won their independence from Spain in the 1820s and later separated into the countries of Guatemala, El Salvador, Nicaragua, and Costa Rica, endured continual internal revolution and made American and British policy tenuous. Both powers sought to curry favor with the fledgling governments of these countries to gain access to canal regions. Americans were concerned that the British might use their colony as a springboard into the area, especially Nicaragua, considered the most promising area for a canal.

The British justified these fears by adopting an aggressive policy along the Mosquito Coast, on the Atlantic side of Nicaragua. The Mosquito Indians lived within the borders of Nicaragua but were not recognized as citizens of that country. The British had taken little interest in the Mosquitos until the United States began to seek a treaty with the Nicaraguan government regarding a canal effort. The British, eyeing an opportunity to stake a claim in the region, declared the Mosquitos an independent state, recognized a new king of the Mosquitos, and seized control of the coastal town of San Juan, renaming it Greytown. President Polk, reacting to the British move, secured a treaty with Nicaragua, negotiated by a Kentucky lawyer named Elijah Hise, that provided Americans with free movement in the country. The United States had made a great stride in obtaining rights to a canal zone; the British were seen as the one potential obstruction.

Relations between England and the United States became more strained. The British seized the island of El Tigre, a possession of Honduras, off the Pacific coast of Nicaragua. This act was justified as a response to a large debt owed the British by the government of Honduras; Americans, however, saw the action as an effort to bolster the British presence around the canal region. To complicate the matter, the Polk administration claimed that El Tigre actually had been ceded by the Honduran government to the United States. For a time, a tiny island off the coast of Central America might have sparked war between the two powers.

President Taylor entered office in the midst of this controversy. His position from the outset was one that stressed cooperation with the British. He feared a situation in which either the United States, Britain, or both became compelled to annex or colonize parts of Latin America. Expansionists in the United States, in fact, entertained such ideas. Taylor and Secretary of State John M. Clayton believed that a treaty with England could be obtained that guaranteed independence for Latin American countries and that could give Americans the upper hand in building a canal. Clayton met with British Foreign Minister Henry Bulwer and articulated the administration's position. Neither country should be allowed to occupy or control territory in Central America.

The treaty signed by Clayton and Bulwer on April 19, 1850, was by design a vague document. The agreement declared that neither government would obtain exclusive control over any part of Central America. Taylor, in presenting the treaty to the Senate for ratification, explained that the treaty would establish commerce between all "great maritime states" and protect Nicaragua. Of course, the British already occupied parts of Central America, and it was unclear as to whether the agreement included British Honduras, El Tigre, or the Mosquito Coast—which meant that the British would be forced to give up these areas. A treaty that addressed these issues directly probably would never have been agreed upon by both countries. Despite the lack of detail in the document, President Taylor believed that securing a treaty between the two nations was the most important act of his presidency. He signed the treaty from his deathbed, on July 5, 1850.

The Clayton-Bulwer Treaty, and Taylor's foreign policy toward Britain generally, met with fierce opposition from expansionist Democrats who feared that the United States was being bullied. While the speech by Senator Stephen A. Douglas of Illinois focuses on the treaty, it also expresses a much more aggressive plan of American involvement in Central America than that of Taylor. Douglas believed that expansion into Latin America might be a future possibility and perhaps a natural continuation of Manifest Destiny that had led America into the West. In a rousing speech, Douglas warns of British designs in Central America while placing any American movement into the region as a continuation of the nation's historic expansion.

President Taylor's policies were defended in Congress by his Secretary of State. In the following rebuttal to the remarks of Douglas (by this time Clayton was back in the Senate), he argues that such agreements were necessary between the commercial powers and rejects the notion that the United States should avoid agreements with England or other European powers. Clayton explains that the United States had a history of successful agreements with foreign states and that the American Revolution depended on such an alliance with France. Clayton, as did Taylor and other Whigs, attempted to portray expansionist Democrats as dangerous warmongers who would put the nation in harm's way for immoral and expensive land grabs.

The Clayton-Bulwer Treaty was only the beginning of conflict between the two powers over rights in Central America. In some respects, the views of Democrats such as Douglas foreshadowed American expansionism in the decades following the Civil War. In 1900, Britain ceded all rights to build a canal in Central America and opened the door for American canal ventures without the threat of hostilities. In the years following, the United

States would spend great amounts of time and money to complete a canal, not in Nicaragua, as had been expected, but in Panama. The Panama Canal opened in 1914 under United States control.

SENATOR JOHN M. CLAYTON (W-DE), SPEECH IN SUPPORT OF THE TREATY WITH GREAT BRITAIN (WASHINGTON, DC, MARCH 15, 1852)

All the objections of the Senator dwindle down at last, as I have said, to a single point—that the treaty ought to have been a treaty for the exclusive right of way across the isthmus; that the error of the treaty of 1850 is, that while it obtains protection from all nations, it makes a navigable highway for all nations on the same terms; and we see that if he had negotiated the treaty, he would have obtained an exclusive right; and he stood up here in defense of the treaty of Mr. Hise, which would have secured to this government (if it had been ratified by Nicaragua and the United States) an exclusive right. What sort of exclusive right is it that he demands? He thinks that the Government of the United States should have obtained the grant—the rights to make a canal, and an exclusive right to navigate it; that forts should be built at both ends to protect it; and of course that we should protect it by every other means necessary. When the Government shall have made it, and when the Government shall have established the forts, the canal, he says, will be open to everybody on the same terms; and thus he seeks the exclusive grant of a right of way! What does he want with it? Why does he prefer it to the plan adopted, of opening the canal to all nations on the same terms? The Senator says he would hold it as a rod—yes, a rod, to compel other nations to keep the peace! He would have no more settling of islands on the coast of Central America! If any government attempted it, he would shut his canal to them! He would also compel all foreign nations to treat us with respect and regard, by means of the tremendous rod which he would hold in his hands. Let us look a little into the justice of this thing, as regards our own country.

The expenses of protecting and taking care of the canal and keeping it in good order, would probably, when added to the interest, make an annual outlay from the Treasury of the United States, in that distant country, of not less than ten millions of dollars. Now, why should we make such an expenditure? Because we want a rod—a rod! Sir, I think it would prove to be a rod to inflict injuries upon ourselves. We want nothing but the right of way there. We proposed that no nation go through that canal, unless she agreed to protect it. In case they agreed to protect it, we should want no forts, no garrisons, and no naval force to guard what none could attack. But, on the other hand, if we were to adopt the plan of the Senator, we should have to keep a standing army in that country to protect it, in the event of a war between us and foreign nations.

We ought, he said, to nullify the treaty of 1850 at once. He now says that some men cannot comprehend the growth of this giant republic. I do not know that there is any man of ordinary intelligence who does not comprehend it. We have grown to such an extent already that we have a country greater than Rome possessed in her palmiest days. We cover a contiguous territory greater, perhaps, than ever was enjoyed by any civilized nation on earth. And yet we are told that we are not capable of binding ourselves even by treaty stipulations to observe our plighted faith, and fulfill our solemn engagement of honor. I remonstrate against the declaration of such a principle, or rather of such a want of all principle. . . ."Treaties cannot fetter us," says he. Sir, the plighted faith of every man of honor binds him at all times, no matter what his interest may be, and the plighted faith of nations equally binds them; and the last place from which a contrary principle should be promulgated, is the Senate of the United States. . . . If there be a country on earth that owes more than any other to treaties, it is ours. We owe our national existence to the old French treaties of 1778. . . . Washington, in the darkest period of the Revolution, at Valley Forge, wintered with his suffering soldiers, when the intelligence reached them that France had entered into an alliance with us, and had guarantied our independence. The glorious news ran through all the ranks of the American army, and the great "Father of his Country" stood up and waved his hat, and shouted for joy, in concert with his troops! Our destiny from that moment became fixed. . . . We owe, I repeat, our national independence to treaties. And now, when we are becoming strong, shall we forget it?

The Senator objects to the treaty of 1850, because, under its provisions, we cannot annex the Central American states. Were there no such treaty, he could not annex them till he had first overrun Mexico, and broken the treaty of Guadalupe Hidalgo. Nay, he must first annex the West India Islands, and British Honduras, too. After "swallowing Mexico," he must take in all the other intermediate countries; and as Great Britain owns many of the islands and dependencies to be devoured, he must include the British lion—a matter not quite so easy of digestion. What an intimation is it for us to make to the world, that we may some day annex these weak little sister Republics, thousands of miles away from us, with a population so different from ours, especially in laws, institutions, and usages! I would much rather other nations of the world know the fact that San Salvador, one of these very Central American States, once applied for admission into our Union, and that our Government not only declined to receive them, but treated the application as one not worthy of a moment's serious regard.

Congressional *Globe*, 32nd Congress, 3rd Session, Appendix, March 15, 1852, 269–270.

SENATOR STEPHEN A. DOUGLAS (D-IL), OPPOSING THE CLAYTON-BULWER TREATY (WASHINGTON, DC, MARCH 10, 1852)

The point that I was coming at was this: that while it has been a matter of boast for years that the Clayton and Bulwer treaty drove Great Britain out of Central America, she has not surrendered an inch: and what is more, she is now proposing negotiations with us with a view to new arrangements, by which she shall hereafter give up her protectorate. . . . I do not understand the congratulation of having accomplished a great and wonderful object, by the expelling of the British lion from the place where Mr. Polk allowed to come and abide, and still a new negotiation or a new arrangement is deemed necessary to secure that which the Senator from Delaware boasts of having accomplished long since.

. . . I know what were the private arguments urged in time which have gone by, and which I trust never will return; and that is, that England and other European Powers never would consent that the United States should have an exclusive right to the canal. Well, sir, I do not know that they would have consented; but of one thing I am certain, I would never have asked their consent. When Nicaragua desired to confer the privilege, and when we were willing to accept it, it was purely an American question with which England had no right to interfere. It was an American question about which Europe had no right to be consulted. Are we under any more obligation to consult European Powers about an American question than the allied Powers were, in their Congress, to consult us, when establishing the equilibrium of Europe by the agency of the Holy Alliance? America was not consulted then. Our name does not appear in all the proceedings. It was a European question, about which it was presumed America had nothing to say. This question of a canal in Nicaragua, when negotiations were pending to give it to us, was so much an American question that the English Government was not entitled to be consulted. England not consent! She will consent to allow you to do that just as long as you consent to allow her to hold Canada, the Bermudas, Jamaica, and her other American possessions. I hope the time has arrived when we will not be told any more that Europe will not consent to that. I heard that argument till I got tired of it when we were discussing the resolutions for the annexation of Texas. I heard it on the California question. It has been said on every occasion whenever we have had an issue about foreign relations, that England would not consent; yet she has acquiesced in whatever we have had the courage and justice to do. And why? Because we kept ourselves in the right. England was so situated with her possessions on this continent, that she dare not fight in an unjust cause. We would have been in the right to have accepted the privilege of making this canal, and England would never had dared to provoke a controversy with us. I think the time has come when America should perform her duty according to our own judgement, and our sense of justice, without regard to what European Powers might say with respect to it. I think this nation is about of age. I think we have a right to judge for ourselves. Let us always do right, and put the consequences behind us.

... Fifty years ago the question was being debated in this Senate whether it was wise or not to acquire any territory on the west bank of the Mississippi river, and it was then concluded that we could never, with safety, extend beyond that river. It was at that time seriously considered whether the Alleghany mountains should not be the barrier beyond which we should never pass. At a subsequent date, after we had acquired Louisiana and Florida, more liberal views began to prevail, and it was thought that perhaps we might venture to establish one tier of States west of the Mississippi; but in order to prevent the sad calamity of an undue expansion of our territory, the policy was adopted of establishing an Indian Territory, with titles of perpetuity, all along the western border of those States, so that no more new states could possibly be created in that direction. That barrier could not arrest the onward progress of people. They burst through it, and passed the Rocky Mountains, and were only arrested by the waters of the Pacific. Who, then, is prepared to say that in the progress of events, having met with the barrier of the ocean in our western course, we may not be compelled to turn to the north and to the south for an outlet?

You may make as many treaties as you please to fetter the limits of this giant Republic, and she will burst them all from her, and her course will press onward to a limit which I will not venture to prescribe. Why the necessity of pledging your faith that you will never annex any more of Mexico? Do you not know that you will be compelled to do it; that you cannot help it; that your treaty will not prevent it, and that the only effect it will have will be to enable the European Powers to accuse us of bad faith and Punic faith as synonymous terms? What is the use of your guarantee that you will never erect any fortification in Central America; never annex, occupy, or colonize any portion of that country? How do you know that you can avoid doing it? If you make the canal, I ask you if American citizens will not settle along its line; whether they will not build up towns at each terminus; whether they will not spread over that country, and convert it into an American state; whether American principles and American institutions will not be firmly planted there? ...

I do not wish to administer to the feeling of jealousy and rivalry that exists between us and England. I wish to soften and smooth it down as much as possible; but why close our eyes to the fact that friendship is impossible while jealousy exists? Hence England seizes every island in the sea and rock upon our coast where she can plant a gun to intimidate us or to annoy our commerce. Her policy has been to seize every military and naval station the world over. Why does she pay such enormous sums to keep her post at Gibraltar, except to keep it *"in terrorem"* over the commerce of the Mediterranean? Why her enormous expense to maintain a garrison at the Cape of Good Hope, except to command the great passage on the way to the Indies? Why is she at the expense to keep her position on that little barren island Bermuda, and the miserable Bahamas, and all the other islands along our coast, except as sentinels upon our actions? Does England hold Bermuda because of any profit it is to her? Has she any other motive for retaining it except jealousy which stimulates hostility to us? Is it not the case with all of her possessions along the coast? Why, then, talk about the friendly bearing of England toward us when she is extending that policy every day? New treaties of friendship, seizure of islands, and erection of new colonies in violation of her treaties, seem to be the order of the day. In view of this state of things, I am in favor of meeting England as we meet a rival; meet her boldly, treat her justly and fairly, but make no humiliating concession for the sake of peace.

Congressional *Globe*, 32nd Congress, 3rd Session, Appendix, March 10, 1852, 260–262.

RECOMMENDED READINGS

Bauer, Jack P. *Zachary Taylor: Soldier, Planter, Statesman of the Old Southwest.* Baton Rouge: Louisiana State University Press, 1985.

Grayson, Benson Lee. *The Unknown President: The Administration of President Millard Fillmore.* Lanham, MD: University Press of America, 1981.

Holt, Michael F. *The Political Crisis of the 1850s.* New York: Wiley Publishers, 1978.

Potter, David M. *The Impending Crisis, 1848–1961.* New York: Harper & Row, 1976.

Scurry, Robert J. *Millard Fillmore.* Jefferson, NC: MacFarland, 2001.

Smith, Elbert B. *The Presidencies of Zachary Taylor and Millard Fillmore.* Lawrence: University of Kansas Press, 1988.

2

FRANKLIN PIERCE

(1853–1857)

INTRODUCTION

Franklin and Jane Pierce were shocked when they received the news. They had been traveling in New Hampshire in the summer of 1852 when word arrived that Pierce would likely be the Democratic Party's presidential candidate in the coming election. No one was more unhappy than Jane, who allegedly fainted. Even Franklin Pierce was less than overjoyed. He reluctantly had agreed to allow his name to be considered because he had no expectations of winning and had refused even to attend the convention. Nevertheless, the unthinkable had happened, and soon Pierce was planning a trip to Washington to prepare for the campaign that lay ahead.

Pierce's nomination was to many Democrats a sign of weakness. Surely there were other candidates who were more qualified to carry the party's banner. Since Whigs Zachary Taylor and Millard Fillmore had held the presidency for the past four years, Democrats hungered to win back the White House. There was no shortage of possibilities. Lewis Cass of Michigan, a party leader who perhaps was the most seasoned Democrat at the convention, stood as the most likely candidate to win a national election. There were other high-profile names, including the upstart Illinois Senator Stephen A. Douglas, James Buchanan of Pennsylvania, and William L. Marcy, who dominated the party in the all-important state of New York. Yet Pierce of New Hampshire had carried the day, and unhappy but desperate Democrats had to line up in support of his candidacy if they held any hopes of defeating the incumbent Whigs.

The opposition immediately recognized that Pierce's anonymity was his greatest limitation, as Whigs trumpeted in jest the question, "Who is Franklin Pierce?" Despite a lack of notoriety, he was a man with considerable political experience, although his career had taken several strange turns. He was born in 1804, in Hillsborough, New Hampshire, to a prominent family. His father Benjamin had a distinguished record of military service, having risen to the rank of general during the Revolutionary War. In later years, Benjamin Pierce served in the New Hampshire state legislature and was elected governor in 1827 and again in 1829. Franklin would capitalize on the family name to launch his own career in local politics in the 1830s.

Franklin Pierce attended Bowdoin College in Maine, an institution reserved for the children of New England's most prominent families. Among his classmates were Henry Wadsworth Longfellow and Nathaniel Hawthorne, the latter of whom befriended Pierce throughout his life. Franklin as a young man showed unlimited promise. Attractive, polished, and outgoing, he was remembered by classmates more for his social skills than his scholarship. Nevertheless, Pierce graduated fifth in his class (of thirteen) and soon became among the more eligible bachelors in all of New England. In 1834, well after his political career was launched, he married Jane Means Appleton, the daughter of Bowdoin College's president. Like Pierce, Jane had grown up in a privileged environment, receiving the finest education available to a young woman in antebellum America. At the same time, Jane was a frail, somewhat sickly, and erratic woman who suffered from bouts of tuberculosis and deep depression. In many respects they made an unlikely couple. The Appletons were "old money" in New England, and Jane always was critical of politics and politicians. Nevertheless, the two enjoyed a successful, if at times difficult, marriage.

Despite Jane's hatred of politics, Pierce ended up following his father into the political arena. After graduating from Bowdoin, he studied law and apprenticed with Levi Woodbury, who later became a power in the state's Democratic Party. Pierce evidently had no ambitions of pursuing a long career in the legal profession. In the late 1820s, he became an ardent supporter of Andrew Jackson, and the popularity of Jackson, combined with Pierce's family name, swept Pierce into the state legislature in 1833. He proved himself a capable legislator with powerful allies; he was elected Speaker of the House at the age of twenty-eight. During the next few years, Pierce rode the tide of Jacksonian success to a seat in the U.S. House of Representatives, and, in 1837, won election to the U.S. Senate. Franklin Pierce, young, articulate, handsome, and gifted in social affairs, was in the late 1830s among the most promising young political leaders in the country.

Yet underneath this success lay personal problems that challenged Pierce throughout his life. There is strong evidence that Pierce abused alcohol for much of his early career at a time when drinking was often at the center of social life in Washington. In fact, alcoholism evidently forced him out of Senate in the late 1830s; for the remainder of his life Pierce was a staunch supporter of temperance organizations. The fact that he was able to come to terms with his addiction and salvage his career indicates a strength of character often overlooked in Pierce.

There also was the problem of Mrs. Pierce, whose condition continued to worsen. She never accepted her husband's career and opposed most of his attempts to climb the political ladder. Most who encountered her described Jane as humorless, even morose. The Pierce's first child, Franklin, died before the age of one, and a second, Frank Robert, died as a young boy. However, it was the loss of their third child, Benjamin, that pushed Jane's disposition from eccentric to hysterical. The event was horrific. In January 1853, the Pierces were traveling in Massachusetts, on a trip that would eventually take them to Washington, D.C., for the inauguration, when their train jumped the track. Franklin and Jane were uninjured, but eleven-year-old Bennie was crushed to death in another car; the two parents witnessed the event but could do nothing to avert the tragedy. Jane was disconsolate; she tended to blame her husband, at least indirectly, for the loss and often wrote letters to her deceased son while living in the White House. She refused to participate in the social life of Washington and offered Franklin little support.

Given these challenges, Franklin Pierce's ascendancy to the presidency was more than the result of the advantages of his birth. A strength of character and sense of purpose were necessary to rejuvenate a career that had all but collapsed by the early 1840s. In 1842, he resigned from the Senate and returned to New Hampshire and withdrew from public life. Despite his personal troubles, Pierce continued to draw the attention of powerful people who saw him as a promising leader. In 1845, he declined a nomination from President Polk to serve as attorney general of the United States. Democrats in New Hampshire also pegged Pierce as their candidate for governor, another honor that Pierce rejected. For a few years, Pierce had made it clear that he had no plans to re-enter the political scene at any level.

But even as Pierce declined these opportunities, he was growing restless. In 1846, with the onset of war with Mexico, Pierce saw an opportunity to start afresh by enlisting in the army. He began as a private but soon was promoted to the rank of colonel. By war's end, Pierce was a brigadier general. His resolve often belied his abilities as a soldier. He volunteered for combat and led troops into Mexico City but was injured after being thrown from his horse. Yet Pierce did show courage, refusing to withdraw and continuing to lead his troops while in considerable pain. Not exactly a war hero, Pierce did return home with his reputation intact, and no doubt enhanced, by his participation in the war.

Pierce, now a decorated veteran, returned to New Hampshire after the war, resuming his law practice and continuing his ambivalence regarding politics. He turned down an opportunity to re-enter the Senate in 1848, when Democrats offered him the nomination. In 1850, however, he did agree to preside over a state constitutional convention, and during the next two years did not reject completely the notion of placing his name in nomination as the Democratic Party's presidential candidate in the next election. However, when his name came up as a potential vice presidential candidate in 1852, he followed his wife's wishes and refused to allow his candidacy to be discussed.

What finally brought Pierce around to the notion of running for president in 1852 is difficult to say. Behind the scenes, and quite removed from Pierce himself, New Hampshire Democrats worked energetically to keep his name in circulation. In the spring of 1852, a longtime political insider named Edmund Burke convinced Pierce that his participation in the party's convention in the coming summer would help the Democrats and might result in Pierce's nomination. Pierce finally relented, and quietly agreed that if nominated for president he would indeed run in the general election. From that point forward, a small but well-organized group of Democrats, including Burke, began to maneuver in an effort to win Pierce the nomination. Pierce placated Jane by assuring her that his nomination was highly unlikely and would serve only to obtain the right candidate for the party.

Pierce's views on public office might have been confused, but his political philosophy was quite clear. He was, above all, a proponent of states' rights and limited federal authority, which made him appealing to those who sought a Northerner with Southern political leanings. Another plus was his strong support for the Compromise of 1850 and particularly the controversial Fugitive Slave Law. Pierce maintained that Northern attempts to block the recapture of escaped slaves was an affront the right of Southerners to their personal property. For Democrats who sought a candidate that might attract voters in both regions, Pierce offered an interesting, if somewhat unpredictable, possibility.

The threat of a sectional split within the Democratic Party clearly was the greatest concern entering the June 1852 convention, which was held in Baltimore. For party stalwarts, the 1848 election had provided valuable lessons about the need for unity. Northern Democrats who sided with the Wilmot Proviso's exclusion of slavery from new territories bolted from the party and nominated New York's favorite son Martin Van Buren under the Free Soil banner. Loyalists blasted those "barnburners" who seemed willing to destroy the party over singular issues, but the split in New York and other Northern states resulted in Whig victory. Four years later, the same issues again threatened the party. Those at the center of the party's power understood the need to find a candidate who could placate both regions.

Party unity meant, first and foremost, finding a candidate who supported the Compromise of 1850 but did not alienate the party's Northern wing. The strongest possibilities, perhaps naturally, were Westerners who might strike a moderate position. For this reason, two individuals from that region were seen by many as the most appropriate candidates. Lewis Cass, the party elder from Michigan, was for most the best possibility, yet there were important drawbacks to his candidacy. For one, he was over seventy years old; secondly, he seemed to be uninterested in campaigning for the presidency once again. To make matters more difficult, the ebullient Stephen A. Douglas was emerging as a challenger to Cass as the party's favorite in the Western states. The rift between Cass supporters and those of Douglas posed a real challenge in offering either as a national candidate.

If Western Democrats split their support between Cass and Douglas, there were other attractive candidates. William L. Marcy, former governor of New York, was the candidate with the most experience. Marcy had been a party leader for decades, had served as secretary of war under President Polk, and enjoyed the support of the New York City business establishment. Furthermore, like Cass, Marcy had worked for some time to build a base of support outside his region—in his case, the South. Also like Cass, however, Marcy's years of experience brought with it political baggage. Rivals in his own party in New York had over time built up an animosity for Marcy that could not be smoothed over during the convention. A split in the New York delegation between Cass and Marcy ultimately denied both the nomination.

Finally, there was James Buchanan of Pennsylvania, who insiders believed had the greatest chance of winning. Better yet, many Democrats believed that Buchanan, more than any other candidate, could carry the fall election against the Whig candidate. Buchanan had a strong record of national service. The former U.S. senator had been Polk's secretary of state and had also served as minister to Russia. His actions during the debates over the Compromise of 1850 had boosted his political fortunes. He was a Northerner who supported with great energy the Fugitive Slave Act and publicly attacked abolitionism as a threat to national security. Buchanan had allies throughout the South and offered that wing of the party a viable candidate. Buchanan also very much wanted the nomination and worked actively to win broad support for his candidacy.

Given such strong candidates, few expected the name of Franklin Pierce to emerge at the convention, not to mention carry the day. But from the outset of the convention, delegates were somewhat pessimistic about the prospects of any of the leading candidates managing a victory. As experienced politicos knew, such an atmosphere meant that an unknown could emerge with the nomination. When the selection process began, none of the candidates received the necessary two-thirds majority. Cass, Buchanan, Douglas, and Marcy all had their supporters, and none was willing to budge. The small group of Pierce supporters then went into action, visiting with various groups of delegates and offering their candidate as a viable compromise. The timing was perfect, for by the third day of voting frustration was on the rise. Delegates began to side with Pierce, and on the forty-ninth ballot he was named the party's nominee. William R. King of Alabama was selected as the vice presidential candidate, both as a means to appease Southerners in the party and to achieve regional balance in the general election.

The Whigs also met in Baltimore that summer. They, too, were frustrated in their attempts to find a strong and nationally popular candidate. Millard Fillmore had served admirably since Zachary Taylor's death in the summer of 1850 but had indicated to those close to the administration that he had little desire to run for re-election. Yet Fillmore, for most Whigs, was the best candidate, for he had followed Taylor in attempting to position himself as a "Union Whig"—refusing to side with one section and supporting the Compromise of 1850. Ultimately, Fillmore agreed to run for the nomination, but he was challenged by others who actively sought the position. One was Major General Winfield Scott, "Old Fuss and Feathers," who like Taylor emerged from the Mexican War a hero in the eyes of many Americans. Perhaps the most seasoned and experienced Whig hopeful was the senior statesman and gifted orator from Massachusetts, Senator Daniel Webster. Mirroring the career of Henry Clay of Kentucky, Webster had forged a distinguished congressional career and had for years sought to use his renown as a springboard into the White House. However, Webster also was in the twilight of his career and suffered from poor health. The election of 1852 would certainly be his last opportunity to become president.

If the Democrats were beset by sectional division, the Whigs faced disintegration. Southerners had no intentions of voting for Webster of Massachusetts; most sided with Fillmore in gratitude for his support of the Fugitive Slave Act. Yet Scott posed an interesting challenge to Fillmore's nomination. The former war hero also was a slaveholder and promised strong support for the Fugitive Slave Act as well. Whigs in the South were split between Scott and Fillmore; in the North they were divided between Webster and Fillmore. Predictably, the nomination process was long and arduous. After the forty-sixth ballot, Webster finally agreed to bow out and expected his supporters to turn to Fillmore. Surprisingly, enough of Webster's supporters sided with Scott to give him the victory on the fifty-third ballot. Fillmore's pride was hurt, but he also was somewhat relieved. Webster was outraged to the point of suggesting that New England Whigs actually vote for Franklin Pierce in the general election.

Pessimistic Whigs, who proclaimed that the party would suffer greatly from its internal and regional divisions, proved in the end to be realists. Northern Whigs generally were unimpressed with Scott as a candidate; many turned to third-party candidates as an alternative. Most notable was an antislavery party formed from the former Free Soilers, called the Free Democrats, who ran John P. Hale. More extreme abolitionists supported a Liberty Party ticket with the writer and activist William Goodell as its champion. The result of this divide among Northerners was a landslide victory for Pierce—the final electoral tally was 254 for Pierce to only 24 for Scott. Revealingly, the popular vote was close and less than 50,000 votes separated Pierce and all other opponents combined. The Whigs had lost their national cohesion and would collapse completely before the next presidential election.

Meanwhile, the somewhat stunned Pierce faced the daunting task of leading the nation during these difficult times. His primary task, maintaining sectional unity, challenged and perhaps overwhelmed his political acumen. Pierce also faced other issues. As an ardent supporter of state political power, the issue of the federal government's responsibilities came up time and again. To his credit, he was consistent in his policy of limited federal authority. To his discredit, however, Pierce was politically tone-deaf, failing to grasp the volatility of partisan politics during the 1850s and eschewing moderation and negotiation. Foreign policy also presented difficulties and placed his states' rights views to the test by raising the question of the federal government's role in territorial acquisition in the West.

By most accounts, Pierce was less than impressive as the nation's leader. On his watch, sectional disputes were blown open by the question of slavery in the Kansas and Nebraska territories. By the end of his term, violence in Kansas resembled a small war. Democrats might have been temporarily pleased with the collapse of the Whigs, but the party was losing its Northern base by failing to appease its supporters in that region. By 1856, the Democrats had come to view Pierce as a liability. His party had lost in almost every local and state election during his presidency, including those in his own state of New Hampshire. The new Republican Party was already enjoying political success, and when Democrats met in Cincinnati during the summer of 1856, most party leaders knew that Pierce would fail to win his party's nomination for a second time. With the nomination of James Buchanan, Pierce left public life and returned home. He lived through the Civil War and died in his Concord, New Hampshire, home on October 8, 1869.

THE KANSAS-NEBRASKA ACT

The acquisition of California and the Southwest as a result of the Mexican War raised the possibility of a transcontinental railroad. While most could agree that a rail line linking the Pacific Coast to the eastern United States offered unlimited economic potential, there was widespread debate as to the location of such a line. Predictably, the debate was drawn along sectional lines. Southerners, particularly in Texas, envisioned a railroad that would traverse the Lone Star State and cut through the Southwest with its terminus in southern California. Southerners were heartened by the Gadsden Purchase of 1853, which acquired for the United States a large swath of territory in the remote Southwest just for such a purpose.

Those north of the Mason-Dixon Line held different views. Senator Stephen A. Douglas of Illinois was perhaps the most vocal of those who advocated a line extending westward from Chicago. Douglas was motivated by politics and economics. Powerful constituents in Chicago pushed for a northern line, and Douglas himself had invested in real estate in Illinois and Michigan that would offer great returns if his plans came to fruition. As deliberations continued in the early 1850s, Douglas began to lay the political groundwork to obtain his Chicago-based line.

The first major obstacle for the railroad was the organization of the Nebraska territory, which had been reserved for Native American tribes. Douglas and others had been at work on the organization of a territorial government there since the 1840s but had found little support outside his own region for such action. In the spring of 1853, a bill to organize Nebraska was defeated soundly in the Senate, led by Southerners who saw little gain in the organization of the region. For one thing, a Nebraska territory would strengthen the argument for a northern-based railroad. Additionally, and perhaps most important, Nebraska lay north of the 36° 30' line of the Missouri Compromise, which meant that according to federal law the territory would exclude slavery. Douglas realized early on that if Nebraska were to become a territory, Southerners would have to be placated.

By January 1854, Douglas had discovered a means of attracting Southerners to a Nebraska bill with the concept of "popular sovereignty," the notion that territorial governments should decide on the issue of slavery regardless of location. Popular sovereignty was not a new idea; since the end of the Mexican War in 1848 had brought slavery back into politics there had been a contingent in favor of the concept. Westerners tended to support it, and Southerners might go along with such a plan because at least it opened up the idea that territories north of the Mason-Dixon Line would permit slavery. Douglas also believed that popular sovereignty was the most advantageous means of deciding the difficult question by removing the debate from Washington and encouraging local governments to come to terms with the issue.

With all of this in mind, Douglas presented a bill for the organization of a territorial government in the Nebraska territory with the provision that slavery be determined by the territorial legislature. Northerners who opposed the extension of slavery into new territories screamed correctly that, if passed, the Missouri Compromise had been destroyed. During deliberations, the bill was expanded to include two separate territories, one for a territory west of Missouri and Iowa called Kansas and another for territory west of Minnesota all the way to the Canadian border to be called Nebraska. For opponents of slavery's extension, the division of the region into two territories seemed a strategy to encourage a compromise.

Southerners came out in support of the Kansas-Nebraska bill and aligned with Westerners to pass the bill in the Senate by a vote of 37 to 14. Opposition in the House of Representatives was stronger; after months of debate the bill passed in May by a margin of 13 votes and was signed into law by President Pierce eight days later. In the following passage, Pierce explains his support of the bill by accusing Northerners of reneging on the Missouri Compromise years earlier by opposing annexation of Texas and the extension of slavery in the Southwest back in the 1840s. Echoing the Southern position, Pierce claimed that Northerners wanted it both ways by supporting the Missouri Compromise when it benefited their wishes.

Predictably, the reaction among Northerners was outrage. A manifesto signed by "Independent Northern Democrats" claimed that Missouri had been brought into the Union a slave state only through the Compromise. Now Southerners had aligned with Westerners such as Douglas to render the Compromise obsolete and to open up all territories, northern or southern, to slavery.

Historians often view the Kansas-Nebraska Act as a turning point in the history of the United States. In a single act, Congress reopened the divisive issue of slavery in the West and polarized debate even further. After 1854, as these disputes became more protracted, Northern Whigs split from those in the South. This move both ushered in the demise of the Whig Party and laid the groundwork for a new, exclusively Northern-based Republican Party. Only six years later, disagreements over slavery erupted in Southern secession and the Civil War.

FRANKLIN PIERCE, IN SUPPORT OF THE KANSAS-NEBRASKA ACT (WASHINGTON, DC, DECEMBER 2, 1856)

It is by the agency of such unwarrantable interference, foreign and domestic, that the minds of many otherwise good citizens have been so inflamed into the passionate condemnation of the domestic institutions of the Southern States as at length to pass insensibly to almost equally passionate hostility toward their fellow-citizens of those States, and thus finally to fall into temporary fellowship with the avowed and active enemies of the Constitution. . . . A question which is one of the most difficult problems of social institution, political economy, and statesmanship they treat with unreasonable intemperance of thought and language. Extremes beget extremes. Violent attack from the North finds its inevitable consequence in the growth of a spirit of angry defiance at the South. . . .

I confidently believe that the great body of those who inconsiderately took this fatal step are sincerely attached to the Constitution and the Union. They would upon deliberation shrink with unaffected horror from any conscious act of disunion or civil war. But they have entered into a path which leads nowhere unless it be civil war and disunion, and which has no other possible outlet. . . .

In the long series of acts of indirect aggression, the first was the strenuous agitation by citizens of the Northern States, in Congress and out of it, of the question of negro emancipation in the Southern States.

The second step in this path of evil consisted of acts of the people of the Northern States, and in several instances of their governments, aimed to facilitate the escape of persons held in service in the Southern States and to prevent their extradition when reclaimed according to law and in virtue of express provisions of the Constitution. . . .

The third stage of this unhappy sectional controversy was in connection with the organization of Territorial governments and the admission of new States into the Union. When it was proposed to admit the State of Maine, by separation of territory from that of Massachusetts, and the State of Missouri, formed of a portion of the territory ceded by France to the United States, representatives in Congress objected to the admission of the latter unless with conditions suited to particular views of public policy. The imposition of such a condition was successfully resisted; but at the same period the question was presented of imposing restrictions upon the residue of the territory ceded by France. That question was for the time disposed of by the adoption of a geographical line of limitation. . . .

The enactment which established the restrictive geographical line was acquiesced in rather than approved by the States of the Union. It stood on the statute book, however, for a number of years; and the people of the respective States acquiesced in the reenactment of the principle as applied to the State of Texas, and it was proposed to acquiesce in its further application to the territory acquired by the United States from Mexico. But this proposition was successfully resisted by the representatives from the Northern States, who, regardless of the statute line, insisted upon applying restriction to the new territories generally, whether lying north or south of it, thereby repealing it as a legislative compromise, and, on the part of the North, persistently violating the compact, if compact there was. . . .

Such was the state of this question when the time arrived for the organization of the Territories of Kansas and Nebraska. In the progress of constitutional inquiry and reflection it had now at length come to be seen clearly that Congress does not possess constitutional power to impose restrictions of this character upon any present or future State of the Union. In a long series of decisions, on the fullest argument and after the most deliberate consideration, the Supreme Court of the United States had finally determined this point in every form under which the question could arise, whether as affecting public or private rights—in question of the public domain, of religion, of navigation, and of servitude. . . .

The argument of those who advocate the enactment of new laws of restriction and condemn the repeal of old ones in effect avers their particular views of government have no self-extending or self-sustaining power of their own, and will go nowhere unless forced by act of Congress. And if

Congress do but pause for a moment in the policy of stern coercion; if it venture to try the experiment of leaving men to judge for themselves what institutions will best suit them; if it not be strained up to perpetual legislative exertion on this point—if Congress proceed thus to act in the very spirit of liberty, it is at once charged with aiming to extend slave labor into all new Territories of the United States.

Of course, these imputations on the intentions of Congress in this respect, conceived, as they were, in prejudice and disseminated in passion, are utterly destitute of any justification in the nature of things and contrary to all the fundamental doctrines and principles of civil liberty and self-government.

A Compilation of the Messages and Papers of the Presidents, vol. 6, James D. Richardson, ed. (New York: Bureau of National Literature, Inc., 1897), 2932–2937.

CONGRESSIONAL OPPOSITION TO THE KANSAS-NEBRASKA ACT (WASHINGTON, DC, JANUARY 30, 1854)

FELLOW CITIZENS: As Senators and Representatives in the Congress of the United States, it is our duty to warn our constituents whenever imminent danger menaces the freedom of our institutions or the permanency of our Union.

Such danger, as we firmly believe, now impends, and we earnestly solicit your prompt attention to it.

At the last session of Congress, a bill for the organization of the Territory of Nebraska passed the House of Representatives with an overwhelming majority. That bill was based on the principle of excluding slavery from the new Territory. It was not taken up for consideration in the Senate, and consequently failed to become a law.

At the present session, a new Nebraska bill has been reported by the Senate Committee on Territories, which, should it unhappily receive the sanction of Congress, will open all the unorganized territory of the Union to the ingress of slavery.

We arraign this bill as a gross violation of a sacred pledge; as a criminal betrayal of precious rights; as part and parcel of an atrocious plot to exclude from a vast unoccupied region immigrants from the Old World, as free laborers from our own States, and convert it into a dreary region of despotism, inhabited by masters and slaves.

Take your maps, fellow citizens, we entreat you, and see what country it is which this bill, gratuitously and recklessly, proposes to open to slavery. . . .

Nothing is more certain in history than the fact that Missouri could not have been admitted as a slave State had not certain members from the free States been reconciled to the measure by the incorporation of this prohibition into the act of admission. Nothing is more certain that this prohibition has been regarded and accepted by the whole country as a solemn compact against the extension of slavery into any part of the territory acquired from France, lying north of 36° 30', and not included in the new State of Missouri. The same act—let it be ever remembered—which authorized the formation of a constitution for the State, without a clause forbidding slavery, consecrated, beyond question, and beyond honest recall, the whole remainder of the territory to freedom and free institutions forever. For more than thirty years—during more than half the period of our national existence under our present Constitution—this compact has been universally regarded and acted upon as inviolable American law. In conformity with it, Iowa was admitted as a free state, and Minnesota has been organized as a free territory.

It is a strange and ominous fact, well calculated to awaken the worst apprehensions, and the most fearful forebodings of future calamities, that it is now deliberately purposed to repeal this prohibition, by implication or directly—the latter certainly manlier way—and this to subvert this compact, and allow slavery in all the yet unorganized territory. . . .

In 1820 the slave States said to the free States: "Admit Missouri with slavery and refrain from positive exclusion south of 36° 30', and we will join you in perpetual prohibition north of that line." The free States consented. In 1854 the slave States say to the free States: "Missouri is admitted; no prohibition of slavery south of 36° 30' has been attempted; we have received the full consideration of our agreement; no more is to be granted by adherence to it on our part; we therefore propose to cancel the compact." If this not be Punic faith, what is it? Not without the deepest dishonor and crime can the free States acquiesce in this demand. . . .

We appeal to the people. We warn you that the dearest interests of freedom and the Union are in imminent peril. Demagogues may tell you that the Union can be maintained only by submitting to the demands of slavery. We tell you that the safety of the Union can only be insured by the full recognition of the just claims of freedom and man. The Union was formed to establish justice, and secure the blessings of liberty. When it fails to accomplish these ends, it will be worthless; and when it becomes worthless, it cannot long endure.

We entreat you to be mindful of that fundamental maxim of Democracy—EQUAL RIGHTS AND EXACT JUSTICE FOR ALL MEN. Do not submit to become agents in extending legalized oppression and systematized injustice over a vast Territory yet exempt from these terrible evils. . . .

Whatever apologies may be offered for the toleration of slavery in the States, none can be urged for its extension into Territories where it does not exist, and where that extension involves the repeal of ancient law, and the violation of solemn compact. Let all protest, earnestly and emphatically, by correspondence, through the press, by memorials, by resolutions of public meetings and legislative bodies, and in whatever other mode may seem expedient, against this enormous crime.

For ourselves, we shall resist it by speech and vote, and with all the abilities which God has given us. Even if overcome in the impending struggle, we shall not submit. We shall go home to our constituents, erect anew the standard of freedom, and call on the people to come to the rescue of the country from the domination of slavery. We will not despair; for the cause of human freedom is the cause of God.

S.P. Chase, Senator from Ohio
Charles Sumner, Senator from Mass.
J.R. Giddings [Mass.]
Edward Wade, Representative from Ohio
Gerrit Smith, Representative from New York
Alex. De Witt, Representative from Massachusetts

Congressional *Globe*, 31st Congress, 1st Session, January 30, 1854, 281–282.

INDIAN REMOVAL

Franklin Pierce inherited from his predecessors an Indian policy marked by alternating periods of aggression and apathy. Before the 1840s, the United States government had followed through with a policy of establishing reservations for Native Americans—mostly in the Midwest. Yet in the years leading up to the Mexican War, this policy began to change. As Americans began to look westward in the age of Manifest Destiny, the potential for confrontation between settlers and Native American tribes increased. The Mexican War perhaps was a watershed in U.S.–Native American relations. With the acquisition of new territory in the Southwest, business leaders and policy makers began to contemplate a transcontinental railroad. Such ventures could mean huge profits. For the government, a rail line traversing the continent meant more settlement in the West and increased access to lucrative trade in the Pacific, particularly in the Far East. The one thing standing in the way of American expansion West seemed to be Native Americans on their reservations.

Administrations from the 1840s onward tended to view relations with Native Americans as a nuisance rather than a crisis. Beginning with the Polk administration, attempts were made to renegotiate treaties in an effort to move Native Americans without sparking hostilities. Pierce continued the policy. His Secretary of State, Jefferson Davis of Mississippi, equated Indian relations with warfare and operated under the assumption that the United States government was engaged in hostile conflict over these areas.

Native Americans who were forced yet again from their homes in the 1840s and 1850s became frustrated with the United States government. Perhaps the most eloquent expression came from the pen of Chief Seattle of the

Duwamish. Like many Indian leaders, he had made agreements with the government in good faith. When American policy changed and the Duwamish were urged to leave the land which had been allotted to them as a reserve, Seattle felt betrayed. His letter to Pierce, which first appeared in print in a Seattle, Washington newspaper years later, offers insight into the difficult position that Native American leaders faced in the nineteenth century. As a spokesman for his people, Seattle clearly seeks to soften relations between the Duwamish and the United States by warning that some of his followers, particularly younger and more militant tribesmen, were becoming bellicose. Seattle writes to Pierce as one statesman to another, informing the president that any American proposals would receive careful and sober consideration. At the same time, the address is full of lamentation, as Seattle explains how his people were becoming separated from their ancestral homelands in poetic language.

If Chief Seattle treated Pierce with the respect of a fellow statesman, the same cannot be said of Pierce in his dealings with Native American leaders. The difference in the ways in which Seattle and Pierce viewed one another may be gleaned from the statement made by Pierce during one of his inaugural speeches. Pierce made few extended public remarks about Native Americans; those he did make indicate that Pierce thought little of the plight of the Indian. Pierce echoes the vast majority of Americans by describing Indians in the West as "predatory," "wild," and "savage." Pierce makes clear that his administration is committed to settling the West with American settlers, at the point of a gun, if necessary. "Indian removal" continued as official policy throughout the 1850s. By 1854, the Kansas and Nebraska territories had been opened up for settlement; by the early 1860s, disputes between some Indian tribes and the United States government had reached a state of war. In the decades following the Civil War, the United States military devoted many of its resources to maintaining order in the West. By the turn of the century, most Native Americans in the West were living in government-established reservations.

FRANKLIN PIERCE, ON RELATIONS WITH WESTERN INDIAN TRIBES (WASHINGTON, DC, DECEMBER 4, 1854)

The experience of the last year furnishes additional reasons, I regret to say, of a painful character, for the recommendation heretofore made to provide for increasing the military force employed in the Territory inhabited by the Indians. The settlers on the frontier have suffered much from the incursions of predatory bands, and large parties of emigrants to our Pacific possessions have been massacred with impunity. The recurrence of such scenes can only be prevented by teaching these wild tribes the power of and their responsibility to the United States. From the garrisons of our frontier posts it is only possible to detach troops in small bodies; and though these have on all occasions displayed a gallantry and a stern devotion to duty which on a larger field would have commanded universal admiration, they have usually suffered severely in these conflicts with superior numbers, and have sometimes been entirely sacrificed. All the disposable force of the Army is already employed on this service, and is known to be wholly inadequate to the protection which should be afforded. The public mind of the country has been recently shocked by savage atrocities committed upon defenseless emigrants and border settlements, and hardly less by the unnecessary destruction of valuable lives where inadequate detachments of troops have undertaken to furnish the needed aid. Without increase of the military force these scenes will be repeated, it is feared, on a larger scale with more disastrous consequences. Congress, I am sure, will perceive that the plainest duties and responsibilities of Government are involved in this question, and I doubt not that prompt action may be confidently anticipated when delay must be attended by such fearful hazards.

. . . Information has recently been received that the peace and settlements in the Territories of Oregon and Washington is disturbed by the hostilities on the part of the Indians, with indications of extensive combinations of a hostile character among the tribes in that quarter, the more serious in their possible effect by reason of the undetermined foreign interests existing in those territories, to which your attention has already been especially invited. Efficient measures have been taken, which, it is believed, will restore quiet and afford protection to our citizens.

A Compilation of the Messages and Papers of the Presidents, vol. 6, James D. Richardson, ed. (New York: Bureau of National Literature, Inc., 1897), 2819–2826.

CHIEF SEATTLE, MESSAGE TO PRESIDENT PIERCE (SEATTLE, WA, 1854)

Yonder sky that has wept tears of compassion upon my people for centuries untold, and which to us appears changeless and eternal, may change. Today is fair. Tomorrow it may be overcast with clouds. My words are like the stars that never change. Whatever Seattle says, the great chief at Washington can rely upon with as much certainty as he can upon the return of the sun or the seasons. The white chief says that Big Chief at Washington sends us greetings of friendship and goodwill. This is kind of him for we know he has little need of our friendship in return. His people are many. They are like the grass that covers vast prairies. My people are few. They resemble the scattering trees of a storm-swept plain. The great—and I presume—good, White Chief sends us word that he wishes to buy our land but is willing to allow us enough to live comfortably. This indeed appears just, even generous, for the Red Man no longer has rights that he need respect, and the offer may be wise, also, as we are no longer in need of an extensive country.

There was a time when our people covered the land as the waves of a wind-ruffled sea cover its shell-paved floor, but that time long since passed away with the greatness of tribes that are now but a mournful memory. I will not dwell on, nor mourn over, our untimely decay, nor reproach my paleface brothers with hastening it, as we too may have been somewhat to blame.

Youth is impulsive. When our young men grow angry at some real or imaginary wrong, and disfigure their faces with black paint, it denotes that their hearts are black, and that they are often cruel and relentless, and our old men and old women are unable to restrain them. Thus it has ever been. Thus it was when the white man began to push our forefathers ever westward. But let us hope that the hostilities between us may never return. We would have everything to lose and nothing to gain. Revenge by young men is considered gain, even at the cost of their own lives, but old men who stay at home in times of war, and mothers who have sons to lose, know better.

Our good father in Washington—for I presume he is now our father as well as yours, since King George has moved his boundaries further north—our great and good father, I say, sends us word that if we do as he desires he will protect us. His brave warriors will be to us a bristling wall of strength, and his wonderful ships of war will fill our harbors, so that our ancient enemies far to the northward—the Haidas and Tsimshians—will cease to frighten our women, children, and old men. Then in reality he will be our father and we his children. But can that ever be? Your God is not our God! Your God loves your people and hates mine! He folds his strong protecting arms lovingly about the paleface and leads him by the hand as a father leads an infant son. But, He has forsaken His Red children, if they really are His. Our God, the Great Spirit, seems also to have forsaken us. Your God makes your people wax stronger every day. Soon they will fill all the land. Our people are ebbing away like a rapidly receding tide that will never return. The white man's God cannot love our people or He would protect them. They seem to be orphans who can look nowhere for help. How then can we be brothers? How can your God become our God and renew our prosperity and awaken in us dreams of returning greatness? If we have a common Heavenly Father He must be partial, for He came to His paleface children. We never saw Him. He gave you laws but had no word for His red children whose teeming multitudes once filled this vast continent as stars fill the firmament. No; we are two distinct races with separate origins and separate destinies. There is little in common between us.

To us the ashes of our ancestors are sacred and their resting place is hallowed ground. You wander far from the graves of your ancestors and seemingly without regret. Your religion was written upon tablets of stone by the iron finger of your God so that you could not forget. The Red Man could never comprehend or remember it. Our religion is the traditions of our ancestors—the dreams of our old men, given them in solemn hours of the night by the Great Spirit; and the visions of our sachems, and is written in the hearts of our people. . . .

A few more moons, a few more winters, and not one of the descendants of the mighty hosts that once moved over this broad land or lived in happy homes, protected by the Great Spirit, will remain to mourn over the graves of a people once more powerful and hopeful than yours. But why should I mourn at the untimely fate of my people? Tribe follows tribe, and nation follows nation, like the waves of the sea. It is the order of nature, and regret is useless. Your time of decay may be distant, but it will surely come, for even the White Man whose God walked and talked with him as friend to friend, cannot be exempt from the common destiny. We may be brothers after all. We will see.

We will ponder your proposition and when we decide we will let you know. But should we accept it, I here and now make this condition that we will not be denied the privilege without molestation of visiting at any time the tombs of our ancestors, friends, and children. Every part of this soil is sacred in the estimation of my people. Every hillside, every valley, every plain and grove, has been hallowed by some sad or happy event in days long vanished. Even the rocks, which seem to be dumb and dead as the swelter in the sun along the silent shore, thrill with memories of stirring events connected with the lives of my people, and the very dust upon which you now stand responds more lovingly to their footsteps than yours, because it is rich with the blood of our ancestors, and our bare feet are conscious of the sympathetic touch. Our departed braves, fond mothers, glad, happy-hearted maidens, and even the little children who lived here and rejoiced here for a brief season, will love these somber solitudes and at eventide they greet shadowy returning spirits. And when the last Red Man shall have perished, and the memory of my tribe shall have become a myth among the White Men, these shores will swarm with the invisible dead of my tribe, and when your children's children think themselves alone in the field, the store, the shop, upon the highway, or in the silence of the pathless woods, they will not be alone. In all the earth there is no place dedicated to solitude. At night when the streets of your cities and villages are silent and you think them deserted, they will throng with the returning hosts that once filled them and still love this beautiful land. The White Man will never be alone. Let him be just and deal kindly with my people, for the dead are not altogether powerless.

First published in Seattle, *Sunday Star*, October 29, 1887, 1.

FEDERAL FUNDING FOR THE MENTALLY ILL

While sectional disputes over slavery dominated politics during the Pierce administration, a broader question as to the role and scope of the federal government continued to come under scrutiny. Democrats generally took the position that the powers of the government should be limited to those specifically enumerated in the Constitution; Whigs tended to argue that powers not explicitly stated could be implied from the document. This classic question of republican government appeared and reappeared throughout the antebellum era.

This debate became the focal point of a bill sponsored by Dorothea Dix and others during the Pierce administration. Dix spent her career championing support of the indigent and mentally ill and had by 1850 become renowned internationally for her work in these areas. As the United States expanded westward in the 1840s, and the amount of land held by the United States government increased exponentially, questions arose as how to distribute this acreage. In 1848, working in conjunction with Dorothea Dix, Senator John Dix of New Hampshire (no relation to the former) proposed that Congress set aside 12 million acres of public lands for the purpose of constructing hospitals for the "indigent insane." Up to this time, there were few such facilities, and most of these were owned and operated by private charities or religious organizations. Dorothea Dix worked for years to expose the poor quality of these institutions and raised awareness of the lack of sanitation and, at times, complete lack of regard for the lives of the mentally ill who spent their lives in asylums.

The Dix bill received support from Democrats and Whigs, most on humanitarian grounds and some for the less admirable reason of gaining more federally held lands for their constituents. In several instances, politicians were encouraged by land speculators and contractors who saw financial gain in the venture. In 1854, the Dix bill passed both houses of Congress and arrived on Pierce's desk for approval. Despite support from both parties, Pierce vetoed the legislation on the basis of federalism and the powers of the federal government. His veto message points out that the Constitution is silent on the authority of Congress to fund ventures of "public beneficence." The president attempted to support the cause of the indigent mentally ill on moral grounds, but warned that such a "novel and vast field of legislation" would serve to broaden significantly the role of the federal government with respect to the states and local governments. Arguing that the Dix bill would be a slippery slope to fund other causes of public welfare, Pierce explained that only private resources should be used to purchase lands for such facilities.

Supporters of the Dix bill disagreed with Pierce's reasoning on several counts. For those who accepted a more flexible reading of the Constitution, Pierce's veto message was an incorrect interpretation of the founders' intent. Others, including Senator Solomon Foot of Vermont, questioned the argument that a set-aside of public lands in any way expanded the role of government. Foot goes further in his response to the veto message by pointing out that the federal government, often with support of "strict-constructionist"

Democrats, had few qualms about setting aside lands for other purposes. Foot argues rightly that in past decades Congress had set aside lands for a variety of purposes—for Native American reserves, for canals, shipyards, and other internal improvements, and for veterans.

A case may be made that Pierce's veto of the Dix initiative might have exacerbated sectionalism, as a majority of supporters in the North equated strict interpretation of the Constitution with Southerners who they believed dominated the Congress and played too great a role in Pierce's administration. Regardless, the veto of the Dix bill indicates that disagreements over the responsibilities of the federal government were not reserved solely for the issue of slavery in the 1850s.

FRANKLIN PIERCE, VETO MESSAGE ON FEDERAL FUNDING FOR HOSPITALS FOR THE INSANE (WASHINGTON, DC, MAY 3, 1854)

The bill entitled "An act making a grant of public lands to the several States for the benefit of indigent insane persons," which was presented to me on the 27th ultimo, has been maturely considered, and is returned to the Senate, the House in which it originated, with a statement of the objections which have required me to withhold from it my approval.

In the performance of this duty, prescribed by the Constitution, I have been compelled to resist the deep sympathies of my own heart in favor of the humane purpose sought to be accomplished and to overcome the reluctance with which I dissent from the conclusions of the two Houses of Congress, and present my own opinions in opposition to the action of a coordinate branch of the Government which possesses so fully my confidence and respect. . . .

It can not be questioned that if Congress has power to make provisions for the indigent insane without the limits of this District it has the same power to provide for the indigent who are not insane, and thus to transfer to the Federal Government the charge of all the poor in all the States. It has the same power to provide hospitals and other local establishments for the care and cure of every species of human infirmity, and this to assume all that duty of either public philanthropy, or public necessity to the dependent, the orphan, the sick, or the needy which is now discharged by the States themselves or by corporate institutions of private endowments existing under the legislation of the States. The whole field of public beneficence is thrown open to the case and culture of the Federal Government. General impulses no longer encounter the limitations and control of our imperious fundamental law; for however worthy may be the present object in itself, it is only one of a class. It is not exclusively worthy of benevolent regard. Whatever considerations dictate sympathy for this particular object apply in like manner, if not in the same degree, to idiocy, to physical disease, to extreme destitution. If Congress may and ought to provide for any one of these objects, it may and ought to provide for them all. And if it be done in this case, what answer shall be given when Congress shall be called upon, as it doubtless will be, to pursue a similar course of legislation in the others? It will obviously be vain to reply that the object is worthy, but that the application has taken a wrong direction. The power will have been deliberately assumed, the general obligation will by this act have been acknowledged, and the question of means and expediency will alone be left for consideration. The decision upon the principle in any one case determines it for the whole class. The question presented, therefore, clearly is upon the constitutionality and propriety of the Federal Government assuming to enter a novel and vast field of legislation, namely, that of providing for the care and support of all those among the people of the United States who by any form of calamity become fit objects of public philanthropy.

I readily and, I trust, feelingly acknowledge the duty incumbent on us all as men and citizens, and as among the highest and holiest of our duties, to provide for those who, in the mysterious order of Providence, are subject to want and to disease of body or mind; but I can not find any authority in the Constitution for making the Federal Government the great almoner of public charity throughout the United States. To do so would, in my judgement, be contrary to the letter and spirit of the Constitution and subversive of the whole theory upon which the Union of these States is founded. . . . Are we not too prone to forget that the Federal Union is the creature of the States, not they of the Federal Union? We were the inhabitants of the colonies distinct in local government one from the other before the Revolution. By that Revolution the colonies each became an independent State. They achieved that independence and secured its recognition by the agency of a consulting body, which, from being an assembly of the ministers of distinct sovereignties instructed to agree to no form of government which did not leave the domestic concerns of each State to itself, was appropriately denominated a Congress. . . . Can it be claimed that any of these functions of local administration and legislation are vested in the Federal Government by any implication? I have never found anything in the Constitution which is susceptible to such a construction. Not one of the enumerated powers touches the subject or has even a remote analogy to it. The powers conferred upon the United States have reference to federal relations, or to the means of accomplishing or executing things of federal relation. So also of the same character are the powers taken away from the States by enumeration. In either case the powers granted and the powers restricted were so granted or so restricted only where it was requisite for the maintenance of peace and harmony between the States or for protecting their common interests and defending their common sovereignty against aggression from abroad or insurrection at home. . . .

The general result at which I have arrived is the necessary consequence of those views of the relative rights, powers, and duties of the States and of the Federal Government which I have long entertained and often expressed and in reference to which my convictions do but increase in force with time and experience.

I have thus discharged the unwelcome duty of respectfully stating my objections to this bill, with which I cheerfully submit the whole subject to the wisdom of Congress.

A Compilation of the Messages and Papers of the Presidents, vol. 6, James D. Richardson, ed. (New York: Bureau of National Literature, Inc., 1897), 2780–2789.

SENATOR SOLOMON FOOT (W-VT), IN SUPPORT OF THE DIX BILL (WASHINGTON, DC, MAY 3, 1854)

The chief and controlling objection of the President to this bill, as I understand from his message, rests upon constitutional considerations. He regards it as an infringement on the Constitution! His heart approves the object of the bill, but the exercise of his best intellectual powers does not enable him to find authority under the Constitution to make the grant! He seems painfully anxious to approve the bill for the vast amount of good it would accomplish, but the Constitution forbids! This bill, which makes a grant of ten millions of acres of public lands, to be equitably apportioned among all the States, and its proceeds applied for the relief and support of the indigent insane of the country, he thinks is a violation of the Constitution! I am unable to concur in this opinion. I dissent from it entirely, with all due respect to the authority from which it emanates. This bill, I undertake to say, more nearly than any which has been passed by Congress, and presented to the consideration of any Executive, carries out, according to its spirit and its letter, the original contract by which the public lands were ceded to the Federal Government by the States. It differs from hundreds of acts which have received the sanction of every Congress and of every President almost from the foundation of the Government, only insomuch as it is more general, more universal, if not more beneficent in its operation. Yet, in the opinion of our President is it unconstitutional? This, after all, is but the opinion of one man, though that man be the President of the United States. But I suppose that Presidents are not always infallible expositors of the Constitution; then even President Pierce may fall into error on a question of constitutional construction. . . .

Mr. President, we have been accustomed to hear a great deal about the limited powers of this Federal Government, and of the reserved powers of the State governments—of the danger of enlarging the one, and of encroaching the other—of the beauty and harmony of the system, provided each department be kept within its own proper sphere of action; and a great deal about the injustice of casting burdens upon one portion of the people for the benefit of the other; and all that sort of learned twaddle, as though it had some bearing upon this question, or as though somebody had denied the truth of these common and thread-worn axioms. I am not aware that anybody proposes, just now, to enlarge the delegated powers of the Federal Government, or to encroach upon the reserved powers of the State governments! And, surely, this bill, so far from imposing any burdens upon one portion of the people for the benefit of another, is the only land bill passed by Congress which effectually extends its benefits alike to all, and relieves the burdens of all alike, by an equitable and general distribution. . . .

This is a sufficient answer to the common objection suggested in the message, that Congress has no power to give lands or money for eleemosynary or charitable purposes; that Congress cannot be made the almoner of the Government bounty, or the dispenser of public charities. Or, if Congress had this power, it is insisted that it ought not to be exercised for such purposes; that the precedent would be dangerous; that if you give to one object, you must give to another; if you give to the indigent insane, you must give to the poor and needy generally, and that applications will multiply, and be pressed upon Congress for all manner of objected purposes. But, sir, it ought not to be forgotten, that these applications always have been, and always will be made. Not a few of them have received the favor of Congress. . . . The objection, however, is based upon the assumption that Congress, upon whom the Constitution confers the jurisdiction, will not properly discriminate between meritorious applications, and those which are unworthy of favor . . .

Sir, if I felt called upon to discuss the question of the expediency of this measure, its relative merit, its relative claims upon your favorable consideration, I imagine it would be found to be no very difficult task to show about as much of merit, or public unity, of enduring beneficence, in a grant of land, which has for its object the relief of thirty thousand American citizens, suffering under the most fearful malady that afflicts the human race, as could be shown in the grant of land for the improvement of streets and alleys in Tuscarawas, or for the improvement of the river bank in Shawneetown, or even in the grant of land for an academy in the State of my friend, near me, from Florida [Mr. Morton,] or for a court-house and jail in Arkansas. But I will not weary the patience of the Senate in this preliminary debate upon the message, by going into a discussion of the relative merits and claims of this, compared with other grants which have received the favor of Congress and of the Executive.

With all due deference and respect, I submit that, with the Constitution before you, and in the face of your legislation of half a century upon this subject, it is idle, it is little short of the ridiculous, to talk about the want of authority in Congress to pass this bill. I have only to express the hope that it may receive the sanction of a constitutional majority in both Houses, and become a law of the land, notwithstanding the objections of the President.

Congressional *Globe*, Appendix, 33rd Congress, 1st Session, May 3, 1854, 550–552.

THE GADSDEN PURCHASE

Westward expansion continued to divide Americans during the Pierce administration. Democrats, particularly in the South, continued to support an aggressive foreign policy in the Western Hemisphere. Despite the territorial gains made in the Southwest as a result of the Mexican War, a vocal group of politicians called for the acquisition of more land in the region. Economics played as much a role as nationalism. Railroad investors had begun consideration of a transcontinental railroad that would pass though Texas and New Mexico, with southern California as its terminus. Southerners in Congress were pressured to acquire lands still held by Mexico in order to carry out such a venture.

By the early 1850s, private interests had sought in many ways to extricate more territory from Mexico's northernmost region. The most notable of these was an expedition in 1853 led by filibusterer William Walker, who led a group of armed followers into Baja California and declared the area an independent republic. The Mexican government managed to drive Walker out, but other Americans arrived in Mexico City to negotiate the sale of territory to the United States. While Mexicans were unenthusiastic about the prospects of losing even more land to the United States, the government was in dire straits financially, buried under massive foreign debt. During the age of filibusters, American foreign policy south of the border often was chaotic and unregulated, and the Mexican government found itself negotiating with more than one group of Americans who claimed to be representing the United States government.

Filibusters made President Pierce's policy in Mexico difficult. As a Democrat, he tended to agree with attempts to acquire more territory for purposes of development. In 1853, he deployed James Gadsden, a railroad developer from South Carolina, to Mexico to negotiate a treaty for the purchase of land in northern Mexico. The treaty, completed in December, offered $15 million for 39 million acres of land. Additionally, the United States agreed to assume responsibility for all private claims against the Mexican government. The treaty also ended American responsibility for preventing raids by Native Americans in United States territory across the border in Mexico. Finally, the treaty provided for free travel of Americans across the Isthmus of Tehuantepec.

Democrats faced strong resistance to the Gadsden Purchase in Congress. Thomas Hart Benton, a Whig Senator from Missouri, opposes the treaty on several grounds. He not only finds fault with the price of the purchase, which he argues is far too high, but also points out that the United States already has ample territory in the West to use for railroad construction. Benton describes the area of the purchase as a wasteland that would never attract American settlers in numbers required to develop the area fully. Benton's attack on the treaty goes further, however, by questioning the constitutionality of acquiring lands through purchase without the consent of the entire Congress. For Benton, the Gadsden Purchase was another example of Southern Democrats hoping to strengthen their numbers in the future by adding more Southern territory to the United States.

The response to such criticisms also was rooted in constitutional principles. T.S. Bocock, a Democratic Representative from South Carolina, maintains that the treaty followed the proper legal and political procedures and was consistent with past governmental acquisition of territory. Bocock, speaking in support of the Pierce administration, also questions the claim that the price secured for the territory was too high. In his estimation, the treaty had satisfied both sides and therefore was a legitimate transaction between states.

Debate in Congress over the Gadsden purchase was heated, and the result of congressional negotiation was a revised treaty that reduced the size of the land grant and cut the price to $10 million. This ratified treaty resulted in acquisition of land in the southernmost areas of present-day New Mexico and Arizona. The railroad that had fueled the Gadsden Purchase was delayed as the United States moved close to civil war. In the decades to follow, the Texas and Pacific Railroad was constructed in the region.

REPRESENTATIVE T.S. BOCOCK (D-VA), IN SUPPORT OF THE GADSDEN PURCHASE (WASHINGTON, DC, JUNE 27, 1854)

... The treaty here has been approved by the President, and not only ratified by two thirds of the Senate, but actually shaped by that body. It is the Senate's treaty. It agrees to give Mexico ten millions of dollars for land and other benefits granted by her. It is fair on its face. It involves no express violation of the Constitution. That there was no fraud or corrupt collusion in its negotiation, results almost necessarily from the fact already stated that it was shaped by the Senate. Only one question remains. Does it embrace stipulations which are properly subjects of treaty regulation? In other words, does the treaty power legitimately extend to the contradicting of debts for lands purchased. This I had supposed would scarcely be doubted at this day. How many treaties have been made by the United States for precisely such a purpose? The treaty for the purchase of Louisiana, the treaty for the cession of Florida, the treaty for the acquisition of California and New Mexico, and various of our Indian treaties, are cases in point.

The idea of exchanging benefits of unequal value necessarily implies the payment of money on one side or the other. That lands should be one of the benefits so transferred results from the necessity of settling boundaries by treaty. How can it be otherwise? It is common; I may perhaps say it is universal. The fact that our Constitution does not expressly provide for acquiring territory in this way, caused Mr. Jefferson and Mr. Madison at first to hesitate and doubt the subject. It was apparent, however, that the power "to make treaties" interpreted by the usage of nations, included this right. The requirements of international intercourse, and the pressing exigencies of the occasion persuaded them strongly in that direction. They yielded to their doubts, and since then the question has been considered settled. As to the previous consultation of the House of Representatives, which has been spoken of, that appears to me to be all fancy, "all moonshine," whether we look to the reason of the case or the history of the country. A little money has sometimes been needed in the progress of a treaty, and has been asked for. That is the whole matter. Good has resulted to us thus far from the exercise of this power. See what we have added to the extent and greatness of our country by treaty! Behold and admire! But this good work may not yet be done. These may be but the first fruits which usher in a rich harvest. We hope by friendly negotiation again judiciously employed, soon to lead Cuba, the region of the Antilles, into the sisterhood of the republic. Again and again, as proper occasion shall offer, the arms of our diplomacy may be extended, till our greatness shall culminate and our destiny shall be accomplished. Who will now set bounds to our grandeur? Who would cripple and destroy the peaceful means of its accomplishment? The doctrines of the present may tell weightily on the future of our country. Let gentlemen look to it.

This treaty being such as I have said, I hold that we are not at liberty, in the exercise of good faith, to refuse this appropriation, or will not be after the ratifications shall have been exchanged. This ten million debt, if not paid, will be an obligatory upon us as any other that we owe. If we then refuse still to pay, we will repudiate our debt, deny the obligation of good faith, tarnish the honor of the country, and give Mexico just cause of war. This is my judgement of this question.

Congressional *Globe*, Appendix, 33rd Congress, 1st Session, June 27, 1854, 1047–1048.

SENATOR THOMAS HART BENTON (W-MO), OPPOSING THE GADSDEN PURCHASE (WASHINGTON, DC, JUNE 26, 1854)

When this Federal Government was formed, and while it was yet supposed that the working of the Government would be according to the terms of the Constitution which created it, there were many sagacious and patriotic men who believed that the Government was too strong—that is would be an overmatch for the people and the States, and that in the single grant of power to Congress to raise money by loans and taxes without limitation, and to raise fleets and armies equally without limitation—in that single feature a dangerous power was given to the new Government, by help of which all other powers might be seized. Foremost among these objectors was the famous orator, Patrick Henry, whose sagacious mind was the first to take alarm at this portentous union of the purse and the sword. He declaimed against it; and that while he believed these powers were to be exercised, as written in the Constitution—by the Congress itself, composed of the immediate and responsible representatives of the people. What would that sagacious man and his compeers have said if they had foreseen that these two tremendous powers were to pass from the hands of Congress into the hands of the President and the Senate, and some foreign potentate—a monarch in old Europe, or some would-be monarch in new America? What would Patrick Henry have said to such a conjunction in such hands? But he could not conceive of such a thing. . . .

The war power—the power to make war—is, as a grant to Congress, a mere illusion—a form without substance. To be sure, Congress is called upon to issue the declaration, as it is now called upon to pass this bill; but the real power of making the war resides elsewhere—resides in the Executive Government alone—which, in its power to conduct our foreign relations, has power to make a quarrel with any nation that it pleases; and when the quarrel is gone up, our people will fight. This is what I was accustomed to hear aged men say when I first came to the public councils; and my own observations since I have been in them have confirmed their opinion. I consider the war power now as being substantially in the hands of the President, and that it depends upon him to make war, or not, when he pleases.

The sword is then gone from Congress, and if this bill passes, I shall consider the purse as having gone along with it; and both sword and purse to be at this day in the hands of the Executive Government. What is the bill? It is a bill to take $10,000,000 of the people's money without their previous consent, and as a matter or right, by virtue of an agreement between the President, the Senate, and Santa Anna—the House of Representatives being ignored in the transaction, except as a machine to be worked by the other party, and called in at the last moment to go through a form:—in fact, to give its check for the money. . . .

Left without information, and confined to the view of the treaty itself, I think it should be rejected for its own demerits visible on its fact. Its principal features are an acquisition of a string of territory, in the States of Chihuahua and Sonora for a railroad, and the payment of ten million dollars. I have many objections to this railroad provision. It is a subject which belongs to Congress; and the Representatives of the people are more proper judges of what would suit the people than the President, Senate, and Santa Anna. In the next place, we have routed for roads within our own territory, without paying ten millions for one. We have a fine national route on the parallels of 38 and 39, by Coo-cha-tope, corresponding with the centre of the Union; a sectional route of the parallels of 34 and 35, by Albuquerque, corresponding with the centre of the southern States. The route gained by the treaty is not even a sectional route. It is too far South to be southern. It is not only beyond the centre, but beyond the limits and latitudes of the southern States; and is besides, a thousand miles out of the way to San Francisco; and through a country so utterly desolate, desert, and God-forsaken, that Kit Carson says a wolf could not make his living upon it—and outside, besides.

The acquisition of foreign territory is not provided for in the Constitution; it is an act beyond the Constitution, and requires the concurrence of both the legislative and Executive authorities to complete it. It is known to everybody that Mr. Jefferson, in the acquisition of Louisiana, held the purchase to be entirely beyond all the powers of the Government; and he only satisfied that doubt by coming, as near as he could, to an original act from the people. He submitted the question to their immediate representatives, and so united both the legislative and diplomatic power in the making of the acquisition.

. . . The purse of the American people lies at the mercy of a secret presidential resolve, a secret senatorial vote, and a secret bargain with any foreign potentate, legitimate or illegitimate. The principle of such a thing is sufficient to startle all thinking people: the extent to which it has been carried should alarm the most thoughtless. Ten millions are in the bill, for which was purchased for only $6,500. Twenty millions were in the treaty as negotiated: fifty millions were authorized to be given: and two hundred and fifty millions more for another purchase conducted with the same secrecy. I say again, farewell to the money and property of the people if these things be done! Farewell to the clause in the Constitution, which gave the string of the public purse to the people's representatives! Farewell to a Constitution which is nothing but the empty skin of an immolated victim!

Congressional *Globe*, Appendix, 33rd Congress, 1st Session, June 26, 1854, 1031–1036.

THE OSTEND MANIFESTO

Few events illustrated the growing division over American foreign policy in the 1850s than the controversial Ostend Manifesto. At issue was the island of Cuba. Despite the attempts of adventurers and filibusters, Cuba remained a Spanish possession—a fact that frustrated a number of expansionist Democrats who saw the island as a clear candidate for acquisition and perhaps annexation. The fiasco of the Narciso Lopez expedition, a flawed attempt to liberate Cuba from Spanish rule that had ended in embarrassment for the United States government, failed to deter others who were committed to seeing the Spanish removed. President Pierce tended to side with the expansionists, as evidenced by some of his foreign policy appointments. His choice of minister to The Hague, for example, was the banker August Belmont, who had made as his personal goal the purchase of Cuba from Spain. Pierce's minister to Spain, Louisiana lawyer Pierre Soulé, also sought the acquisition of Cuba and in the past had met with Cuban exiles in New York who shared the same objective. While the president remained, for the most part, publicly silent on the issue of Cuba, these appointments made clear where his sympathies lay.

After a few years of relative quiet regarding Cuba, in 1854 relations between the United States and Spain once again became strained due to actions of American adventurers. In March, the *Black Warrior*, an American ship, was seized by Spanish officials off the coast of Cuba and its crew arrested for violating harbor regulations. Expansionists at home sought to use the action for political gain and cried out for war against Spain for her ill treatment of Americans on the high seas. Cool heads prevailed, however, and another crisis with Spain was averted.

In July 1854, however, Spanish-American relations almost reached a breaking point due to the issuance of the Ostend Manifesto. Secretary of State William L. Marcy had instructed Soulé to discuss with other American leaders abroad a strategy for purchasing Cuba from Spain. Soulé jumped at the chance and arranged a meeting in Ostend, Belgium, that was attended by Soulé, Ambassador to France John Y. Mason, and Ambassador to Great Britain James Buchanan. Although the meeting was supposed to be secret, the meeting attracted scores of reporters and the "secret message" that was to travel back to Marcy was distributed to the press and widely published.

The Ostend Manifesto spelled out the reasons why the United States should purchase Cuba from Spain. The three Americans did not hesitate to use firm language, pointing out that insurrection in Cuba against the Spanish colonial government was a strong possibility. The manifesto also claims that if Spain refuses to sell Cuba, the United States would be justified in using force to take the island.

If Pierce agreed with the sentiment of the Ostend Manifesto, publicly he could ill afford to support the controversial statement. Eighteen fifty-four was an election year, and extreme voices of expansion would result in the alienation of Northern Democrats, who were crucial to the success of the party. In fact, political opposition to the acquisition of Cuba could be found in all regions of the country. Representative William W. Boyce of South Carolina offers in the following speech his reasons for opposing any actions in Cuba. For Boyce, the annexation of Cuba would not strengthen the defenses of the nation but rather weaken them. Annexation also would mean that the Cubans themselves would become American citizens; Boyce, as a Southerner, was particularly concerned about the prospect of granting citizenship to nonwhites who, in his view, were "the worst kind of material" for democratic government.

Pierce managed to downplay the Ostend Manifesto and backed off from attempts to purchase Cuba. While relations between Spain and the United States would never warm completely, final resolution of the Cuban question would not occur until the Spanish-American War of 1898, when, upon defeating Spain, the United States claimed Cuba as a protectorate.

EXCERPT FROM THE OSTEND MANIFESTO (OSTEND, BELGIUM, OCTOBER 1854)

We firmly believe that, in the progress of human events, the time has arrived when the vital interests of Spain are as seriously involved in the sale, as those of the United States in the purchase, of the island and that the transaction will prove equally honorable to both nations.

Under these circumstances we cannot anticipate a failure, unless possibly through the malign influence of foreign powers who possess no right whatever to interfere in the matter.

We proceed to state some of the reasons which have brought us to this conclusion, and, for the sake of clearness, we shall specify them under two distinct heads:

1. The United States ought, if practicable, to purchase Cuba with as little delay as possible.

2. The probability is great that the government and Cortes of Spain will prove willing to sell it, because this would essentially promote the highest and best interests of the Spanish people.

Considerations exist which render delay in the acquisition of this island exceedingly dangerous to the United States.

Besides, the commercial nations of the world cannot fail to perceive and appreciate the great advantages which would result to their people from a dissolution of the forced and unnatural connexion between Spain and Cuba, and the annexation of the latter to the United States. The trade of England and France with Cuba would, in that event, assume at once an important and profitable character, and rapidly extend with the increasing population and prosperity of the island.

We know that the President is justly inflexible in his determination to execute the neutrality laws; but should the Cubans themselves rise in revolt against the oppression which they suffer, no human power could prevent citizens of the United States and liberal-minded men of other countries from rushing to their assistance. Besides, the present is an age of adventure, in which restless and daring spirits abound in every portion of the world.

It is not improbable, therefore, that Cuba may be wrested from Spain by a successful revolution; and in that event she will lose both the island and the price which we are now willing to pay for it—a price far beyond what was ever paid by one people to another for any province.

It is certain that, should the Cubans themselves organize an insurrection against the Spanish government, and should other independent nations come to the aid of Spain in the contest, no human power could, in our opinion, prevent the people and government of the United States from taking part in such a civil war in support of their neighbors and friends.

But if Spain, dead to the voice of her own interest, and actuated by stubborn pride and a false sense of honor, should refuse to sell Cuba to the United States, then the question will arise, What ought to be the course of the American government under such circumstances? Self-preservation is the first law of nature, with States as well as with individuals. All nations have, at different periods, acted upon this maxim. Although it has been made the pretext for committing flagrant injustice, as in the partition of Poland and other similar cases which history records, yet the principle itself, though often abused, has always been recognized.

After we shall have offered Spain a price for Cuba far beyond its present value, and this shall have been refused, it will then be time to consider the question, does Cuba, in the possession of Spain, seriously endanger our internal peace and the existence of our cherished Union?

Should this question be answered in the affirmative, then, by every law, human and divine, we shall be justified in wresting it from Spain if we possess the power, and this upon the very same principle that would justify an individual in tearing down the burning house of his neighbor if there were no other means of preventing the flames from destroying his own home.

Under such circumstances we ought neither to count the cost nor regard the odds which Spain might enlist against us. We forbear to enter into the question, whether the present condition of the island would justify such a measure? We should, however, be recreant to our duty, be unworthy of our gallant forefathers, and commit base treason against our posterity, should we permit Cuba to be Africanized and become a second St. Domingo, with all its attendant horrors to the white race, and suffer the flames to extend to our own neighboring shores, seriously to endanger or actually to consume the fair fabric of our Union.

We also forbear to investigate the present condition of the questions at issue between the United States and Spain. A long series of injuries to our people have been committed in Cuba by Spanish officials and are unredressed. But recently a most flagrant outrage on the rights of American citizens and on the flag of the United States was perpetrated in the harbor of Havana under circumstances which, without immediate redress, would have justified a resort to measures of war in vindication of national honor. That outrage is not only unatoned, but the Spanish government has deliberately sanctioned the acts of its subordinates and assumed the responsibility attaching to them.

But this course cannot, with due regard to their own dignity as an independent nation, continue; and our recommendations, now submitted, are dictated by the firm belief that the cession of Cuba to the United States, with stipulations as beneficial to Spain as those suggested, is the only effective mode of settling all past differences and of securing the two countries against future collisions.

We have already witnessed the happy results for both countries which followed a similar arrangement in regard to Florida.

Yours, very respectfully,
JAMES BUCHANAN
J.Y. MASON
PIERRE SOULÉ

House Executive Documents, 33rd Congress, 2nd Session, 127–136.

REPRESENTATIVE W.W. BOYCE (D-SC), OPPOSITION TO THE OSTEND MANIFESTO (WASHINGTON, DC, JANUARY 15, 1855)

Mr. Chairman, I propose to make some observations on the annexation of Cuba. I consider it the great question of our foreign relations.

A feverish impatience seems to be seizing upon our people for territorial extension. In some quarters the cry is for the Canadas. Upon these points, we have been informed by a leading member from Ohio [Mr. Campbell] that the people upon the northern frontier took with deep feeling to the annexation of the British Provinces of North America. In other quarters the cry is for the Sandwich Islands; some are wishing for another partition of Mexico; others are looking to the regions watered by the mighty Amazon; more are bent upon the acquisition of Cuba, and some have such inordinate stomachs that they are willing to swallow the entire continent. These are all but various phases of the manifest destiny idea. I must confess, I do not sympathize with this idea. I think our true mission is conservatism, not indefinite extension. . . .

It is very clear that, do what else we may, we have nothing to gain by annexing more territory, to increase our population by a foreign supply. If we do not need any more territory, or any extraordinary addition of population by acquisition of territory, then the annexation of Cuba cannot be urged on either these grounds. Then upon what grounds can it be urged? Perhaps it may be urged on the ground that it is necessary to us as a military position to protect our commerce. But I cannot admit this; and, in considering this point, I must assume that it is the settled policy of our Government not to permit Cuba to pass from Spain into the hands of any of the great European Powers. Taking this for granted, I say we have nothing to fear from Cuba. We have strong positions at Key West and Tortugas, which we are now fortifying, and which can be rendered impregnable. Our naval power is infinitely superior to that of Spain; we can effectually command the outlets of the Gulf of Mexico; and the idea of our commerce being in any danger from Cuba is, I think, without significant foundation. . . .

But I go further; so far from the acquisition of Cuba strengthening us in a military point of view, I think it would be a source of infinite weakness. And if the history of the contests in Europe, between the great Powers, demonstrate any fact, it is that maritime colonies to a nation of secondary naval force are great drawbacks. . . .

The whole argument for the annexation of Cuba, in a national point of view, may be summed up in the four propositions I have been considering:

1. More territory.
2. More population.
3. Military position.
4. More commerce.

The first three have no merit; on the contrary, they are full of disadvantages. The last has some merit, but it is entirely outweighed by other adverse considerations. I conclude, therefore, on national grounds, that it is inexpedient to annex Cuba. . . .

Would Cuba be a stable political community, or, in other words, competent to self-government? I doubt it. Self-government involves two considerations—the race, and the training. There is only one race of people in modern times who have shown the capability of self-government, that is the Anglo-Saxon race, the race to which we belong; and with us it is still, in some degree, an experiment. But whatever question there may be as to other races, there can be but one opinion as to the incompetency of the Spanish race. At no time, and under no circumstances, have they been able to preserve republican institutions. The Spanish-American republics, whose populations are of the same race and grade as the whites of Cuba, have become the by-word of history; every step in their insane career has been the melancholy blot and blur of free institutions. The Spanish Creole race of Cuba are the worst kind of materials with which to build up republican institutions. . . .

It may be said, suppose England and France seize Cuba, what then? There are some things so improbable that they need hardly be considered, and this is one. After England and France are done with Russia, they will not be in a mood to disturb anybody, much less will they want to jar on the United States. But neither England nor France want Cuba; in their hands it would be necessarily a free negro colony, and, therefore, worthless; but if either of them should want it, their mutual jealousy would prevent either from taking it. But if, in violation of all possibility, they should make the attempt, I say at once I would draw the sword and drive them into the sea. . . .

Mr. Chairman, the acquisition of Cuba will open a new volume in our history. Former acquisitions were the necessities of location, or of circumstance. This is not. By this step we are fairly launched in the career of conquest, from which there is no outlet but to storm the future, sword in hand. From this career we have nothing to hope, and everything to fear; for our greatest success would be our greatest disaster.

Congressional *Globe*, Appendix, 33rd Congress, 2nd Session, January 15, 1855, 91–94.

RECOMMENDED READINGS

Gara, Larry. *The Presidency of Franklin Pierce*. Lawrence: University of Kansas Press, 1991.

Holt, Michael F. *The Political Crisis of the 1850s*. New York: Wiley Publishers, 1978.

Levine, Bruce. *Half Slave, Half Free*. New York: Hill & Wang, 1992.

Nichols, Roy F. *Franklin Pierce: Young Hickory of the Granite Hills*. Philadelphia: University of Pennsylvania Press, 1958.

Potter, David M. *The Impending Crisis, 1848–1961*. New York: Harper & Row, 1976.

3

JAMES BUCHANAN

(1857–1861)

INTRODUCTION

The celebrations, with parades, dancing, and other forms of revelry had lasted for two full days, but James Buchanan knew that serious times lay ahead. He had arrived at Wheatland, his estate in Pennsylvania, only a few days earlier after having served as the United States Ambassador to England for almost three years. Although he never married and had no children, Buchanan did have a large extended family of nieces and nephews and their children, and all were thrilled at his return. Friends from the area of Lancaster, Pennsylvania, where Buchanan had spent most of his early life, also arrived at Wheatland that spring of 1856, along with those made throughout a long and distinguished political career. Everyone there, including Buchanan, knew that this carnival-like atmosphere was more than a welcome-home party. Newspaper reporters lurked, seeking opportunities to speak with Democratic Party leaders. Strategists met behind closed doors and spoke quietly of future plans. Eighteen fifty-six was an election year, and even though the incumbent Franklin Pierce had served only a single term, few expected him to survive the convention to receive the nomination again. Consequently, Buchanan stood as the most probable replacement for Pierce, as the Democratic candidate and as president.

While insiders assured Buchanan that the nomination was his for the taking, the "Sage of Wheatland" understandably had his doubts. In the prior three presidential elections he had been among the leading candidates for the party's nomination; in each of these Buchanan failed to win. The 1852 primary was the most frustrating, as the dark horse Pierce not only won the party contest but went on to win the White House. Yet the

Pierce administration had been an embattled one and Pierce himself had proclaimed from the outset that he had no intentions of seeking the presidency for a second term. Naturally, party leaders sought out other prospects. Buchanan was an obvious choice. He enjoyed a rare combination of experience, affability, charm, and political acumen that had guided him throughout an impressive career.

Buchanan grew up with the nation itself. He was born near Mercersburg, Pennsylvania, in April 1791 to a Scotch-Irish farming family. Buchanan's father, James, Sr., had migrated to the United States from Ireland in 1783, and held great hopes that his son would enjoy the opportunities available in America to rise above his station. There were times, in fact, when the father's expectations evidently became overbearing, yet Buchanan and his father always remained on good terms. James, Sr. oversaw his son's early education, then sent him to Dickinson College, where he graduated in 1809. During his college years, Buchanan's personality as an extroverted, talented, and at times quite arrogant man emerged. He achieved high grades but also compiled a record of disciplinary problems that nearly led to his expulsion. Nevertheless, Buchanan left Dickinson one of the more accomplished students of his class.

By this time, Buchanan was intent on a career in politics and law. He apprenticed with James Hopkins, a noted attorney in Lancaster, Pennsylvania, which at that time served as the state's capital. Buchanan was admitted to the bar in 1812 and only two years later ran for a seat in the state assembly. Buchanan began his political life as a member of the Federalist party, a product more of tradition than political philosophy. From the outset, he tended to support the Democratic elements of his state in central and western Pennsylvania more than the Federalists of Philadelphia. For the time being, however, Buchanan was proud of his membership in the party of George Washington and John Adams.

Buchanan's early life was one of unbridled success until his tragic relationship with Ann Coleman. Buchanan's success made him one of the more eligible bachelors in Lancaster. He became entranced with the striking daughter of wealthy iron magnate and Dickinson College trustee Robert Coleman. Ann Caroline Coleman had many suitors, however, and initially was unimpressed with the aggressive and sometimes overbearing Buchanan. Also, Ann's parents were aware of Buchanan's disciplinary problems while a student at Dickinson. Nevertheless, young James Buchanan never gave in, and in the end Ann succumbed to his indefatigable pursuits. The couple announced their engagement in 1819.

Trouble appeared from the start of the tortured engagement. Few would deny that the class divide in America was more fluid than in Old Europe, but certainly it was there, particularly in small towns and cities where one's social rank was of utmost importance. The socialites of Lancaster, of which the Colemans were among the most prominent, began to circulate rumors that Buchanan was interested more in attaching himself to the Coleman family fortune than in Ann's affections. Close friends managed to convince her that there were some doubts as to James Buchanan's intentions; she made him aware of these concerns forthrightly. Buchanan was undeterred and sought to repair any damage done to the fragile relationship.

Despite his efforts, the relationship was doomed. Part of it was his own doing. Already under the suspicious watch of the Coleman family, Buchanan committed a breach in etiquette in visiting the wife of a close friend whose unmarried young sister, Miss Grace Hubley, was visiting. Buchanan's visit was innocent, but lasted very late and became the focus of gossip in Lancaster. Ann Coleman was offended, and also hurt, for Buchanan had been away on business for several days and had chosen to make this visit before calling on the Colemans. This perceived slight, combined with the potential damage to Miss Coleman's reputation, compelled her to call off the engagement. Refusing to see Buchanan at all, she traveled to Philadelphia to see family and to recuperate from an illness. Five days later, a stunned Lancaster received word that she had died. Rumors of suicide, brought on by her difficulties with Buchanan, circulated through town. Buchanan was crushed. The Coleman family refused to allow him to attend a private viewing of the body and continued to hold him somewhat responsible for her death. Buchanan came away from the incident heartbroken and changed. He remained a bachelor for the duration of his life; close friends asserted that Buchanan's entire demeanor took on an air of seriousness and urgency after these events.

Perhaps accusations of opportunism provided Buchanan with even more resolve to excel. Over the next several decades, Buchanan ascended from local assemblyman to president of the United States. His first foray into national politics was in 1820, when Buchanan won a seat in the House of Representatives in the Seventeenth Congress. This was the time of the "Era of Good Feelings," in which a single political party, the Democratic-Republican Party, controlled the Congress. "Good Feelings," however, did not mean complete agreement. By the early 1820s, factions had begun to form within the party, based primarily on region. Two major groups emerged. The first was the National Republicans, who followed Kentuckian Henry Clay's American System and were linked closely to the Hamiltonians of an earlier age. This union of Northeastern financial interests and those in the Western states advocated tariffs to protect domestic industry, promoted a centralized banking system, and asserted national responsibility for "internal improvements"—the development of infrastructure such as roads, canals, and ports.

Buchanan had always considered himself a direct descendent of the Federalists. However, as he worked his way through political debates in the early 1820s he found himself most often in agreement with another faction, which stressed local political authority, particularly the doctrine of states' rights, and personal property rights. As Andrew Jackson emerged as a political phenomenon, Buchanan attached his own fortunes to those of "Old Hickory." When in the late 1820s the Jacksonians formed a new political party, the Democratic Party, Buchanan joined enthusiastically and remained a staunch Democrat for the remainder of his career. The move proved to be prescient, as the party came to dominate national politics from the time of Jackson to the Civil War.

Jackson's rise in politics was a boon to Buchanan. He was persuaded to serve as United States minister to Russia in 1831, which launched Buchanan's career as a diplomat. He served well in the post and returned in 1834 to fill a vacancy in the United States Senate. For the remainder of the 1830s, Buchanan was a strong voice of support for Jackson and his successor Martin Van Buren. In 1837, he declined a request to serve as the United States Attorney General for Van Buren and remained in the Senate. In 1843 he was elected to that body for the third time.

During these years, despite or perhaps because of his marital status, Buchanan enjoyed a close relationship with extended family and became somewhat of a patriarch. Now well-to-do and highly regarded, he welcomed a large number of less fortunate relatives. By the early 1850s, he had over thirty nieces, nephews, grandnieces, and grandnephews that looked to him for advice and financial support. At any given time several of these were living under his roof. After he purchased the Wheatland estate in 1848, his role as family provider grew. Harriet Lane, a niece orphaned at the age of nine, moved there and grew into a beautiful and vibrant young woman. As Buchanan's political fortunes increased, Ms. Lane took on the role as social hostess for the estate. In later years, Harriet Lane became world-renowned as mistress of the White House, entertaining and dazzling heads of state and dignitaries from all parts of the globe.

Meanwhile, Buchanan had moved out of the Senate and into new positions of leadership. As a leading Democrat, he was mentioned as a possible presidential candidate in the election of 1844, the first of several occasions when the party would consider him for the role. Instead, he was tapped as James K. Polk's secretary of state, a position in which he served in a historic capacity. Buchanan oversaw the settlement of the Oregon boundary dispute, the annexation of Texas, and the war with Mexico. At the end of Polk's administration, and with the election of Whig Zachary Taylor to the presidency in 1848, Buchanan retired with his reputation as a skilled statesman intact.

Retirement was short-lived, however. Buchanan expected to re-enter the political fray with the 1852 election. President Fillmore hardly could be considered a lock for re-election, and once again Buchanan's name was at the top of the list of potential Democratic competitors. During the tumult of the Taylor-Fillmore years, Buchanan skillfully established himself as a voice of moderation. Always maintaining good relations with Southern

Democrats, he supported the Compromise of 1850 and urged support for the Fugitive Slave Act as fair and necessary for the protection of Southern slaveholders. At the Democratic convention of June 1852, Buchanan was seen as a candidate who could hold the party's sectional wings together. However, while Buchanan had made many friends during his political career, he also had his share of rivals. Among these was Senator Stephen A. Douglas of Illinois. Douglas also campaigned as a national candidate and managed to split the party's support enough to create gridlock at the convention. After continual balloting, the Democrats finally went with a compromise candidate in Pierce. Pierce went on to win the general election; Buchanan had to feel somewhat spurned by his party.

To President Pierce's credit, he recognized Buchanan's influence and talents and offered him the position of minister to England in April 1853. Once again Buchanan served energetically, and this time somewhat controversially, as an American diplomat. As a Democrat with Southern sympathies, he promoted expansionism and continued to advocate an aggressive foreign policy. Along with the American ministers to France and Spain, Buchanan signed the Ostend Manifesto that announced in direct terms the nation's intent to acquire Cuba from Spain. He also dealt effectively with the British seizure of the Bay Islands off the Honduran Coast and managed to take a firm stance toward England without sparking conflict. By Spring 1856, Buchanan's name again was being mentioned as a candidate for president, even though Pierce was completing only his first term. His happy return to the Wheatland estate, far from a restful event, began his most important political journey.

Much had happened since Buchanan had left for England. The Whig Party, having fought for years to hold together its various factions, dissolved in the wake of the debates over the Kansas-Nebraska Act. In its place came the Republican party, born of an alliance between antislavery elements in the Northwest with Free Soilers, abolitionists, and anti-immigrant Know-Nothings. Outraged by the abandonment of the Missouri Compromise and with the possibility of slavery entering territory above the Mason-Dixon Line, Northerners flocked to the new party. Republican leaders worked energetically to focus on more than the slavery question. At the 1856 convention, the party announced a platform of economic development and internal improvements. However, its strongest language was reserved for territorial issues. The Republicans made it clear that their aim was to prohibit slavery in the West and charged the Pierce administration with criminal behavior in the recent Kansas debacle. The new party ran the popular "Pathfinder," the explorer John C. Frémont, for president.

Democrats had reason to believe that the White House would remain in their hands if care were taken to keep its faction united. From the beginning of the convention, which began on June 2, 1856, in Cincinnati, that goal was far from assured. The past few months had been among the most chaotic in

American political history. On May 22, South Carolina Senator Preston Brooks had attacked Charles Sumner of Massachusetts with a cane on the floor of the Senate in retaliation for remarks Sumner had made in the heat of debates over slavery in the territories. Two days later, at Pottawatomie Creek, Kansas, abolitionist John Brown and his sons had brutally murdered five proslavery men in response to earlier violence at Lawrence. With the convention to meet only a few days later, slavery and sectional politics threatened to shatter the party.

There was serious debate during the convention, but most of it was over the candidate, not the platform. Franklin Pierce hesitantly agreed to run for re-election and faced challenges from all sides. Pierce should have listened to his own conscience. Few in the party believed he could win and the contest came down to Buchanan and Douglas. When Pierce removed himself from the balloting, it became a two-man race. After more balloting, with Buchanan leading on each but falling short of a majority, Douglas bowed out with an eye on the 1860 nomination. In the end, the fact that Buchanan had been out of the country for two years may have given him the edge. Pierce and Douglas had fought for the Kansas-Nebraska Act and won, but in the process had generated a great deal of criticism. Buchanan, something of an outsider when it came to these recent political battles, enjoyed an air of impartiality.

The Democratic Party platform sought to strike a middle ground on the issues of the day but offered more for the Southern wing. In addition to nominating the proslavery John C. Breckenridge for the vice presidency, the party announced its support of the Kansas-Nebraska Act and popular sovereignty in the territories. The platform also affirmed the Compromise of 1850 and criticized those who would agitate on the slave issue as dangerous to the Union. Buchanan stayed at Wheatland for most of the election, traveling across Pennsylvania in the final stages to ensure victory in his home state. Despite the fact that the Republican Party was engaged in its first election and running against the highly regarded Buchanan, the results were strikingly close. Buchanan won a narrow victory in the electoral college; his home state might have been pivotal. If nothing else, the 1856 campaign indicated that the Republicans were a force with which to be reckoned and that Democrats' attempts to dismiss them as extremist "Black Republicans" would not work.

Buchanan entered the White House committed to overcoming regional strife. As did many Americans at the time, he believed that far more important problems faced the nation than slavery. There were questions regarding settlement and development of the frontier. There were foreign policy issues, on which Buchanan was most focused. His inaugural address of March 1857 assured Americans that the territorial disputes would resolve themselves in the courts and in Congress along constitutional lines. Much of his speech addressed other issues—tariffs and trade, defense of the frontier, and relations with other nations. His words are reminders to students of history that the patterns and causal links applied to the past often obscure the fact that, to the participants, events were far from inevitable. Buchanan certainly was aware of the explosive nature of the regional dispute, but secession and war were the farthest things from his and most Americans' minds.

If regional balance was a high priority for the new administration, Buchanan did little to achieve it in his cabinet selections. In an effort to avoid controversy, he selected Lewis Cass, the aged and infirm elder of the party, as secretary of state. As his other cabinet choices were announced, the influence of Buchanan's Southern friends became evident. In all, there was little variety in the choices. Four were Southerners who were unapologetic about slavery in the South or in the territories; three were from Northern states but for the most part held Southern views on the issues. Also crucial was Buchanan's refusal to make a cabinet-level appointment from among Douglas's supporters, a move that created much hostility toward Buchanan within his own party. Presidents enjoy the privilege of selecting their respective cabinets; however, Buchanan failed to show any political sensitivity in these important decisions.

In fact, insensitivity characterized Buchanan's presidency as a whole. He was talented and certainly experienced in politics. Buchanan was headstrong and had a clear understanding that politics was as much practical as ideological. However, Buchanan never understood the depth of opposition to slavery, and particularly its westward expansion, in the North. Buchanan's views on slavery were in effect Southern. Slavery, he believed, was a question of property rights. As such, when Southerners claimed that any prohibition on slavery anywhere was an affront to the basic right of property guaranteed by the Constitution, Buchanan understood. Northerners, increasingly, saw the issue in moral terms. As crises mounted, Buchanan took stances he believed to be supported clearly by the Constitution. Only this way, he assumed, could the Union be maintained. The tragedy of Buchanan's presidency was that each decision made in the name of constitutional rights to property and due process provoked more anger and hostility in the North. When secession occurred, Buchanan still clung to the hope that there could be a political or legal resolution. Even in later years, following the Civil War, he pointed to Northern agitators who had little regard for constitutional principles as the instigators of the conflict.

THE LECOMPTON CONSTITUTION

The most immediate crisis Buchanan faced upon entering the White House was in Kansas. During the Pierce administration, a controversy over government in the territory had grown to the point that Eastern reporters were writing sensationalized stories about "bleeding Kansas." The problems had existed since 1854, when residents of the territory were to establish a government by way of "popular sovereignty" as required by the newly enacted Kansas-Nebraska Act. In the weeks preceding the election of a territorial legislature and a delegate to Congress, the region became the center of national attention. Free Soilers, outraged at the repeal of the Missouri Compromise that would have guaranteed the exclusion of slavery in the region, were convinced that Southerners would stop at nothing to ensure the westward spread of slavery. Groups in the Northeast began to raise funds to send antislavery settlers to Kansas to ensure a free-state population there, although such efforts met with little success.

Southerners, for their part, believed that a free Kansas would provide yet another outlet for escaped slaves; many somehow convinced themselves through tortured logic that the future of the slave system everywhere lay in the balance. Prior to the November 1854 election, proslavery Missourians, perhaps as many as two thousand, crossed the border to vote illegally, and Northern cries of "border ruffians" who sought to undermine the voice of the people rang out across the North. Free Soilers eventually formed their own political party, centered at Topeka, and developed their own legislature which they claimed to be the legitimate government of the territory. To make matters worse, sporadic violence between those who supported slavery and those opposed to it threatened to spark a full-scale civil war in the region.

In 1855, antislavery advocates in Kansas met in Topeka for a convention to draft a constitution for statehood that excluded slavery (and also contained a provision to exclude free blacks from the territory as well). The proslavery legislature denounced the convention as illegal and illegitimate; Pierce agreed and refused to recognize the convention on the grounds that it did not have the sanction of the territorial legislature. In early 1857, the day after Buchanan entered office, the proslavery legislature met at Lecompton, Kansas, for the purpose of forming another constitutional convention. The governor of the territory resigned in protest, claiming that the vast majority of citizens in Kansas did not recognize the Lecompton convention as a voice of the voters.

Buchanan was resolved to remedy the problem in Kansas by recognizing the Lecompton convention as legitimate so as to achieve statehood for the territory as quickly as possible. Buchanan himself probably cared little as to whether slavery would be allowed there or not, but Southerners close to the president urged him to work actively to sustain the Lecompton constitution.

The proslavery constitution drafted at Lecompton was put to the voters in December 1857. Despite the attempts of the new territorial governor, Buchanan appointee Robert J. Walker, to sell the document as legitimate, Free Soilers refused to support it. First, they argued that all elections in Kansas had been unlawful, and that any vote on the constitution would be tainted as a result. Second, the opposition criticized the fact that the ballot only allowed voters to accept the new constitution with slavery or without; voters did not have the option to reject the constitution altogether. The outcome of the voting justified the concerns of the Free Soilers. Even though the vast majority of Kansas residents opposed slavery in the territory, the proslavery version of the document won easily, primarily because most Free Soilers refused to vote at all.

President Buchanan then made a crucial decision to recognize the outcome of the Lecompton vote. In the following speech, he argues that the constitution was formed legitimately and placed blame for any difficulties in Kansas squarely on the shoulders of antislavery advocates. Buchanan's support for a constitution that clearly did not reflect the views of most citizens of Kansas resulted in outrage in several quarters. Governor Walker resigned; soon the antislavery legislature sponsored their own election, which allowed voters to support the constitution or reject it outright. In a landslide, voters rejected the document, although this time supporters of the constitution refused to participate in what they viewed was an illegal and unnecessary election.

Buchanan's dogged support of the Lecompton constitution met with sharp criticism from the Republicans and further alienated antislavery Democrats. Most significantly, the crisis drove a wedge between Buchanan and Stephen A. Douglas, the powerful Democratic senator from Illinois and a champion of popular sovereignty in the Western territories. Douglas and Buchanan had been rivals for years; Buchanan's actions pushed Douglas to declare a complete break with the administration. In the following congressional address, Douglas explains that the Lecompton constitution violated the basics precepts of popular sovereignty and lacked legitimacy. In the end, the Lecompton constitution was approved by both the House of Representatives and the Senate, but then was rejected by the voters of Kansas when it was returned to the state for a vote on ratification. Soon disputes over slavery would engulf the entire nation.

JAMES BUCHANAN, IN SUPPORT OF THE LECOMPTON CONSTITUTION (WASHINGTON, DC, FEBRUARY 2, 1858)

I have received from J. Calhoun, esq., president of the late constitutional convention of Kansas, a copy, duly certified by himself, of the constitution framed by that body, with the expression of a hope that I would submit the same to the consideration of Congress "with the view of the admission of Kansas into the Union as an independent State." In compliance with this request, I herewith transmit to Congress, for their action, the constitution of Kansas, with the ordinance respecting the public lands, as well as the letter of Mr. Calhoun, dated at Lecompton on the 14th ultimo, by which they were accompanied. Having received but a single copy of the constitution and ordinance, I send this to the Senate.

A great delusion seems to pervade the public mind in relation to the condition of parties in Kansas. This arises from the difficulty of inducing the American people to realize the fact that any portion of them should be in a state of rebellion against the government under which they live. When we speak of the affairs of Kansas, we are apt to refer merely to the existence of two violent political parties in that Territory, divided on the question of slavery, just as we speak of such parties in the States. This presents no adequate idea of the true state of the case. The dividing line there is not between two political parties, both acknowledging the lawful existence of the government, but between those who are loyal to this government and those who have endeavored to destroy its existence by force and by usurpation—between those who sustain and those who have done all in their power to overthrow the territorial government established by Congress. This government they would long since have subverted had it not been protected from their assaults by the troops of the United States. Such has been the condition of affairs since my inauguration. Ever since that period a large proportion of the people of Kansas have been in a state of rebellion against the government, with a military leader at their head of a most turbulent and dangerous character. . . .

This Topeka government, adhered to with such treasonable pertinancy, is a government in direct opposition to the existing government prescribed and recognized by Congress. It is a usurpation of the same character as it would for a portion of the people of any State of the Union to undertake to establish a separate government within its limits for the purpose of redressing any grievance, real or imaginary, of which they might complain against the legitimate State government. Such a principle, if carried into execution, would destroy all lawful authority and produce universal anarchy.

From this statement of facts the reason becomes palpable why the enemies of the government authorized by Congress have refused to vote for delegates to the Kansas constitutional convention, and also afterwards on the question of slavery, submitted by it to the people. It is because they have ever refused to sanction or recognize any other constitution than that framed at Topeka. . . .

From this review it is manifest that the Lecompton convention, according to every principle of constitutional law, was legally constituted and was invested with power to frame a constitution.

The sacred principle of popular sovereignty has been invoked in favor of the enemies of law and order in Kansas. But in what manner is popular sovereignty to be exercised in this country if not through the instrumentality of established law? In certain small republics of ancient times the people did assemble in primary meetings, passed laws, and directed public affairs. In our country this is manifestly impossible. Popular sovereignty can be exercised here only through the ballot box; and if the people will refuse to exercise it in this manner, as they have done in Kansas at the election of delegates, it is not for them to complain that their rights have been violated.

The Kansas convention, thus lawfully constituted, proceeded to frame a constitution, and, having completed their work, finally adjourned on the 7th day of November last. They did not think it proper to submit the whole of this constitution to a popular vote, but they did submit the question whether Kansas should be a free or a slave state to the people. This was the question which had convulsed the Union and shaken it to its very center. This was the question which had lighted up the flames of civil war in Kansas and had produced dangerous sectional parties throughout the Confederacy. It was of a character so paramount in respect to the condition of Kansas as to rivet the anxious attention of the people of the whole country upon it, and it alone. . . .

The people of Kansas have, then, "in their own way" and in strict accordance with the organic act, framed a constitution and State government, have submitted the all important question of slavery to the people, and have selected a governor, a Member to represent them in Congress, members of the State legislature, and other State officers. They now ask admission into the Union under this constitution, which is republican in its form. It is for Congress to decide whether they will admit or reject the State which has thus been created. For my own part, I am decidedly in favor of its admission, and thus terminating the Kansas question. This will carry out the great principle of nonintervention recognized and sanctioned by the organic act, which declares in express language in favor of "nonintervention by Congress with slavery in the States or Territories," leaving "the people thereof perfectly free to form and regulate their domestic institutions in their own way, subject only to the Constitution of the United States." In this manner, by localizing the question of slavery and confining it to the people whom it immediately concerned, every patriot anxiously expected that this question would be banished from the halls of Congress, where it has always exerted a baneful influence throughout the whole country.

A Compilation of the Messages and Papers of the Presidents, vols. 6–7, James D. Richardson, ed. (New York: Bureau of National Literature, Inc., 1897), 3002–3009.

SENATOR STEPHEN A. DOUGLAS (D-IL), IN OPPOSITION TO THE LECOMPTON CONSTITUTION (WASHINGTON, DC, MARCH 22, 1858)

In 1854, when it became necessary to organize the Territories of Kansas and Nebraska, the question arose, what principle was to apply to those Territories? It was true they both lay north of the line of 36° 30'; but it was also true that four years before, the policy of a geographical line had been abandoned and repudiated by the Congress of the United States, and in lieu of it the plan of leaving each Territory free to decide the question for itself had been adopted. I felt it to be my duty, as a Senator from the State of Illinois, and I will say as a member of the Democratic Party, to adhere in good faith to the principles of the compromise measures of 1850, and to apply them to Kansas and Nebraska as well as to the other Territories. To show that I was bound to pursue this course, it is only necessary to refer to the public incidents of those times. In the presidential election of 1852, the great political parties of that day each nominated its candidate for the presidency upon a platform which indorsed the compromise measures of 1850, and both pledged themselves to carry them out in good faith in all future time in the organization of all new Territories. The Whig party adopted that platform at Baltimore, and placed General Scott, their candidate, upon it. The Democratic Party adopted a platform identical in principle, so far as this question was concerned, and elected General Pierce President of the United States upon it. Thus the Whig party and the Democratic party each stood pledged to apply this principle in the organization of new Territories. Not only was I a Democrat—as a Senator who voted for their adoption—bound to apply their principle to this case; but as a Senator from Illinois, I was under an imperative obligation, if I desired to obey the will and carry out the wishings of my constituents, to apply the same principle. . . .

We are told that it was made by a convention assembled at Lecompton in September last, and has been submitted to the people for ratification or rejection. How submitted? In a manner that allowed every man to vote for it, but precluded the possibility of any man voting against it. We are told that there is a majority of about five hundred thousand five hundred votes recorded in its favor under these circumstances. I refrain from going into the evidence which has been taken before the commission recently held in Kansas to show what proportion of these votes were fraudulent; but, supposing them all to have been legal, *bona fide* residents, what does that fact prove, when the people on that occasion were allowed only to vote for, and could not vote against, the constitution? On the other hand, we have a vote of the people in pursuance of law, on the 4th January last, when this constitution was submitted by the Legislature to the people for acceptance or rejection, showing a majority of more than ten thousand against it. If you grant that both these elections were valid, if you grant that the votes were legal and fair, yet the majority is about two to one against this constitution. Here is evidence to my mind conclusive that this Lecompton constitution is not the embodiment of the popular will of Kansas. How is this evidence to be rebutted? By the assumption that the election on the 21st of December, where the voters were allowed to vote for it but not against it, was a legal election; and that the election on the 4th of January, where the people were allowed to vote for or against the constitution as they chose, was not a legal and valid election. . . .

Sir, we have heard the argument over and over again, that the Lecompton convention was justified in withholding this constitution from submission to the people, for the reason that it would have been voted down if it had been submitted to the people for ratification or rejection. We are told that there was a large majority of Free-Soilers, of Abolitionists, of Free-State men in the Territory, who would have voted down the constitution if they had got a chance, and that is the excuse for not allowing the people to vote upon it. That is an admission that this constitution is not the act and deed of the people of Kansas; that it does not embody their will; and yet you are called upon to give it force and vitality; to make it the fundamental law of Kansas with a knowledge that it is not the will of the people, and misrepresents their wishes. I ask you, sir, where is your right, under our principles of Government, to force a constitution upon an unwilling people? You may resort to all the evidence that you can obtain, from every source that you please, and you are driven to the same conclusion, that this constitution is not the will of the people. . . .

But we are told that it is a matter of but small moment whether the constitution embodies the public will or not, because it can be modified and changed by the people of Kansas at any time as soon as they are admitted into the Union. Sir, it matters not whether this constitution is to be the permanent fundamental law of Kansas, or is to last only a day, a month, or a year; because, if it is not their act and deed you have no right to force it upon them for a single day. If you have the power to force it upon this people for one day, you may do it for a year, for ten years, or permanently. The principle involved is the same. It is as much a violation of fundamental principle, a violation of popular sovereignty, a violation of the Constitution of the United States, to force a State constitution on an unwilling people for a day, as it is a year or for a longer time. . . .

The President of the United States tells us that he sees no objection to inserting a clause in the act of admission declaratory of the right of the people of Kansas, with the consent of the first Legislature, to change this constitution notwithstanding the provision which it contains, that it shall not be changed until after the year 1864. Where does Congress get power to intervene and change a provision in the constitution of a State? If this constitution declares, as I insist it does, that it shall not be changed until after 1864, what right has Congress to intervene, to alter, or annul that provision prohibiting alteration? If you can annul one provision, you may another, and another, and another, until you have destroyed the entire instrument.

Congressional *Globe*, 35th Congress, 1st Session, March 22, 1858, 194–196.

THE HOMESTEAD BILL

The means by which Western lands were to be settled had been a controversy since initial settlement in the seventeenth century. During the colonial era, and into the early national period, as the United States expanded its boundaries, concerns arose as to how to encourage settlement yet achieve a reasonably fair means of distributing land. Often this was a difficult task. Low prices often resulted in land speculation rather than settlement. In the era of Manifest Destiny, as the United States acquired enormous new territories, problems relating to settlement arose once again. As had been the case in prior times, one problem was encouraging Americans to uproot and take their families to new locales.

Republicans promoted a bill that offered very inexpensive or even free land, usually 160 acres, to settlers who occupied and "improved" the land for a period of five years. Such homestead laws, supporters argued, provided lands to average Americans who otherwise could not secure the funds necessary to purchase lands for a new home. The Republican Party had several reasons to support such a plan. Homesteading allowed the new party to position itself as friend to the common man and the "yeoman farmer," a cherished symbol in American culture. Also, the Homestead Bill, as it was presented in Congress, included immigrants as well as residents of the United States in an effort to undercut the image of nativism attached to the Republicans. The bill also gave the Republicans a means of promoting themselves as more than a single-issue party and could assure voters that the party had a vision for the nation's future.

As Senator James Doolittle of Wisconsin illustrates all too well, slavery and racial sentiments permeated this issue as well. Republicans, particularly in the Western states, were most concerned with keeping slaves and free blacks out of Western territories. The Homestead Law, the argument ran, would encourage the populating of these areas with whites and keep out slaveholders who might develop large plantations and transport slave labor into the region. Doolittle's speech is valuable in showing that most Republicans were less concerned with slavery in the Southern states and more concerned with the settlement of large numbers of blacks in the West. Doolittle makes clear that one result of the Homestead Bill would be to guarantee racial purity through the exclusion of blacks in Western territories north of the Mason-Dixon Line.

Debate over the issue was regional, but not exclusively along the lines of North and South that most at the time believed it to be. Southerners tended to oppose the measure, but Americans in the Southwest, particularly Texas, supported the law. Northeasterners and a significant number of those in the Southeast tended to oppose the measure. As the bill was a Republican initiative, Democrats voiced strong opposition. However, the bill gained enough support among Westerners of both parties to clear both the House of Representatives and the Senate in 1860. Buchanan vetoed the measure; the bill did not have the support necessary to override his action. In his veto message to the Senate, Buchanan offers an exhaustive list of reasons for his opposition to the bill. Foremost among his concerns, not surprisingly, was the question of federal responsibility. The president argues that Congress would exceed its authority in regulating the sale of public lands so closely. Buchanan also claims that the law favored farmers over other Americans and in the end actually would promote speculation rather that end it.

Buchanan's veto was only a temporary setback for supporters of the Homestead Bill. In 1862, during the Civil War, a Republican-dominated Congress passed a new version of the bill that was signed into law by President Lincoln. Settlers began to move west in large numbers, taking advantage of free land in the years following the war.

JAMES BUCHANAN, VETO MESSAGE ON HOMESTEAD BILL (WASHINGTON, DC, JUNE 22, 1860)

I return with my objections to the Senate, in which it originated, the bill entitled "An act to secure homesteads to actual settlers on the public domain, and for other purposes," presented to me on the 20th instant.

This bill gives to every citizen of the United States "who is the head of his family," and to every person of foreign birth residing in the country who has declared his intention to become a citizen, though he may not be the head of a family, the privilege of appropriating to himself 160 acres of Government land, of settling and residing upon it for five years; and should his residence continue until the end of this period, he shall then receive a patent of the payment of 25 cents per acre, or one-fifth of the present Government price. During this period the land is protected from all the debts of the settler.

This bill contains a cession to the States of all the public lands within their respective limits "which have been subject to sale at private entry, and which remain unsold after the lapse of thirty years." This provision embraces a present donation to the States of 12,229,731 acres, and will from time to time transfer to them large bodies of such lands which from peculiar circumstances may not be absorbed by private purchase and settlement.

To the actual settler this bill does not make an absolute donation, but the price is so small that it can scarcely be called a sale. It is nominally 25 cents per acre, but considering this is not to be paid until the end of five years, it is in fact reduced to about 18 cents per acre, or one-seventh of the present minimum price of the public lands. In regard to the States, it is an absolute and unqualified gift.

1. This state of the facts raises the question whether Congress, under the Constitution, has the power to give away the public lands either to States or individuals. . . .

2. It will prove unequal and unjust in its operation among the actual settlers themselves.

The first settlers of a new country are a most meritorious class. They brave the dangers of savage warfare, suffer the privations of a frontier life, and with the hand of toil bring the wilderness into cultivation. The "old settlers," as they are everywhere called, are public benefactors. This class have all paid for their lands the Government price, or $1.25 per acre. They have constructed roads, established schools, and laid the foundation of prosperous commonwealths. Is it just, is it equal, that after they have accomplished all this by their labor new settlers should come in among them and receive their farms at the price of 25 or 18 cents an acre? Surely the old settlers, as a class, are entitled to at least equal benefits with the new. . . .

3. This bill will do great injustice to the old soldiers who have received land warrants for their services in fighting the battles of their country. It will greatly reduce the market value of these warrants. . . .

4. This bill will prove unequal and unjust in its operation, because from its nature it is confined to one class of our people. It is a boon exclusively conferred upon the cultivators of the soil. Whilst it is cheerfully admitted that these are the most numerous and useful class of our fellow-citizens and eminently deserve all the advantages which our laws have already extended to them, yet there should be no new legislation which operates to the injury or embarrassment of the large body of respectable artisans and laborers. The mechanic who emigrates to the West and pursues his calling must labor long before he can purchase a quarter section of land, whilst the tiller of the soil who accompanies him obtains a farm at once by the bounty of the government. . . .

5. This bill is unjust to the old States of the Union in many respects; and amongst these States, so far as the public lands are concerned, we may enumerate every State east of the Mississippi with the exception of Wisconsin and a portion of Minnesota. . . .

6. This bill will open one vast field for speculation. Men will not pay $1.25 for lands when they can purchase them for one-fifth of that price. Large numbers of actual settlers will be carried out by capitalists upon agreements to give them half of their land for the improvement of the other half. This can not be avoided. Secret agreements of this kind will be numerous. In the entry of graduated lands the experience of the Land Office justifies this objection.

The people of the United States have advanced with steady but rapid strides to their present condition of power and prosperity. They have been guided in all their progress by the fixed principle of protecting the equal rights of all, whether they be rich or poor. No agrarian sentiment has ever prevailed upon them. The honest poor man, by frugality and industry, can in any part of our country acquire a competence for himself and his family, and in doing this he feels that he eats the bread of independence. He desires no charity, either from the Government or from his neighbors. This bill, which proposes to give him land at an almost nominal price out of the property of the Government, will go far to demoralize the people and repress

this noble spirit of independence. It may introduce among us those perni-
cious social theories which have proved so disastrous in other countries.

A Compilation of the Messages and Papers of the Presidents, vol. 7, James D. Richardson,
ed. (New York: Bureau of National Literature, Inc., 1897), 3139–3145.

SENATOR JAMES R. DOOLITTLE (R-WI), IN SUPPORT OF THE HOMESTEAD BILL (WASHINGTON, DC, APRIL 10, 1860)

Mr. President, I support this measure because, opening our Territories to
free white men will, in my opinion, tend to prevent their Africanization
through the introduction of negro slaves, and thus secure in the end, what I
believe God in His providence intended, that the temperate regions under
our control shall become the permanent homes of the pure Caucasian race.
The adoption of his policy will, in my judgement, tend to bring on a final
settlement of this whole negro question. By the influence of our example in
opening our territories to the Caucasian race, who are the children of the
temperate zone, and by our treaty arrangements with our neighboring
State upon the south, who occupy the tropical regions of this continent, we
may induce them in these zones to open equally wide their beautiful territories to the children of the tropics, to the descendants of Africa—the men
best adapted to dwell within them, and to cultivate and to develop them.

I believe, sir, that we may, while we open our territories to the Caucasian
race, induce those tropical States which are already in the possession of the
colored races, where color is no degradation either socially or politically, to
open wide their territories for the surplus population of the United States of
African descent. Let us throw wide open our territories, which are within
the temperate latitudes, to become the homes to the free white man, who
are the children of the temperate zone; whom God in His providence has
planted in that zone; who have, through all history, controlled the destinies
of that zone; and at the same time, by the influence of our example and by
treaty, let us induce the tropical States of America to open equally wide
their domain, capable of sustaining hundreds of millions of human beings,
to colored men—the children of the tropics, the children of the sun—and
thus open a way, when, in the providence of God, in the fullness of time,
that destiny must be accomplished: THE PEACE AND GRADUAL SEPA-
RATION OF THE RACES, FOR THE HIGHEST GOOD OF BOTH.

Let no man misunderstand me. I would in no respect infringe on the
rights of the States, nor of individual citizens of the States. By the Constitution of the United States, and by that higher law of reason upon which that
Constitution rests, every State has, and must forever have, the undisputed,
unquestioned right over its own destiny, and to provide for the maintaining
and defending of its own domestic institutions. And, sir, while the policy I
suggest would open a way for States and for individuals by which they

could become free to rid themselves of slaves, if they should choose to do so, it would by no means, nor in the slightest degree, infringe upon their sovereign rights, nor constrain their independent action. It would only make them free to act for themselves, in their own time and in their own way. They would remain free, forever free, to hold or to emancipate their slaves. That is their business, not ours. . . .

Mr. President, as I would give homesteads to the free white laboring men of the Caucasian race in our temperate territories, so would I, both by treaty and by example, induce the tropical States of America to open their domains, and give homes and homesteads and civil and social equality to the free colored men who are among us. . . .

This solution of the negro question, to which I have referred, is a solution to which gentlemen must come. It is not to be postponed much longer, either. I submit, that nineteen twentieths of the people of the free States—I mean the white people of the slave States—would today be in favor of providing some place where these people can live on God's earth, and enjoy life, and enjoy their wives and children. I do not believe that the people of the South would deny to them that boon.

Congressional *Globe*, 36th Congress, 1st Session, Tuesday, April 10, 1860, 1632–1633.

THE *DRED SCOTT* CASE

Among the several crises Buchanan faced during the first months of his administration was the long-awaited *Dred Scott* v. *Sandford* decision. The United States Supreme Court's ruling, issued only two days after his inauguration, on March 6, 1857, resulted in even more sectional hostility over slavery. Scott's case had been tied up in the courts for over a decade and by this time had attracted national attention. Despite Buchanan's efforts to defuse the passions wrought by the slavery issue, the Court's controversial decision sparked outrage across the Northern states and energized the Republican Party.

Scott's case was complex. He was born a slave in Virginia about 1800 and had lived on a plantation there until 1818, when his master moved to Alabama and finally came to rest in St. Louis, Missouri, in 1830. In 1833, Scott was sold to Dr. John Emerson, a United States Army surgeon, who took Scott to Fort Armstrong in the state of Illinois where they lived for almost three years. In 1836, Emerson took Scott to the area of present-day Minnesota, where they lived until 1838. Ultimately, Scott ended up in St. Louis, where he lived at the time of Dr. Emerson's death in 1843. Emerson's widow inherited both Scott and his wife, whom he had married while in Minnesota in 1837, and the Scotts remained in the service of Mrs. Emerson (she hired the two of them out) until 1846, when Dred Scott decided to sue for his freedom in a St. Louis court. He claimed that having lived in a free region of the Northwest Territory, as well as in the free state of Illinois, qualified him for freedom.

Scott's case languished in the courts for years due to technicalities. After several delays, the case went to trial in 1850 and a jury soon arrived at a decision in his favor. The decision, based on several prior cases of similar circumstances, surprised few. However, the case took an interesting turn in 1852, when the Missouri Supreme Court reversed the decision and affirmed Scott's status as a slave. The case was then appealed to the United States Circuit Court, which in 1854 upheld the state court decision. Finally, the case reached the United States Supreme Court in early 1857.

The High Court's decision to affirm the lower court ruling was expected; seven out of nine justices agreed that Scott should remain a slave. In addition, however, Chief Justice Roger B. Taney of Maryland wrote an opinion that not only upheld the earlier verdict, but addressed the constitutional basis on which slavery was determined in territories. Taney's controversial decision first stated that Scott, as a slave, had no legal standing and could not sue in court at all, which nullified the case. He went further to argue that no African Americans legally could be counted as citizens and justified this on the grounds that blacks historically had been considered inferior to whites. Finally, and perhaps most controversial at the time, Taney claimed that the Missouri Compromise of 1820, which had established a north-south line separating "slave" and "free" territories, was unconstitutional because it deprived slaveholding citizens the right of property in federally regulated areas.

Taney's decision, which represented the entire Court, not only affirmed the repeal of the Missouri Compromise that had been achieved by the Kansas-Nebraska Act but also challenged the concept of popular sovereignty in any Western territory. As Southern Senator John C. Calhoun had argued, Taney stated that any move to block the rights of slaveholders to own slaves in a territory violated the due process clause of the Fifth Amendment. Supporters of slavery rejoiced at the decision, while those opposed to the expansion of slavery saw Taney's work as further evidence that national politics was firmly under the control of Southern apologists. In the end, the *Dred Scott* case only fueled the already growing flames of sectional mistrust.

Northern abolitionists, of course, were outraged by the decision. The former slave and leading abolitionist Frederick Douglass provides a powerful indictment of the decision in the following speech, delivered in New York on May 11, 1857. Douglass rejects the argument made by advocates of slavery that the Constitution protects slavery and explains to his audience that slavery could be prevented from spreading into the West without subverting the laws of the land.

President Buchanan had hoped all along that the Court would find in favor of Southern interests and supported the Court's ruling. He made brief mention of the case in his March 4 inaugural speech but said little about the decision after the fact. One may gain a glimpse of Buchanan's views by considering an article from the pro-Buchanan newspaper, the Washington *Un-*

ion. The article attempts to strike a concilatory tone, urging both sides to accept the decision as a means of maintaining national unity. However, the decision did anything but promote appeasement. Northerners who before had cared little about slavery in the South now assumed that the slaveocracy was bent on expansion into new territories. As Taney's decision rang out across the North, the ranks of the Republican Party grew considerably. In the march toward sectional crisis, the *Dred Scott* case stands as one of the more pivotal events.

THE WASHINGTON *UNION* ON THE *DRED SCOTT* CASE (WASHINGTON, DC, MARCH 12, 1857)

We cherish a most ardent and confident expectation that this decision will meet a proper reception from the great mass of our intelligent countrymen; that it will be regarded with soberness and not with passion; and that it will thereby exert a mighty influence in diffusing sound opinions and restoring harmony and fraternal concord throughout the country. It comes at an auspicious period. Had it been pronounced—which could hardly have been possible—during the excitement of the presidential canvass, its useful effect, for the present at least, would have been lost. Though no less just and constitutional than it is, it would have been temporarily overwhelmed in the surges of party clamor. Now, however, the excitement and strife of the late canvass are happily abated. The sober second thought has returned to the people; and they are well prepared to receive the judgement of the highest tribunal in the land, even if it, in many instances, differs from their own favorite political opinions.

The court which has settled the vexed constitutional question as to the power of Congress over Territories is entirely independent of the legislative branch of the government. It is elevated above the schemes of party politics, and shielded alike from the effects of sudden passion and of popular prejudice. Little motive, therefore, can the venerable jurists who compose that tribunal have to deviate from the true principles of law.

It would be fortunate, indeed, if the opinion of that court on this important subject could receive the candid and respectful acquiescence which it merits. Such an exhibition of the moral conservatism of the people would well correspond with that sublime example of the fitness of the people for self-government lately witnessed in the laying down and taking up of high executive trusts in the midst of orderly enthusiasm. But we expect this decision will for a while be questioned, and even ridiculed by the antislavery press. The judges who concurred in it will be abused. . . .

Many men supported the Nebraska-Kansas act who believed Congress had the right to exclude slavery from the Territories, but who deemed it inexpedient to have the right exercised. They wished to keep the subject out of Congress. They thought as Mr. Webster did when he favored the organization of New Mexico without the application of the Wilmot proviso. There men may be unprepared for this decision. We know that in the non-slaveholding States there are many who sincerely deprecated the repeal of the Missouri Compromise. There are many who have been brought up in the faith of the Wilmot proviso. They, perhaps, have not examined both sides of the question, and will feel a regret at this decision as deep at the pleasure of our southern friends is ardent. . . .

Never perhaps, in the history of the country, has there existed so much bitterness between the North and the South as within the past year. And it is remarkable that this bitterness has resulted not from measured so much as from transient excesses. The troubles in Kansas and some other accidental acts contributed to this state of things. But the chief cause of alienation was the unbridled license of a portion of the press and the intemperate language employed by many of our public speakers. It has been common for some of the ablest journals of the North to represent and vilify the institutions and the people of the South. And these attacks have been reciprocated by some of the radical papers of the South. Orators have resorted to the same practice. Under such circumstances, what else but bitterness and alienation could follow? What else but distrust be excited? . . .

It is gratifying to see that a better feeling is beginning to exist between both sections of the country; and we invoke the temperate and intelligent public opinion of the country, so potent for wise purposes, to withhold every vestige of support from that class whose livelihood is to create sectional animosity. In this way their shafts will fall impotent in the dust, and the wounds they have before made will become healed.

The Washington *Union*, March 12, 1857, 1.

FREDERICK DOUGLASS, IN REACTION TO THE *DRED SCOTT* V. *SANDFORD* DECISION (BOSTON, MA, JUNE 12, 1857)

Mr. Chairman, Friends, and Fellow Citizens:

While four millions of our fellow countrymen are in chains—while men, women, and children are bought and sold on the auction-block with horses, sheep, and swine—while the remorseless slave-whip draws the warm blood of our common humanity—it is meet that we assemble as we have done to-day, and lift up our hearts and voices in earnest denunciation of the vile and shocking abomination. It is not for us to be governed by our hopes or our fears in this great work; yet it is natural on occasions like this, to survey the position of the great struggle which is going on between slavery and freedom, and to dwell upon such signs of encouragement as may have been lately developed, and the state of feeling these signs or events have occasioned in us and among the people generally. It is a fitting time to take an observation to ascertain where we are, and what our prospects are. . . .

In one view the slaveholders have a decided advantage over all opposition. It is well to notice this advantage—the advantage of complete organization. They are organized; and yet were not at the pains of creating their organization. The State governments, where the system of slavery exists, are complete slavery organizations. The church organizations in those States are equally at the service of slavery; while the Federal Government, with its army and navy, from the chief magistracy in Washington, to the Supreme Court, and thence to the chief marshalship at New York, is pledged to support, defend, and propagate the crying curse of human bondage. The pen, the purse, and the sword, are united against the simple truth, preached by humble men in obscure places.

This is one view. It is, thank God, only one view; there is another, and a brighter view. David, you know, looked small and insignificant when going to meet Goliath, but looked larger when he had slain his foe. . . .

This infamous decision of the Slaveholding wing of the Supreme Court maintains that slaves are within the contemplation of the Constitution of the United States, property; that slaves are property in the same sense that horses, sheep, and swine are property; that the old doctrine that slavery is a creature of local law is false; that the right of the slaveholder to his slave does not depend upon the local law, but is secured wherever the Constitution of the United States extends; that Congress has no right to prohibit slavery anywhere; that slavery may go in safety anywhere under the star-spangled banner; that colored persons of African descent have no rights that white men are bound to respect; that colored men of African descent are not and cannot be citizens of the United States. . . .

I have no fear that the National Conscience will be put to sleep by such an open, glaring, and scandalous tissue of lies as that decision is, and has been, over and over, shown to be.

The Supreme Court of the United States is not the only power in this world. It is very great, but the Supreme Court of the Almighty is greater. Judge Taney can do many things, but he cannot perform impossibilities. He cannot bale out the ocean, annihilate the firm old earth, or pluck the silvery star of liberty from our Northern sky. He may decide, and decide again; but he cannot reverse the decision of the Most High. He cannot change the essential nature of things—making evil good, and good evil. . . .

Such a decision cannot stand. God will be true though every man be a liar. We can appeal from this hell-black judgement of the Supreme Court, to the court of common sense and common humanity. We can appeal from man to God. If there is no justice on earth, there is yet justice in heaven. You may close your Supreme Court against the black man's cry for justice, but you cannot, thank God, close against him the ear of a sympathising world, nor shut up the Court of Heaven. All that is merciful and just, on earth and in Heaven, will execrate and despise this edict of Taney. . . .

But I come now to the great question as to the constitutionality of slavery. The recent slaveholding decision, as well as the teachings of the anti-slavery men, make this a fit time to discuss the constitutional pretensions of slavery. . . .

"We, the people of the United States, in order to form a more perfect Union, establish justice, insure domestic tranquility, provide for the common defense, promote the general welfare, and secure the blessings of liberty to ourselves and our posterity, do ordain and establish this constitution for the United States of America."

Neither in the preamble nor in the body of the Constitution is there a single mention of the term *slave* or *slave holder*, *slave master* or *slave state*, neither is there any reference to the color, or the physical peculiarities of any part of the people of the United States. Neither is there anything in the Constitution standing alone, which would imply the existence of slavery in this country.

"We, the people"—not we, the white people—not we, the citizens, or the legal voters—not we, the privileged class, and excluding all other classes but we, the people; not we, the horses and cattle, but we the people—the men and women, the human inhabitants of the United States, do ordain and establish this Constitution, &c. . . .

In conclusion, let me say, all I ask of the American people is, that they live up to the Constitution, adopt its principles, imbibe its spirit, and enforce its provisions.

When this is done, the wounds of my bleeding people will be healed, the chain will no longer rust on their ankles, their backs will no longer be torn by the bloody lash, and liberty, the glorious birthright of our common humanity, will become the inheritance of all the inhabitants of this highly favored country.

Frederick Douglass Papers, June 12, 1857. Library of Congress, speech file, reel 14, 32.

JOHN BROWN'S RAID

Few could deny that slavery had become the central political controversy of the nation by the late 1850s. For many on both sides, what had been mainly a political issue was evolving into one of morality. For Northerners, the abolitionists who had for years decried slavery as a blight on all Americans were attracting more sympathy. In the South, the fight to gurantee slavery in the territories was becoming a cause for preserving a way of life. In the midst of growing passions, John Brown's raid on Harpers Ferry, Virginia, in October 1859 forced the issue even more.

John Brown already was a known entity to many Americans. A fiery Free-Soiler considered insane by some, Brown had led four of his sons and three other men on a killing spree in May 1856 that came to be called the

"Pottawatomie Massacre." In retaliation for the sacking of the free-soil town of Lawrence by a mob, Brown and his followers pulled five men from their homes on the night of May 24 and brutally murdered them while the victims' families watched in horror. Brown went into hiding, and emerged again in Maryland, where he planned a raid on a federal arsenal at Harpers Ferry, Virginia, in present-day West Virginia. Brown and his band of followers, about twenty in all, planned to spark a slave insurrection by providing them with weapons and establishing an armed compound in the mountains of Virginia. Brown was convinced that they could incite slave rebellions throughout the South.

The raid went badly for Brown and his men. They managed to overtake the arsenal, but the swarms of liberated slaves ready to take up arms never materialized. Local militia and angry townspeople surrounded the arsenal and shot two of the group. On October 18, President Buchanan ordered Lieutenant-Colonel Robert E. Lee to lead marines on an attack of the arsenal and capture Brown. The siege of the arsenal was brief and violent. Ten of Brown's men were killed and Brown was taken into custody.

John Brown's trial attracted national attention. He was found guilty of treason and conspiracy to incite insurrection; he and six others were hanged for their crimes. Southerners reacted strongly to John Brown's raid. While some observers referred to Brown as a madman, most in the South took the view that Brown was representative of the fanatical abolitionism spreading across the Northern tier. The raid on Harpers Ferry signaled to Southerners that attempts to incite slave rebellions and to abolish the slave system altogether would increase in the future.

While such exaggerations bordered on paranoia, Northerners were ambivalent about John Brown. Abolitionists made a martyr of Brown. Those who were opposed to slavery approached the incident in different ways. Some rejected him as insane; others admired his bravery.

John Brown's raid was significant for both sides. A considerable number of Northerners, impressed with the boldness of Brown's actions, were forced for the first time to see the slavery issue as a moral cause and not simply a political disagreement to be negotiated in Congress. Among those who were moved by Brown was the essayist and orator Ralph Waldo Emerson. His speech in Boston in the wake of the trial paints a portrait of Brown as a patriot, rooted in virtue and the American tradition of freedom. Of course, words like these sparked outrage in the South. President Buchanan, unimpressed with Brown's attack on federal property, attempted to strike a conciliatory tone in his annual message of 1860. Whether Buchanan actually misread the passions generated on both sides by Brown's raid, or whether the president merely was seeking to offer words of calm during a time of danger is difficult to say. Regardless, given the sequence of events that followed, Buchanan's reaction seems tragically detached. In his address, the president suggests that the current crisis over slavery would soon pass and actions such as those by John Brown would fade in public memory.

JAMES BUCHANAN, REACTION TO JOHN BROWN'S RAID (1859)

Whilst it is the duty of the President "from time to time to give Congress information of the state of the Union," I shall not refer in detail to the recent sad and bloody occurrences at Harpers Ferry. Still, it is proper to observe that these events, however bad and cruel in themselves, derive their chief importance from the apprehension that they are but symptoms of an incurable disease in the public mind, which may break out in still more dangerous outrages and terminate at last in an open war by the North to abolish slavery in the South.

Whilst for myself I entertain no such apprehension, they ought to afford a solemn warning to us all to beware of the approach of danger. Our Union is a stake of such inestimable value as to demand our constant and watchful vigilance for its preservation. In this view, let me implore my countrymen, North and South, to cultivate the ancient feelings of mutual forebearance and good will toward each other and strive to allay the demon spirit of sectional hatred and strife now alive in the land. This advice proceeds from the heart of an old public functionary whose service commenced in the last generation, among the wise and conservative statesmen of that day, now nearly all passed away, and whose first and dearest earthly wish is to leave his country tranquil, prosperous, united, and powerful.

We ought to reflect that in this age, and especially in this country, there is an incessant flux and reflux of public opinion. Questions which in their day assumed a most threatening aspect have now nearly gone from the memory of men. They are "volcanoes burnt out, and on the lava and ashes and squalid scoria of old eruptions grow the peaceful olive, the cheering vine, and the sustaining corn." Such, in my opinion, will prove to be the fate of the present sectional excitement should those who wisely seek to apply the remedy continue always to confine their efforts within the pale of the Constitution. If this course be pursued, the existing agitation on the subject of domestic slavery, like everything human, will have its day and give place to other and less threatening controversies. Public opinion in this country is all-powerful, and when it reaches a dangerous excess upon any question the good sense of the people will furnish the corrective and bring it back within safe limits. Still, to hasten this auspicious result at the present crisis we ought to remember that every rational creature must be presumed to intend the natural consequences of his own teachings. Those who announce abstract doctrines subversive of the Constitution and the Union must not be surprised should their heated partisans advance one step further and attempt by violence to carry these doctrines into practical effect. In this view of the subject, it ought never to be forgotten that however great may have been the political advantages resulting from the Union to every portion of our common country, these would all prove to be as nothing should the time ever arrive when they can not be enjoyed without serious danger to the personal safety of the people of fifteen members [states]of the Confederacy. If the peace of the domestic fireside throughout these States should ever be invaded, if the mothers of families within this extensive region should not be able to retire to rest at night without suffering dreadful apprehensions of what may be their own fate and that of their children before the morning, it would be vain to recount to such people the political benefits which result to them from the Union. Self-preservation is the first instinct of nature, and therefore any states of society in which the sword is all the time suspended over the heads of the people must at last become intolerable. But I indulge in no such gloomy forebodings. On the contrary, I firmly believe that the events at Harpers Ferry, by causing the people to pause and reflect upon the possible peril to their cherished institutions, will be the means under Providence of allaying the existing excitement and preventing further outbreaks of a similar character. They will resolve that the Constitution and the Union shall not be endangered by rash counsels, knowing that should "the silver cord be loosed or the golden bowl be broken * * * at the fountain" human power could never reunite the scattered and hostile fragments.

A Compilation of the Messages and Papers of the Presidents, vol. 7, James D. Richardson, ed. (New York: Bureau of National Literature, Inc., 1897), 3084–3085.

RALPH WALDO EMERSON, SPEECH ON JOHN BROWN (BOSTON, MA, NOVEMBER 18, 1859)

Mr. Chairman, and Fellow Citizens: I share the sympathy and sorrow which have brought us together. Gentlemen who have preceded me have well said that no wall of separation could here exist. This commanding event which has brought us together, eclipses all others which have occurred for a long time in our history, and I am very glad to see that this sudden interest in the hero of Harper's Ferry has provoked an extreme curiosity in all parts of the Republic, in regard to the details of his history. Every anecdote is eagerly sought, and I do not wonder that gentlemen find traits of relation readily between him and themselves. One finds a relation in the church, another in the profession, another in the place of his birth. He was happily a representative of the American Republic. Captain John Brown is a farmer, the fifth in descent from Peter Brown, who came to Plymouth in the Mayflower, in 1620. All the six have been farmers. His grandfather, of Simsbury, in Connecticut, was a captain in the Revolution. His father, largely interested as a raiser of stock, became a contractor to supply the army with beef, in the war of 1812, and our Captain John Brown, then a boy, with his father was present and witnessed the surrender of General Hull. He cherishes a great respect for this father, as a man of strong character, and his respect is probably just. For himself, he is so transparent that all men see him through. He is a man to make friends wherever on earth courage and integrity are esteemed, the rarest of heroes, a pure idealist, with no by-end of his own. Many of you have seen him, and every who has heard him speak has been impressed alike by his simple, artless goodness, joined with his sublime courage. He joins that perfect Puritan faith which brought his fifth ancestor to Plymouth Rock and his grandfather's ardor in the Revolution. He believes in two articles, two instruments, shall I say?—the Golden Rule and the Declaration of Independence; and he used this expression in conversation here concerning them, "better that a whole generation of men, women and children should pass away by a violent death than that one word of either should be violated in this country." There is a Unionist—there is a strict constructionist for you. He believes in the Union of the States, and he conceives that the only obstruction to the Union is Slavery, and for that reason, as a patriot, he works for its abolition. The governor of Virginia has pronounced his eulogy in a manner that discredits the moderation of our timid parties. His own speeches to the court have interested the nation in him. What magnanimity, and what innocent pleading, as of childhood! You remember his words: "If I had interfered in behalf of the rich, the powerful, the intelligent, the so-called great, or any of their friends, parents, wives or children, it would have been all right. But I believe that to have interfered as I have done, for the despised poor, was not wrong, but right."

It is easy to see what a favorite he will be with history, which plays such pranks with temporary reputations. Nothing can resist the sympathy which all elevated minds must feel with Brown, and through them the whole civilized world; and if he must suffer, he must drag official gentlemen into an immortality most undesirable, of which they have already some disagreeable forebodings. Indeed, it is the *reduction ad absurdum* of Slavery, when the governor of Virginia is forced to hand over a man whom he declared to be a man of the most integrity, truthfulness and courage he has ever met. Is that the kind of man the gallows is built for? It were bold to affirm that there is within that broad commonwealth, at this moment, another citizen as worthy to live, and as deserving of all private honor, as this poor prisoner.

But we are here to think of relief for the family of John Brown. To my eyes, that family looks very large and very needy of relief. It comprises his brave fellow sufferers in the Charlestown Jail; the fugitives still hunted in the mountains of Virginia and Pennsylvania; the sympathizers with him in all the states; and, I may say, almost every man who loved the Golden Rule and the Declaration of Independence, like him, and who sees what a tiger's thirst threatens him in the malignity of public sentiment in the slave states.

It seems to me that a common feeling joins the people of Massachusetts with him.

I said John Brown was an idealist. He believed in his ideas to the extent that he existed to put them all into action; he said 'he did not believe in moral suasion, he believed in putting the thing through.' He saw how deceptive the forms are. We fancy, in Massachusetts, that we are free; yet it seems the government is unreliable. Great wealth, great population, men of talent in the executive, on the bench,—all the forms right,—and yet, life and freedom are not safe. Why? Because the judges rely on the forms, and do not, like John Brown, use their eyes to see the fact behind the forms. . . .

Miscellanies by Ralph Waldo Emerson (Boston: Houghton Mifflin, 1904), 267–273.

RECOMMENDED READINGS

Johannsen, Robert W. *Stephen A. Douglas.* New York: Oxford University Press, 1973.

Klein, Philip S. *President James Buchanan: A Biography.* University Park: Pennsylvania State University Press, 1962.

Oates, Stephen B. *To Purge This Land With Blood: A Biography of John Brown.* Amherst: University of Massachusetts Press, 1984.

Oates, Stephen B., and Buz Wyeth, *The Approaching Fury: Voices of the Storm, 1820–1861.* New York: HarperCollins, 1997.

Smith, Elbert B. *The Presidency of James Buchanan.* Lawrence: University of Kansas Press, 1975.

4

ABRAHAM LINCOLN

(1861–1865)

INTRODUCTION

A well-known adage claims that only Jesus and William Shakespeare have been the subject of more writing than Abraham Lincoln. For generations he has been a man of controversy, hailed as a saint and denounced as a tyrant. He has received credit for the abolition of slavery in America, but is also depicted as a political opportunist. In the popular imagination, he has been both a down-home, log cabin–reared son of the wilderness and a keen legal thinker who confronted the most difficult constitutional questions in the nation's history. In some respects, the actual Abraham Lincoln has yielded to an icon representing American values and ideals.

But of course Lincoln was a man, not a myth, who served as president during the nation's most perilous hour. Like George Washington, his early life is shrouded in mythology. He did rise from modest, even meager, beginnings, and at times his climb up the political, social, and economic ladders of antebellum America seems the stuff of fiction. As most Americans know, Lincoln was born in Kentucky, in 1809, to Thomas Lincoln and Nancy Hanks Lincoln. His father, a journeyman farmer and laborer, had been born into a well-to-do farming family that hailed from Virginia and had moved to Kentucky in the 1780s. Due to the tradition of primogeniture, the eldest son, Lincoln's uncle Mordecai, inherited the entire family estate upon the death of the father (Lincoln's grandfather, also named Abraham, who in 1786 was killed in an Indian raid his sons witnessed). Thomas received nothing and was forced to make his way in the world on his own. His mother, Thomas Lincoln's second wife, came from poor origins, and, according to Lincoln himself, was born out of wedlock.

Young Abe Lincoln lived a rather unexceptional life. The family lived modestly, managing to stay one step ahead of destitution. Lincoln was one politician who actually lived in a log cabin, during an era when this fact could pay political dividends later in life. Like most boys on the frontier, he did not receive a formal education and spent most of his time hunting, fishing, and dreaming of faraway places. When he was seven years old, the family left Kentucky and settled in Indiana and later near Decatur, Illinois. Lincoln's mother died when he was quite young, but Thomas Lincoln soon remarried, to Sarah Bush Johnston, who raised Abraham and remained close to him in adulthood. In fact, his father's decision to remarry may have been a pivotal event in Lincoln's life. Sarah believed education was important for her children, despite her own lack of schooling, and with his father's approval Abraham entered a log cabin school nearby. The schools Lincoln attended were quite crude, but they introduced him to the world of books that broadened his horizons.

Lincoln lived with his family, who needed his labor and any wages he could provide, until 1831, when at the age of twenty-one he moved to New Salem, Illinois. Already, he displayed his distinctive physical traits. He stood six-feet-four-inches tall, struck a gangly, almost awkward pose, had a shock of dark, curly hair, and a friendly but also thoughtful appearance. The townspeople of New Salem soon came to regard Lincoln as a young man of great talent and wit who was destined for success. Lincoln himself was not short on confidence. Within weeks of living on his own for the first time, he announced his intention to run for the state legislature. While he was unsuccessful in his first political race, he did receive most of the votes of New Salem, an impressive accomplishment for a man in his early twenties who had only been in town for a few months. During the campaign, Lincoln also had volunteered for military service in the Black Hawk War, a series of skirmishes between the United States Army and the Sauk and Fox tribes over territory. Lincoln never saw combat, but came away from the experience with a positive view of the military; he had been named captain of his company and had enjoyed the camaraderie of the soldiers.

When Lincoln returned to New Salem, his career began to take several turns and twists. He entered into a partnership to run a store that quickly failed. He also was hired as a surveyor and was appointed the town's postmaster. Politics, however, continued to exert a pull on him. In 1834, he again ran for the state legislature. By this time, Lincoln had become popular in town and most people in the countryside surrounding New Salem were familiar with his name. His appointment as postmaster also allowed him to meet and make an impression on people in the area. All this came in handy when he launched his second political campaign.

Lincoln came of age during the "Era of Good Feelings," when the Republican, or Democratic-Republican, Party was the only viable party. By the 1820s, the party had divided into factions, and from the beginning Lincoln sided with the "National" wing of the party, which had backed Henry Clay throughout the 1820s. Lincoln agreed with their views of internal improvements to be funded through tariffs. Growing up near rivers, he understood the need for a well-developed transportation system based on rivers and canals. Through economic strength based on trade, Lincoln believed the nation would prosper. When the Whig party was formed in reaction to Andrew Jackson's administration, which opposed nationalist economic policy and attacked the Bank of the United States, most National Republicans, including Lincoln, joined with enthusiasm.

Lincoln's identification with the Whigs made sense in New Salem, where most agreed with Clay's ideas. However, anyone with statewide political aspirations would find it rough going in a staunchly pro-Jackson state. Even in the area outside New Salem, farmers tended to support Democratic candidates. Lincoln may have learned important lessons in his initial electoral defeat, for in the 1834 contest he kept his comments against Old Hickory to a minimum, hoping not to alienate Jacksonians in the region who otherwise would vote for the likeable Lincoln. The strategy worked. Lincoln was elected to the legislature and soon departed for the capital, located at that time in Vandalia. He served as a state representative for seven years.

Lincoln also began to prepare for a career in law. With the aid of friends, but primarily through arduous self-study, Lincoln educated himself and was admitted to the Illinois Bar in 1837. By then he had served in the state legislature for three years and had won a re-election bid a year earlier. He entered into legal partnership with John Todd Stuart in Springfield, where the state capital had been relocated. In time his law practice, as well as his political career, flourished. By the end of the decade, Lincoln was a leader of Illinois Whigs in the legislature. In 1840, he campaigned energetically for the Whig presidential candidate, William Henry Harrison.

By then Lincoln's political philosophy had begun to crystallize. He continued advocate federal support for infrastructure and a nationalist economic strategy. Lincoln also indicated that he considered slavery to be immoral, a belief he probably inherited from his father. Thomas Lincoln detested slavery both for religious and economic reasons and belonged to a sect of Baptists who openly opposed slavery. Like many settlers in the West, he also believed that slave labor took opportunities away from whites and provided wealthy slaveholders with an unfair advantage in the marketplace.

Lincoln was not an abolitionist. The thought of emancipating slaves probably never occurred to him during his early career. Instead, he took for granted that the peculiar institution was entrenched in the South but should be blocked from other areas. Lincoln agreed with the majority of Americans in both sections that African Americans innately were inferior to whites. Even as late as the 1850s, as a rising national figure, Lincoln rejected the notion that free blacks should be granted the right to vote.

This most eligible bachelor courted and then married the spirited Mary Todd, the daughter of wealthy businessman Robert S. Todd of Lexington, Kentucky. Lincoln first met her at social gatherings in Springfield, where Mary had relatives. At first sight Lincoln was overwhelmed by the short, pretty, refined, educated, and extroverted woman of twenty-two. Despite their very different backgrounds, they had a great deal in common, particularly their interest in politics. Todd was impressed with Lincoln's intelligence, sobriety, ambition, and the prospects that come with such attributes. After a courtship that had its share of turns, the wedding took place in November 1842.

In 1846, Lincoln's patience and party loyalty finally paid off. In 1844, the party had nominated for Congress Edward Baker, a friend of Lincoln's who declared his intention to serve only one term. As the end of Baker's service approached, Lincoln worked energetically to guarantee party support for his nomination for the upcoming election. He won his party's support in late summer and prevailed in the fall election. Soon Abraham and Mary Todd Lincoln were making preparations to leave for Washington. The Thirtieth Congress convened in December 1847 with Lincoln, now thirty-eight years old, in the freshman class.

This was a challenging time to launch a congressional career. Democratic President James K. Polk's expansionist policies in the West, including the Mexican War, inflamed sectional disputes. In the early stages of the war, Lincoln and most other Whigs said little in opposition to a war that had the support of a majority of Americans. Criticism of the war, Lincoln knew, would be damaging and perhaps fatal to his candidacy for Congress. However, by the end of the war, Whigs had become more vocal in their opposition to Polk's policies, particularly as the military engagement wound down and focus shifted to postwar negotiations. Lincoln, now safely elected to his congressional seat, echoed other Whigs in attacking the administration for a reckless foreign policy.

His willingness to confront Democrats may have impressed fellow Whigs in Washington, but it failed to sit well with supporters back in Illinois who tended to view opposition to the war as a sign of lack of patriotism. Yet Lincoln was not without political skill. He avoided falling into the quagmire of the Wilmot Proviso debates, which forced a number of politicians in both parties to confront the slavery issue. Lincoln evidently was little concerned with the question of slavery in the territories and considered the debate to be a minor one. He spent most of his time in Congress working for the election of a Whig president in 1848. Lincoln also sensed the declining fortunes of his party, both in Illinois and nationally.

A more immediate problem was that his congressional term was coming to an end. Lincoln had received the nomination with the understanding that he would step aside after a single term and allow another of the Whig politicians in his Illinois district to run. After entertaining the possibility of a presidential appointment as governor of the Oregon Territory, Lincoln returned to Springfield in 1849 and resumed his legal practice. There was now a family to consider. He was the father of two boys—Robert Todd Lincoln, born in 1843, and Edward Baker "Eddie" Lincoln, born in 1846.[1] The return to Illinois gave Lincoln time to build up his legal practice and become more secure financially. In 1854, now a renowned attorney, events pulled him back into politics.

At issue was the Kansas-Nebraska Act, which did away with the Missouri Compromise and opened up the possibility that slavery would enter this Northern region. Lincoln and most Northern Whigs were aghast by what was viewed as an attempt by Southerners to create numerous new slave states. To make matters worse, longtime Democratic rival Stephen A. Douglas had sponsored the bill and was instrumental in pushing it through the Senate. Lincoln may have been itching to return to public life anyway, but this inflammatory legislation drew him out. He announced his candidacy for a seat in the state legislature and began to speak out publicly against Douglas. In the process, Lincoln and Douglas began an intense and historic rivalry that lasted for the remainder of the decade.

Events moved rapidly in 1854. All across the North, protests rang out against the new legislation as politicians joined the "anti-Nebraska" movement. More extreme Northern Whigs abandoned the party for its refusal to voice opposition to the measure and formed the Republican Party. The result was the collapse of the Whig Party. Early on, Lincoln attempted to maintain his ties with the Whigs, fearing that more conservative Illinois voters would reject the extremism of the new party. However, he soon experienced the opposite problem. Opponents began to paint Lincoln as sympathetic to the South; he was, after all, born in a slave state and had married the daughter of a slaveholder. Attitudes in Illinois and elsewhere were polarizing; politicians found it difficult to maintain a moderate position.

Lincoln had been loyal to the Whigs during difficult times, but after his election to the state legislature he joined the Republicans. The new party was a better fit, for he represented the moderate wing that would have to prevail if the party had national aspirations. The party differed from the Whigs a great deal. First, it was an exclusively Northern party with a Northern perspective. In the 1856 presidential election, its platform called for repeal of the Kansas-Nebraska Act and the Fugitive Slave Act. The party nominated John C. Frémont as its first candidate for president.

Lincoln was a party leader from the outset. In the 1856 Republican convention, the Illinois delegation pushed for his nomination as Frémont's running mate. Nationally, however, Lincoln was an unknown entity and failed to receive sufficient support to be placed on the ticket. He did campaign energetically for Frémont in Illinois and in the end was quite pleased with the outcome. As most Americans, even Republicans, had anticipated, Frémont lost to the Democrat James Buchanan. However, the success of the new party was stunning. In Illinois, a longtime bastion of the Democratic Party, Frémont received one-third of the votes and won most northern counties. In only its first national election, the Republicans had made inroads in Illinois and made it clear that they were a legitimate political force.

Lincoln's active leadership won him the party's nomination for the United States Senate in 1858. His opponent was Senator Stephen A. Douglas, the controversial but quite popular Democrat. Unseating an incumbent of the majority party would be a difficult task in any case. In this race, the fiery Douglas, adoringly known to supporters as the "Little Giant," would be formidable. He was known for his oratorical talents, combining clever phrases with a theatrical stage presence. Moreover, Douglas was a powerful force in the Democratic Party and had been considered a candidate for president.

The 1858 Illinois Senate race was historic. Both candidates were seasoned and intelligent political veterans. The two met for seven debates over the course of three months and attracted national attention. Both men agreed that slavery was wrong. The main points of controversy had to do with slavery in the territories, the Fugitive Slave Law, and the controversial *Dred Scott* case. Lincoln stressed in the debates that African Americans were human beings, and as such deserved to receive the legal and political guarantees that all citizens were promised by the Declaration of Independence.

Douglas agreed with much of Lincoln's argument. He was less vocal in his denunciation of slavery, often regretting its existence but accepting it as a reality. He also agreed that slavery should never expand into already-free states and desired to see Western territories established as free states. However, there was one fundamental disagreement between the two. Douglas stressed local rule under the banner of "states' rights." Slavery, he claimed, may be wrong, but states had the authority to determine the matter without restraints from the national government. This had been Douglas's view for a decade and had been the philosophical justification for the Kansas-Nebraska Act. Lincoln, by contrast, stressed the rights guaranteed by the Declaration of Independence to all Americans, regardless of race. This bedrock principle of American democracy could not coexist with a government that allowed for the expansion of slavery. Their debates were a microcosm of the broader disagreement that was pulling the nation apart.

Lincoln lost the election, but the outcome could be viewed as a victory. The polling was very close; in fact, Republicans carried the popular vote of the state in the election but were unable to take over control of the state legislature. As this was decades before states moved to a popular vote for senators, the state legislature then selected Douglas. As the nation moved toward the next presidential election, Lincoln stood as a legitimate Republican candidate.

The year 1860 was pivotal in the nation's history. Much had occurred during President Buchanan's term that contributed to sectional division. The ranks of the Republican Party continued to grow and had became a serious challenge to Democratic dominance in national politics. Moreover, issues surrounding slavery had taken center stage in the public interest. The controversial *Dred Scott* decision, in which the Supreme Court invalidated the Missouri Compromise and claimed that Southerners had a right to transport slaves into any new territory, astounded and outraged many Northerners. In 1859, John Brown's attempted raid on a federal arsenal at Harper's Ferry, Virginia, with the intent of inciting slave insurrections across the South, heightened tensions. Antislavery activists hailed Brown as a hero and a martyr upon his execution; Southerners increasingly were convinced that all Northerners were as aggressive as Brown himself. Buchanan, the hapless Democratic president, attempted to guide the ship of state on a straight course through these very choppy waters, appealing often to Union and castigating those Northerners who he believed were contributing to regional hostility.

As the election approached, Southern partisans began to threaten secession if the Republican party prevailed, arguing that a Northern-based party could never represent the interests of both sections. In the midst of this tense atmosphere, the two parties met for their nominating conventions. The Democratic convention, held in Charleston, South Carolina, was a disaster. Douglas, the clear leader among Northern Democrats, was attacked by Southerners for statements he had made regarding the immorality of slavery during his Senate campaign against Lincoln. Despite efforts to maintain a middle course, Douglas was confronted by a powerful and vocal group of Democratic leaders who ultimately walked out of the convention in protest. After days of frustration, the convention ended with no candidate and planned to reconvene in Baltimore.

Weeks of delay did little to dampen the passions of angry Southern delegates. In Baltimore, Douglas eventually won the party's nomination, but in the process caused even more Southern delegates to leave the convention in protest. Soon a separate Southern convention was organized where the Southern delegation nominated Vice President John C. Breckenridge of Kentucky as their candidate under a Southern Democrat banner. The one remaining national political party finally had given way to sectionalism.

Republicans viewed the disintegration of the Democratic Party as a great opportunity. Their convention, in Chicago, took place amid an atmosphere of confidence and militancy. Lincoln was perfectly positioned to win the nomination. The only other serious candidate was New Yorker William H. Seward, who enjoyed more popularity in the East but was opposed by Westerners. Lincoln opposed slavery but never had been associated with abolitionists, a crucial point in winning the support of moderates. Lincoln won the nomination on the third ballot and chose Hannibal Hamlin of

Maine as his running mate. The party's platform was a sound one. While it openly opposed the extension of slavery into new territories, it also offered a range of policies on economic development, including construction of a transcontinental railroad and legislation to open new territories to settlement through homesteading provisions.

Considering the state of the Democratic Party, Lincoln's victory was unsurprising. He carried every free state, which gave him a majority in the electoral college. Douglas was second in the popular vote, but won only the state of Missouri. Breckenridge, the Southern Democrat candidate, won most of the South except for Tennessee, Kentucky, and Virginia; these border states went for Tennessean John Bell, who ran as a unionist candidate on the Constitutional Union ticket. The election illustrated the extent to which the nation was divided. Lincoln did not appear on the ballot of a single Southern state; Breckenridge received no support in the North. Douglas's attempt to appeal to both regions proved impossible. Lincoln's ability to win a majority in the electoral college without winning a single vote in the South also indicated that the more populous North had an advantage in such a contest.

There was, of course, little celebration after the election. Southerners who threatened secession upon Lincoln's election were committed to carrying out the promise. In December 1860, the South Carolina legislature issued an Ordinance of Secession. Within two months, seven Southern states had left the Union. Lincoln prepared for his inauguration while Buchanan made final appeals to the South to reject secession. His words, however, were far too few and far too late. As the inauguration approached, Buchanan watched and waited as secessionists took hold of federal forts and arsenals in the South. Most critical was Fort Sumter, off the South Carolina coast at Charleston. For weeks, Major Robert Anderson had warned that he could only hold the fort as long as he had provisions and weapons. South Carolina officials made it clear that any attempts to refortify the fort would be met with force. As Lincoln took the oath of office, the situation at Fort Sumter had become critical.

Lincoln faced the crisis at Sumter as he did most others of his embattled presidency—with direct action. He was firm and unmoving in his goal of preserving the Union. His inaugural address of March 1861 rejected the notion that states had a right to secede. He repeated that the administration had no intention of challenging slavery where it existed. He also sought to ease tensions by assuring Southerners that there would be no invasion of their states. However, as Confederates fired on Fort Sumter in April, and as the Confederate government under the leadership of Jefferson Davis began to organize a military, war became likely if Lincoln were to preserve the nation.

Lincoln's wartime record, the subject of ongoing historical debate, cannot be summarized easily. He was committed to winning the war, seeking out military commanders willing to take the offensive against the Confederate Army even if it meant political attacks at home. His first term in office was a very difficult one. Most Northerners expected the war to be brief and relatively bloodless. When it proved otherwise, Democratic opponents attacked Lincoln for ineptitude. Lincoln's decision to broaden the powers of the executive for the duration of the war also met with considerable opposition. His willingness to spend government funds without congressional consent, his decision to blockade Southern ports, his policy of suspending civil rights in hostile locations, and the monumental Emancipation Proclamation all met with opposition.

Much of the political debate during his presidency centered on the question of executive authority. Critics decried the expansion of executive power as authoritarian; Lincoln, an attorney, understood the reasoning behind such complaints but defended his action as necessary to save the nation from ruin. Controversies pertaining to the right of citizens to criticize the administration and the military, the legality of a draft in a democracy, and the authority of the president to make pronouncements on slavery in the rebellious states challenged the administration. In the end, Southerners found that Lincoln was consistent and unswerving in his commitment to preserving the union at any cost. This decisiveness and firm resolve in the face of adversity was crucial in determining the war's outcome.

Shocked Northerners mourned in the wake of Lincoln's assassination, committed by John Wilkes Booth on April 11, 1865. As the years passed, Lincoln's place in history as perhaps the greatest of all presidents became secured. At the time, however, many would have disagreed. Lincoln's years in the White House were beset with criticism, tragedy, and death on all fronts. His son Willie died in 1862, at the age of twelve, most likely of typhoid; he had already lost one son, Eddie, in 1850. The final years of Lincoln's life were shrouded in mourning for his son and the sons of thousands killed in the bloody battles of the war. By early 1865, the war's outcome was assured, but offered cold comfort to the exhausted Lincoln. His final months were consumed by efforts to overcome Northern anger and offer a tone of conciliation and unification with the South. Lincoln, above all else, cherished the Union that he was so instrumental in saving.

NOTE

1. Eddie would die in 1850. That same year, another son, William Wallace "Willie" Lincoln was born.

SLAVERY

Slavery's emergence as a central issue in American politics began decades before the Civil War. Even before the Revolution, thoughtful citizens debated slavery as it related to economics, politics, and morality. During the constitutional convention, slavery generated heated debate, defused only through compromise. Compromise prevented the issue from tearing the nation apart for decades.

In the 1830s, abolitionists forced increasing numbers of Northerners to at least reflect on the broader moral and religious ramifications of slavery. While the movement was slow in growing, the work of reformers gradually placed slavery at the center of debate—not only in Congress but in the homes of Americans in both sections. By 1850, no candidate for public office could avoid the question altogether. Most searched for middle ground by claiming the right of people to disagree without commenting on the moral questions involved. By the time of the 1854 Kansas-Nebraska Act, which once again forced open the question of slavery in the Western territories, such fence-straddling became more difficult.

The Republican Party broke new ground in the 1850s by offering a clear denunciation of slavery. Officially, the party claimed no efforts to abolish slavery in the South but was unabashed in identifying forced servitude as wrong and against democratic principles. Southerners justified the institution on the basis of property rights and heritage.

Abraham Lincoln's views of slavery, like those of most Americans, were subject to change over the course of these turbulent years. However, one constant was his belief that slavery was unjust and with time would disappear. In the 1850s, during his rapid rise onto the national political stage, Lincoln expressed on several occasions his sentiments on the immorality of slavery. His historic 1854 speech at Peoria, Illinois, in reaction to the Kansas-Nebraska Act, provides a clear example of Lincoln's views with respect to slavery. Lincoln, careful to avoid being branded an extremist, assures his audience that Southerners have the right to own slaves within their borders. However, Lincoln also refers to slavery as a "cancer," one that had been recognized by the founders, and one that perhaps would be eradicated in time. Lincoln's speech also indicates that opponents of slavery did not believe that there was equality among the races. Lincoln, echoing most Northerners, stresses that while African Americans, as human beings, are guaranteed basic rights of liberty, they are inferior to whites and ideally would be relocated to Africa.

Southerners responded to growing criticism of slavery by developing justifications for its existence. Among the more interesting of these came from the writer George Fitzhugh, who designed an intellectual defense of slavery and even described the system as more humane than the Northern system of free labor. His major work, *Sociology for the South*, written in 1854, attacks modern capitalism as both predatory and hostile to tradition. In his attempt to champion slavery, Fitzhugh argues that servitude had been in the past the norm in human civilization, and that all societies sanction one form or another of enslavement. Slavery in the South, he explains, had deep roots in Western history and could not be abolished suddenly. He also claims that slavery protects inferior blacks from exploitation by an unforgiving free market. Emancipation, he argues, would result in the ruin of African Americans. Fitzhugh equates the mental capacity of blacks to children and lauds the protective nature of the slave system. Revealingly, both Lincoln and Fitzhugh agree on the assumption of black inferiority. Lincoln, however, grants blacks their humanity and cannot support their enslavement.

Philosophical debates on slavery were significant, for they shaped public opinion and focused national attention on the matter. Ultimately, intellectual exchange gave way to violence before the issue was resolved permanently.

ABRAHAM LINCOLN, ON SLAVERY
(PEORIA, IL, OCTOBER 16, 1854)

When southern people tell us they are no more responsible for the origin of slavery than we; I acknowledge the fact. When it is said that the institution exists; and that it is very difficult to get rid of it, in any satisfactory way, I can understand and appreciate the saying. I surely will not blame them for not doing what I should not know how to do myself. If all earthly power were given me, I should not know what to do, as to the existing institution. My first impulse would be to free all the slaves, and send them to Liberia,—to their own native land. But a moment's reflection would convince me, that whatever of high hope, (as I think there is) there may be in this, in the long run, its sudden execution is impossible. . . .

When they remind us of their constitutional rights, I acknowledge them, not grudgingly, but fully, and fairly; and I would give them any legislation for the reclaiming of their fugitives, which should not, in its stringency, be more likely to carry a free man into slavery, than our ordinary criminal laws are to hang an innocent one. . . .

The doctrine of self-government is right—absolutely and eternally right—but it has no just application, as here attempted. Or perhaps I should rather say that whether it has such just application depends on whether a negro is *not* or *is* a man. If he is *not* a man, why in that case, he who *is* a man may, as a matter of self-government, do just as he pleases with him. But if the negro *is* a man, is it not to that extent, a total destruction of self-government, to say that he too shall not govern *himself*? When the white man governs *another* man, that is *more* than self-government—that is despotism. If the negro is a *man*, why then my ancient faith teaches me that "all men are created equal"; and that there can be no moral right in connection with one man's making a slave of another. . . .

I have quoted so much at this time to show that according to our ancient faith, the just powers of government are derived from the consent of the governed. Now the relation of masters and slaves is, PRO TANTO, a total violation of this principle. The master not only governs the slave without his consent; but he governs him by a set of rules altogether different from those which he prescribes for himself. Allow ALL the governed an equal voice in the government, and that, and that only is self-government.

Let it not be said I am contending for the establishment of political and social equality between the whites and blacks. I have already said the contrary. I am not now combating the argument of NECESSITY, arising from the fact that the blacks are already amongst us; but I am combating what is set up as a MORAL argument for allowing them to be taken where they have never yet been—arguing against the EXTENSION of a bad thing, which where it already exists, we must of necessity, manage as best we can. . . .

I object to it because it assumes that there CAN BE MORAL RIGHT in the enslaving of one man by another. I object to it as a dangerous dalliance for a few [free?] people—a sad evidence that, feeling prosperity we forget right—that liberty, as a principle, we have ceased to revere. I object to it because the fathers of the republic eschewed, and rejected it. The argument of "Necessity" was the only argument they ever admitted in favor of slavery; and so far, and so far only as it carried them, did they ever go. They found the institution existing among us, which they could not help; and they cast blame upon the British King for having permitted its introduction. BEFORE the constitution, they prohibited its introduction into the north-western Territory—the only country we owned, then free from it. At the framing and adoption of the constitution, they forbore to so much as mention the word "slave" or "slavery" in the whole instrument. In the provision for the recovery of fugitives, the slave is spoken of as a "PERSON HELD TO SERVICE OR LABOR." In that prohibiting the abolition of the slave trade for twenty years, that trade is spoken of as "The migration or importation of such persons as any of the States NOW EXISTING, shall think proper to admit," &c. There are the only provisions alluding to slavery. Thus, the thing is hid away, in the constitution, just as an afflicted man hides away a wen or a cancer, which he dares not cut out once, lest he bleed to death; with the promise, nevertheless, that the cutting away may begin at the end of a given time. Less than this our fathers COULD not do; and NOW [MORE?] they WOULD not do. Necessity drove them so far, and farther, they would not go. . . .

Our republican robe is soiled, and trailed in the dust. Let us repurify it. Let us turn and wash it white, in the spirit, if not the blood, of the Revolution. Let us turn slavery from its claims of "moral right," back upon its existing legal rights, and its arguments of "necessity." Let us return it to the position our fathers gave it; and there let it rest in peace. Let us re-adopt the Declaration of Independence, and with it, the practices, and policy, which harmonize with it. Let north and south—let all Americans—let all lovers of liberty everywhere—join in the great and good work. If we do this, we shall not only have saved the Union, but we shall have so saved it, as to make, and to keep it, forever worthy of saving. We shall have so saved it, that the succeeding millions of free happy people, the world over, shall rise up, and call us blessed, to the latest generations.

The Collected Works of Abraham Lincoln, vol. 3., Roy Basler, Marion Dolores Pratt, and Lloyd A. Dunlap, eds. (New Brunswick, NJ: Rutgers University Press, 1953), 247–276.

GEORGE FITZHUGH, JUSTIFICATIONS FOR SLAVERY IN THE SOUTH (RICHMOND, VA, 1854)

But abolish negro slavery, and how much of slavery still remains. Soldiers and sailors in Europe enlist for life; here, for five years. Are they not slaves who have not only sold their liberties, but their lives also? And they are worse treated than domestic slaves. No domestic affection and self-interest extend their aegis over them. No kind mistress, like a guardian angel, provides for them in health, tends them in sickness, and soothes their dying pillow. Wellington at Waterloo was a slave. He was bound to obey, or would . . . have been shot for gross misconduct, and might not, like a common laborer, quit his work at any moment. He had sold his liberty, and might not resign without the consent of his master, the king. The common laborer may quit his work at any moment, whatever his contract; declare that liberty is an inalienable right, and leave his employer to redress by a useless suit for damages. The highest and most honorable position on earth was that of the slave Wellington; the lowest, that of the free man who cleaned his boots and fed his hounds. The African cannibal, caught, christianized and enslaved, is as much elevated by slavery as was Wellington. The kind of slavery is adapted to the men enslaved. Wives and apprentices are slaves; not in theory only, but in fact. Children are slaves to their parents, guardians and teachers. Imprisoned culprits are slaves. Lunatics and idiots are slaves also. Three-fourths of free society are slaves, no better treated, when their wants and capacities are estimated, than negro slaves. . . .

Negro slavery would be changed immediately to some form of peonage, serfdom, or villeinage, if the negroes were sufficiently intelligent and provident to manage a farm. No one would have the labor and trouble of management, if his negroes would pay in hires and rents one-half what free tenants pay in rent in Europe. Every negro in the South would be soon liberated, if he would take liberty on the terms that white tenants hold it. The fact that he cannot enjoy liberty on such terms, seems conclusive that he is only fit to be a slave.

But for the assaults of the abolitionists, much would have been done ere this to regulate and improve Southern society. Our negro mechanics do not work so hard, have many more privileges, and are better fed and clothed than field hands, and are yet more valuable to their masters. The slaves of the South are cheated of their rights by the purchase of Northern manufactures which they could produce. Besides, if he would employ our slaves in the coarser processes of the mechanic arts and manufactures, such as brick making, getting and hewing timber for ships and houses, iron mining and smelting, coal mining, grading railroads and plank roads, in the manufacture of cotton, tobacco, &c., we would find a vent in new employments for their increase, more humane and more profitable than the vent afforded by new states and territories. . . . Free doctrines, not slavery, have made the South agricultural and dependent, given her a sparse and ignorant population, ruined her cities, and expelled her people.

Would the abolitionists approve of a system of society that set white children free, and remitted them at the age of fourteen, males and females, to all the rights, both as to person and property, which belong to adults? Would it be criminal or praiseworthy to do so? Criminal, of course. Now, are the average of negroes equal in information, in native intelligence, in prudence or providence, to well-informed white children of fourteen? We who have lived with them for forty years, think not. The competition of the world would be too much for the children. They would be cheated out of their property and debased in their morals. Yet they would meet every where with sympathizing friends of their own color, ready to aid, advise, and assist them. The negro would be exposed to the same competition and greater temptations, with no greater ability to contend with them, with these additional difficulties. He could be welcome nowhere; meet with thousands of enemies and no friends. If he went North, the white laborers would kick him and cuff him, and drive him out of employment. If he went to Africa, the savages would cook him and eat him. If he went to the West Indies, they would not let him in, or if they did, they would soon make of him a savage and idolater. . . .

We abhor the doctrine of the "Types of Mankind"; first, because it is at war with scripture, which teaches us that the whole human race is descended from a common parentage; and, secondly, because it encourages and incites brutal masters to treat negroes, not as weak, ignorant, and dependent brethren, but as wicked beasts, without the pale of humanity. The Southerner is the negro's friend, his only friend. Let no intermeddling abolitionist, no refined philosophy, dissolve this friendship.

George Fitzhugh, *Sociology for the South, or the Failure of Free Society* (Richmond, VA: A. Morris, 1854), 82–95.

SECESSION

On December 20, 1860, in the wake of Abraham Lincoln's election, the South Carolina legislature met in special session to approve an Ordinance of Secession. The document stated that the Republican party sought to abolish slavery and that the only recourse was to leave the Union. Other Southern states soon held their own conventions. By February 1861, Alabama, Florida, Georgia, Louisiana, Mississippi, and Texas had joined South

Carolina. President James Buchanan stumbled through the remaining days of his term hoping to stave off hostilities. He made few public pronouncements on secession, although he was opposed to the act in principle.

While the act of secession came suddenly, a discussion as to the rights of a state to break from the Union had been ongoing across the South. In some respects, the question was as old as the republic itself. Thomas Jefferson, in the late 1790s, had written about state sovereignty in the Virginia and Kentucky Resolutions. Some New Englanders had pondered secession during the War of 1812. During Andrew Jackson's presidency, disputes between South Carolinians and the administration over tariffs had also brought forth the question. As hostilities increased in the late 1850s, Southerners began to raise the issue again. Could a state legally break from the Union?

The argument in favor of the right to secession was based on the principle of "states' rights." Often drawing from Jefferson, secessionists claimed that the Union was a compact of sovereign states. States had predated the Union, and although each had given up some liberties when entering the nation, each retained its freedom of action. The state commissioner of Alabama, S.F. Hale, in a letter to Kentucky governor Beriah Magoffin, dated December 12, 1860, succinctly outlines the secessionist argument. Additionally, Hale draws from the Declaration of Independence, stressing the rights of individuals in the face of perceived governmental oppression and the fundamental right of revolution when liberties are not guaranteed by the government. The ability of secessionists to draw from the language of the Declaration gave them a powerful voice throughout the Southern states.

Lincoln was firm in his opposition to secession, believing that the states always had been defined by their inclusion in a greater whole. In his historic speech to Congress, on July 4, 1861, Lincoln points out that no state had ever been a true sovereign, even before the time of the Constitution. Prior to the Revolution, the colonists were bound by a common tie to England. Independence had only been won through cooperation between the former colonies, and the Constitution grew out of this union of states. He also argues that only Texas ever had a government separate from the other states, and even in that case the government was short-lived and only existed because of delays in granting the region statehood. Lincoln also raises the interesting problem of how these seceding states could justify forming a new Confederate Union, given their extreme views on the rights of the individual states. If the Southern states came to disagree on any matter, he asks rhetorically, would this government be doomed to collapse as well?

In the end, the answer to these matters could not be found on paper or heard from the pulpit, but rather settled on the battlefield. The Civil War resolved with finality the longstanding question of state sovereignty and federal authority. States might reserve certain responsibilities and liberties but were part of a greater, indivisible whole.

ABRAHAM LINCOLN, IN OPPOSITION TO THE RIGHT OF
STATES TO SECEDE FROM THE UNION
(WASHINGTON, DC, JULY 4, 1861)

It might seem at first thought to be of little difference whether the present movement at the South be called "secession" or "rebellion." The movers, however, well understand the difference. At the beginning they knew they could never raise their treason to any respectable magnitude by any name which implies *violation* of law. They knew their people possessed as much of moral sense, as much of devotion to law and order, and as much pride in and reverence for the history and Government of their common country as any other civilized and patriotic people. They knew they could make no advancement directly in the teeth of these strong and noble sentiments. Accordingly, they commenced by an insidious debauching of the public mind. They invented an ingenious sophism, which, if conceded, was followed by perfectly logical steps through all the incidents to the complete destruction of the Union. The sophism itself is that any State of the Union may *consistently* with the National Constitution, and therefore *lawfully* and *peacefully*, withdraw from the Union without the consent of the Union or of any other State. The little disguise that the supposed right is to be exercised only for just cause, themselves to be the sold of its justice, is too thin to merit any notice.

With rebellion thus sugar coated they have been drugging the public mind of their section for more than thirty years, and until at length they have brought many good men to a willingness to take up arms against the Government the day *after* some assemblage of men have enacted the farcical pretense of taking their State out of the Union who could have been brought to no such thing the day *before*.

This sophism derives much, perhaps the whole, of its currency from the assumption that there is some omnipotent and sacred supremacy pertaining to a State—to each State of our Federal Union. Our States have neither more or less power than that reserved to them in the Union by the Constitution, no one of them ever having been a State out of the Union. The original ones passed into the Union even before they cast off their British colonial dependence, and the new ones each came into the Union directly from a condition of dependence, excepting Texas; and even Texas, in its temporary independence, was never designated a State. The new ones only took the designation of States on coming into the Union, while that name was first adopted for the old ones in and by the Declaration of Independence. Therein the "United Colonies" were declared to be "free and independent States"; but even then the object plainly was not to declare their independence of one another or of the Union, but directly the contrary, as their mutual pledge and their mutual action before, at the time, and afterwards abundantly show. The express plighting of faith by each and all of the original thirteen in the Articles of Confederation, two years later, that the Union shall be perpetual is most conclusive. Having never been States, either in substance or in name, outside of the Union, whence this magical omnipotence of "State rights," asserting a claim of power to lawfully destroy the Union itself? Much is said about the "sovereignty" of the States, but the word even is not in the National Constitution, nor, as is believed, in any of the State constitutions. What is a "sovereignty" in the political sense of the term? Would it be far wrong to define it "a political community without a political superior?" Tested by this, no one of our States, except Texas, ever was a sovereignty, and even Texas gave up the character on coming into the Union, by which she acknowledged the Constitution of the United States and the laws and treaties of the United States made in pursuance of the Constitution to be for her the supreme law of the land. The States have their status in the Union, and they have no other legal status. If they break from this, they can only do so against law and by revolution. The Union, and not themselves separately, procured their independence and their liberty. By conquest or purchase the Union gave each of them whatever of independence and liberty it has. The Union is older than any of the States, and, in fact, it created them as States. . . .

The seceders insist that our Constitution admits of secession. They have assumed to make a national constitution of their own, in which of necessity they have either discarded or retained the right of secession, as they insist it exists in ours. If they have discarded it, they thereby admit that on principle it ought not to be in ours. If they have retained it, by their own construction of ours they show that to be consistent they must secede from one another whenever they shall find it the easiest way of settling their debts or effecting any other selfish or unjust object. The principle itself is one of disintegration, and upon which no government can possibly endure. . . .

The Constitution provides, and all the States have accepted the provision, that "the United States shall guarantee to every State in this Union a republican form of government." But if a State may lawfully go out of the Union, having done so it may also discard the republican form of government; so that to prevent its going out is an indispensable means to an end of maintaining the guaranty mentioned; and when an end is lawful and obligatory the indispensable means to it are also lawful and obligatory.

A Compilation of the Messages and Papers of the Presidents, vol. 7, James D. Richardson, ed. (New York: Bureau of National Literature, Inc., 1897), 3227–3232.

S.F. HALE, STATE COMMISSIONER OF ALABAMA, ON THE RIGHT OF SECESSION (FRANKFURT, KY, DECEMBER 27, 1860)

Although each State, as a sovereign political community, must finally determine these grave issues for itself, yet the identity of interest, sympathy, and institutions, prevailing alike in all the slaveholding States, in the opinion of Alabama, renders it proper that there should be a frank and friendly consultation, by each one, with her sister Southern States, touching their common grievances, and the measures necessary to be adopted to protect the interest, honor, and safety of their citizens. . . .

I therefor[e] submit, for the consideration of your Excellency, the following propositions, which I hope will command your assent and approval:

1. The people are the source of all political power; and the primary object of all good Governments is to protect the citizen in the enjoyment of life, liberty and property; and whenever any form of Government becomes destructive of these ends, it is the inalienable right, and the duty of the people to alter or abolish it.

2. The equality of all the States of this Confederacy, as well as the equality of rights of all the citizens of the respective States under the Federal Constitution, is a fundamental principle in the scheme of the Federal Government. The Union of these States under the Constitution, was formed "to establish justice, insure domestic tranquility, provide for the common defense, promote the general welfare, and secure the blessings of liberty to her citizens and their posterity"; and when it is perverted to the destruction of the equality of the States, or substantially fails to accomplish these ends, it fails to achieve the purposes of its creation, and ought to be dissolved.

3. The Federal Government results from a Compact entered into between separate sovereign and independent States, called the Constitution of the United States, and Amendments thereto, by which these sovereign States delegated certain specific powers to be used by that Government, for the common defense and general welfare of all the States and their citizens; and when these powers are abused, or used for the destruction of the rights of any State or its citizens, each State has an equal right to judge for itself, as well of the violations and infractions of that instrument, as of the mode and measure of redress; and if the interest or safety of her citizens demands it, may resume the powers she had delegated, without let or hindrance from the Federal Government, or any other power on earth.

4. Each State is bound in good faith to observe and keep, on her part, all the stipulations and covenants inserted for the benefit of other States in the Constitutional Compact—the only bond of Union by which the several States are bound together; and when persistently violated by one party to the prejudice of her sister States, ceases to be obligatory on the States so

aggrieved, and they may rightfully declare the compact broken, the Union thereby formed dissolved, and stand upon their original rights, as sovereign and independent political communities; and further, that each citizen owes his primary allegiance to the State in which he resides, and hence it is the imperative duty of the State to protect him in the enjoyment of all his Constitutional rights, and see to it that they are not denied or withheld from him with impunity, by any other State or Government. . . .

The Federal Government has failed to protect the rights and property of the citizens of the South, and is about to pass into the hands of a party pledged for the destruction, not only of their rights and property, but the equality of the States ordained by the Constitution, and the heaven-ordained superiority of the white over the black race. What remains, then, for the Southern States, and the people of these States, if they are loyal to the great principles of civil and religious liberty, sanctified by the sufferings of a seven-year's war, and baptized with the blood of the Revolution? Can they permit the rights of their citizens to be denied and spurned? their property spirited away, their own sovereignty violated, and themselves degraded to the position of mere dependencies, instead of sovereign States? or shall each for itself, judging the infractions of the Constitutional Compact, as well as the mode and measure of redress, declare that the covenants of that sacred instrument, in their behalf, and for the benefit of their citizens, have been willfully, deliberately, continuously and persistently broken and violated by the other parties to the compact, and that they and their citizens are therefore absolved from all further obligations to keep and perform the covenants thereof, resume the powers delegated to the Federal Government, and, as sovereign States, form other relations for the protection of their citizens and the discharge of the great ends of Government? The Union of these States was one of fraternity as well as equality; but what fraternity now exists between the citizens of the two sections? Various religious associations, powerful in numbers and influence, have been broken asunder, and the sympathies that bound together the people of the several States, at the time of the formation of the Constitution, has ceased to exist, and feelings of bitterness, and even hostility, have sprung up in its place. How can this be reconciled, and a spirit of fraternity established? Will the people of the North cease to make war upon the institution of Slavery, and award to it the protection guaranteed by the Constitution? The accumulated wrongs of many years, the late action of the members in Congress in refusing every measure of justice to the South, as well as the experience of all the past, answers, *No, never!* . . .

Your obedient servant, etc.,
S.F. HALE,
Commissioner from the State of Alabama.
Frankfurt, December 27, 1860.

War of the Rebellion: The Official Records of the Union and Confederate Armies, 130 vols. (Washington, DC: U.S. Government Printing Office, 1882–1909), 4: 1, 4–11.

SUSPENSION OF THE WRIT OF *HABEAS CORPUS*

Lincoln never enjoyed unanimous support in the North. Democrats, particularly "Peace Democrats" who opposed the war, constantly held Lincoln under close scrutiny and criticized his decisions. While there was a bipartisan wave of support in the weeks following the fall of Fort Sumter, soon Democrats again began blasting the administration on several fronts.

One area of controversy was Lincoln's record with respect to civil rights during the war, particularly when it came to the writ of *habeas corpus*. This doctrine requires that any citizen placed under arrest be given his day in court in a speedy fashion. During debates over the Constitution, delegates recalled a common complaint that the British often arrested colonists for alleged crimes and detained them indefinitely without bringing them before a magistrate, even if they proved to be innocent. The Seventh Amendment to the Constitution, as part of the Bill of Rights, reinforced this concept that also was mentioned in Article I of the Constitution. Few principles of law have been more cherished in the American legal system.

Yet by the spring of 1861, Lincoln was fully prepared to suspend the writ of *habeas corpus*, a decision that met with strong reaction from opponents. The controversy concerned Maryland. In the weeks after the initial fighting off the coast of South Carolina, Lincoln headed a precarious government in Washington, D.C. Directly to the south was hostile Virginia and the threat of unimpeded rebel troops marching into the capital. Maryland, which surrounded the District of Columbia, remained in the Union, but a large portion of that state sympathized with the Southern cause. This became all too apparent in April, when desperately needed troops from Massachusetts, heading to Washington, were met by violent mobs in Baltimore. Four soldiers were killed before the troops made their way out of the city, and the governor of Maryland informed Lincoln that no more soldiers could be sent through the city. For a time, it seemed as if the national capital had been cut off from the rest of the Union with no reinforcements.

Eventually, troops did begin to make their way into Washington by avoiding Baltimore altogether, but with the state emerging as the primary conduit for Northern troops to enter the capital, attacks on these forces could be crippling. In response to increasing agitation against the government in Maryland, on April 27 Lincoln announced the suspension of the writ of *habeas corpus* on the main military route through the state. The proclamation gave the military the authority to arrest individuals or groups suspected of aiding in the rebellion, and allowed prisoners to be detained indefinitely. Lincoln's opponents denounced the measure as a usurpation of power, and a test case quickly emerged. John Merryman, an active secessionist, was arrested by Union soldiers in Maryland and detained at Fort McHenry in Baltimore. Merryman requested and obtained a writ of *habeas corpus* from Chief Justice of the Supreme Court Roger B. Taney, who also happened to be the district judge presiding over Maryland and no friend of the president. Lincoln commanded the officers in Baltimore to ignore the writ, which would have required the military to bring Merryman before a tribunal or release him.

Lincoln's refusal to submit to the writ moved Taney to write a dissent in the case, titled *Ex Parte Merryman*. In the dissent, the Chief Justice argues that Lincoln clearly overstepped the bounds of his office. The main thrust of Taney's argument rests on his interpretation of the Constitution. The power to suspend the writ did exist in the case of rebellion or threat to national security, he concedes, but this power was included in Article I, which meant that only Congress could do so. The executive, under any circumstances, did not have the authority to suspend the writ of *habeas corpus*.

Lincoln initially ignored Taney's critique, but in time felt moved to confront growing criticism of his wartime policies. In his July 4, 1861, address to Congress, Lincoln took time to address those who accused him of abusing the powers of his office. He maintains that arguments such as those advanced by Taney were guilty of legal hairsplitting and that his opponents were willing to watch the government collapse on the basis of minor legal disputes. Lincoln claims that his primary duty as president is to preserve the Union. "Even in such a case," he asks, "would not the official oath be broken if the Government should be overthrown when it was believed that disregarding the single law would tend to preserve it?" Lincoln further argues limiting the power to suspend the writ to Congress was useless in the present crisis, because Congress could not convene during the early months of the upheaval. In the end, Lincoln might be willing to admit that there were legal questions regarding his actions, but that desperate times called for extreme measures.

Lincoln's wartime policies did not come without cost, as Democrats were able to use disputes such as these to gain more support. However, Lincoln did survive the political battles with his opponents, gaining re-election in 1864. More importantly, Lincoln's decisive actions may have prevented the Confederacy from securing very damaging gains in the early and perhaps most crucial months of the conflict.

ABRAHAM LINCOLN, ON SUSPENDING THE WRIT OF *HABEAS CORPUS* (WASHINGTON, DC, JULY 14, 1861)

Having been conveyed on an extraordinary occasion, as authorized by the Constitution, your attention is not called to any ordinary subject of legislation.

At the beginning of the present Presidential term, four months ago, the functions of the Federal Government were found to be generally suspended within the several States of South Carolina, Georgia, Alabama, Mississippi, Louisiana, and Florida, excepting only those of the Post-Office Department.

Within these States all the forts, arsenals, dockyards, custom-houses, and the like, including the movable and stationary property in and about them, had been seized and were held in open hostility to this Government, excepting only Fort Pickens, Taylor, and Jefferson, on and near the Florida coast, and Fort Sumter, in Charleston Harbor, South Carolina. The forts thus seized had been put in improved condition, new ones had been built, and armed forces had been organized and were organizing, all avowedly with the same hostile purpose. . . .

Recurring to the action of the Government, it may be stated that at first a call was made for 75,000 militia, and rapidly following this a proclamation was issued for closing ports of the insurrectionary districts by proceedings in the nature of blockade. So far all was believed to be strictly legal. At this point the insurrectionists announced their purpose to enter upon the practice of privateering.

Other calls were made for volunteers to serve three years unless sooner discharged, and also for large additions to the Regular Army and Navy. These measures, whether strictly legal or not, were ventured upon under what appeared to be a popular demand and a public necessity, trusting then, as now, that Congress would readily ratify them. It is believed that nothing had been done beyond the constitutional competency of Congress.

Soon after the first call for militia it was considered a duty to authorize the Commanding General in proper cases, according to his discretion, to suspend the privilege of the writ of *habeas corpus*, or, in other words, arrest and detain without resort to the ordinary processes and forms of law such individuals as he might deem dangerous to the public safety. This authority had purposely been exercised but very sparingly. Nevertheless, the legality and propriety of what had been done under it are questioned, and the attention of the country had been called to the proposition that one who is sworn to "take care that the laws be faithfully executed" should not himself violate them. Of course some consideration was given to the questions of power and propriety before this matter was acted upon. The whole of the laws which were required to be faithfully executed were being resisted and failing of execution in nearly one-third of the States. To state the question more directly, Are all laws but one to go unexecuted, and the Government itself go to pieces lest that one be violated? Even in such a case, would not the official oath be broken if the Government should be overthrown when it was believed that disregarding the single law would tend to preserve it? But it was not believed that this question was presented. It was not believed that any law was violated. The provision of the Constitution that "the privilege of the writ of *habeas corpus* shall not be suspended unless when, in cases of rebellion or invasion, the public safety may require it" is equivalent to a provision—is a provision—that such privilege may be suspended when, in cases of rebellion or invasion, the public safety does require it. It was decided that we have suspension of the privilege of the writ which was authorized to be made. Now it is insisted that Congress, and not the Executive, is vested with this power; and as the provision was plainly made for a dangerous emergency, it can not be believed that the framers of the instrument intended that in every case the danger should run its course until Congress could be called together, the very assembling of which might be prevented, as was intended in this case, by the rebellion.

No more extended argument is now offered, as an opinion at some length will probably be presented by the Attorney-General. Whether there shall be any legislation upon the subject, and, if any, what, is submitted entirely to the better judgement of Congress.

A Compilation of the Messages and Papers of the Presidents, vol. 7, James D. Richardson, ed. (New York: Bureau of National Literature, Inc., 1897), 3221–3226.

CHIEF JUSTICE ROGER B. TANEY, ON SUSPENSION OF THE WRIT OF *HABEAS CORPUS* (BALTIMORE, MD, APRIL 1861)

A copy of the warrant or order under which the prisoner was arrested was demanded by his counsel, and refused: and it is not alleged in the return, that any specific act, constituting any offence against the laws of the United States, has been charged against him upon oath, but he appears to have been arrested upon general charges of treason and rebellion, without proof, and without giving the names of the witnesses, or specifying the acts which, in the judgement of the military officer, constituted these crimes. Having the prisoner thus in custody upon these vague and unsupported accusations, he refuses to obey the writ of *habeas corpus*, upon the ground that he is duly authorized by the president to suspend it.

The case, then, is simply this: a military officer, residing in Pennsylvania, issues an order to arrest a citizen of Maryland, upon vague and indefinite charges, without any proof, so far as appears; under this order, his house is entered in the night, he is seized as a prisoner, and conveyed to Fort McHenry, and there kept in close confinement; and when a *habeas corpus* is served on the commanding officer, requiring him to produce the prisoner before a justice of the supreme court, in order that he may examine into the legality of the imprisonment, the answer of the office, is that he is authorized by the president to suspend the writ of *habeas corpus* at his discretion, and in the exercise of that discretion, suspends it in this case, and on that ground refuses obedience to the writ.

As the case comes before me, therefore, I understand that the president not only claims the right to suspend the writ of *habeas corpus* himself, at his discretion, but to delegate that discretionary power to a military officer, and to leave it to him to determine whether he will or will not obey the judicial process that may be served upon him. No official notice has been given to the courts of justice, or to the public, by proclamation or otherwise, that the president claimed this power, and had exercised it in the matter stated in the return. And I certainly listened to it with some surprise, for I had supposed it to be one of those points of constitutional law upon which there was no difference of opinion, and that it was admitted on all hands, that the privilege of the writ could not be suspended, except by act of congress.

When the conspiracy of which Aaron Burr was the head, became so formidable, and was so extensively ramified, as to justify, in Mr. Jefferson's opinion, the suspension of the writ, he claimed, on his part, no power to suspend it, but communicated his opinion to congress, with all the proofs in his possession, in order that congress might exercise at its discretion upon the subject, and determine whether the public safety required it. . . .

But the documents before me show, that the military authority in this case has gone far beyond the mere suspension of the privilege of the writ of *habeas corpus*. It has, by force of arms, thrust aside the judicial authorities and officers to whom the constitution has confided the power and duty of interpreting and administering the laws, and substituted a military government in its place, to be administered and executed by military officers. . . . Up to that time, there had never been the slightest resistance or obstruction to the process of any court or judicial officer of the United States, in Maryland, except by the military authority. And if a military officer, or any other person, had reason to believe that the prisoner had committed any offence against the laws of the United States, it was his duty to give information of the fact and evidence to support it, to the district attorney; it would then have become the duty of that officer to bring the matter before a district judge or commissioner, and if there was sufficient legal evidence to justify his arrest, the judge or commissioner would have issued his warrant to the marshal to arrest him. . . . The constitution provides, as I have before said, that "no person shall be deprived of life, liberty or property, without due process of law." It declared that "the right of the people to be secure in their persons, houses, papers and effects, against unreasonable searches and seizures, shall not be violated; and not warrant shall issue, but upon probable cause, supported by oath or affirmation, and particularly describing the place to be searched, and the persons or things to be seized." It provides that the party accused shall be entitled to a speedy trial in a court of justice. . . .

In such a case, my duty was too plain to be mistaken. I have exercised all the power which the constitution and laws confer upon me, but that power has been resisted by a force too strong for me to overcome. It is possible that the officer who had incurred this grave responsibility may have misunderstood his instructions, and exceeded the authority intended to be given him; I shall, therefore, order all the proceedings in this case, with my opinion, to be filed and recorded in the circuit court of the United States for the district of Maryland, and direct the clerk to transmit a copy, under seal, to the president of the United States. It will then remain for that high officer, in fulfillment of his constitutional obligation to "take care that the laws be faithfully executed," to determine what measures he will take to cause the civil process of the United States to be respected and enforced.

17 Fed. Cas. 144, No. 9487.

THE MILITARY DRAFT

Northerners and Southerners alike had, at the outset of hostilities, expected the war to be brief. On both sides, armies were formed using a standard one-year military enlistment, with bonuses for those soldiers who elected to re-enlist. By early 1862, the status of the Confederate army was becoming desperate. Always outnumbered by Union forces, and with enlistments running out, the Confederate Congress resorted to a draft to replenish its numbers—the first such conscription in the history of the United States.

The state of the Northern military was not much better. By the end of 1862, Union officers were warning the administration and Congress that without a draft, troop levels would fall to dangerous levels. In March 1863, Republicans in Congress pushed through the Conscription Act, otherwise known as the Enrollment Act. The law made all males between the ages of twenty and forty-five eligible for military service and required states to draft numbers to meet quotas not filled through voluntary enlistment. The law included several exemptions. Those employed in vital areas, such as telegraph operators, railroad workers, government officials, and judges were granted automatic exemptions. Additionally, those with physical disabilities were passed over from the lottery system that each state devised. Most controversial was the exemption granted to those willing and able to pay $300.

While many in the North support the draft as necessary to win the war, the policy met with strong opposition. Riots broke out in several cities, the most serious in New York City in July 1863. Mobs of poor city dwellers rioted in the streets, burning down buildings and houses and attacking black neighborhoods with unbridled violence. After four days of chaos, with hundreds dead and incalculable damage to the city, the riots died down. Yet for a brief time many Northerners feared that the rebellion that before had been relegated to the South had come into their own homes.

There also was political opposition to the draft, particularly among Democrats who opposed most of Lincoln's wartime policies. In the following speech, Representative S.E. Ancona, a Democrat from Pennsylvania, complains that the Conscription Act serves to divide rather than unite Northerners, and that the law favors the wealthy who can afford to buy their way out of military service. Lincoln responds to such criticism by arguing that the Constitution grants Congress the right to raise armies—which, he goes on to say, can include a draft—and that any concerns about individual rights pale in comparison to the specter of losing the war.

Lincoln also dismisses complaints that the draft laws are favorable to the wealthy, pointing out that exemptions traditionally were granted only to those who could find a replacement, a far more expensive prospect. If anything, he argued, the $300 exemption would actually widen the range of people who could eliminate themselves from service, if desired.

As opposition to the draft faded, states carried out their task and rejuvenated the Union army. After the Civil War, conscription became a standard policy of the United States military during times of war and occasionally during peacetime. A draft has been instituted in every major war in which the United States has been involved since the Civil War.

ABRAHAM LINCOLN, IN SUPPORT OF CONSCRIPTION
(WASHINGTON, DC, SEPTEMBER 1863)

It is at all times proper that misunderstanding between the public and the public servant should be avoided; and this is far more important now, than in times of peace and tranquility. I therefore address you without searching for a precedent upon which to do so. Some of you are sincerely devoted to the republican institutions, and territorial integrity of our country, and yet are opposed to what is called the draft, or conscription.

At the beginning of the war, and ever since, a variety of motives pressing, some in one direction and some in the other, would be presented to the mind of each man physically fit for a soldier, upon the combined effect of which motives he would, or would not, voluntarily enter the service. Among those motives would be patriotism, political bias, ambition, personal courage, love of adventure, want of employment, and convenience, or the opposites of some of these. We already have, and have had in the service, as appears, substantially all that can be obtained upon this voluntary weighing of motives. And yet we must somehow obtain more, or relinquish the original object of the contest, together with all the blood and treasure already expended in the effort to secure it. To meet this necessity the law for the draft has been enacted. You who do not wish to be soldiers, do not like this law. This is natural; nor does it imply want of patriotism. Nothing can be so just, and necessary, as to make us like it, if it is disagreeable to us. We are prone, too, to find false arguments with which to excuse ourselves for opposing such disagreeable things. In this case those who desire the rebellion to succeed, and others who seek reward in a different way, are very active in accommodating us with this class of arguments. They tell us the law is unconstitutional. It is the first instance, I believe, in which the power of congress to do a thing has ever been questioned, in a case when the power is given by the constitution in express terms. Whether a power can be implied, when it is not expressed, has often been the subject of controversy; but this is the first case in which the degree of effrontery has been ventured upon, of denying a power which is plainly and distinctly written down in the constitution. The constitution declares that "The congress shall have power . . . To raise and support armies; but no appropriation of money to that use shall be for longer term than two years." The whole scope of the conscription act is "to raise and support armies." There is nothing else in it. . . .

It is clear that a constitutional law may not be expedient or proper. Such would be a law to raise armies when no armies were needed. But this is not such. The republican institutions, and territorial integrity of our country can not be maintained without the further raising and supporting of armies. There can be no army without men. Men can be had only voluntarily, or involuntarily. We have ceased to obtain them voluntarily; and to obtain them involuntarily, is the draft—the conscription. If you dispute the fact, and declare that men can still be had voluntarily in sufficient numbers, prove the assertion by yourselves volunteering in such numbers, and I shall gladly give up the draft. Or if not a sufficient number, but any one of you will volunteer, he for his single self, will escape all the horrors of the draft; and will thereby do only what each one of a least a million of his manly brethren have already done. Their toil and blood have been given as much for you as for themselves. Shall it all be lost rather than you too, will bear your part? . . .

Much complaint is made of that provision of the conscription law which allows a drafted man to substitute three hundred dollars for himself; while, as I believe, none is made of that provision which allows him to substitute another man for himself. Nor is the three hundred dollar provision objected to for unconstitutionality; but for inequality—for favoring the rich against the poor. The substitution of men is the provision if any, which favors the rich to the exclusion of the poor. But this being a provision in accordance with an old and well known practice, in the raising of armies, is not objected to . . .

The principle of the draft, which simply is involuntary, or enforced service, is not new. It has been practiced in all ages of the world. It was well known to the framers of our constitution as one of the modes of raising armies, at the time they placed in that instrument the provision that "the congress shall have power to raise and support armies." It has been used, just before, in establishing our independence; and it was also used under the constitution in 1812. Wherein is the peculiar hardship now? Shall we shrink from the necessary means to maintain our free government, which our grandfathers employed to establish it, and our own fathers have already employed once to maintain it? Are we degenerate? Has the manhood of our race run out?

Complete Works of Abraham Lincoln, v. 9, John G. Nicolay and John Hay, eds. (New York: Francis P. Tandy Co., 1905), 74–90.

REPRESENTATIVE S.E. ANCONA (D-PA),
OPPOSING CONSCRIPTION BILL
(WASHINGTON, DC, FEBRUARY 28, 1863)

In consideration of the bill (S. No. 511) entitled "An act for enrolling and calling out the national forces, and for other purposes," now before the House for its deliberation and concurrence, I propose to avail myself of my right as the Representative, in part, of the loyal, patriotic, and conservative people of a great State, to discuss its provisions and to record my solemn protest, in the name and behalf of my constituents, against its passage in the form it is presented. . . .

In view of the policy upon which this war is now conducted, as announced in the proclamations of the President, issued in obedience to and at the behest of the revolutionary element of the Republican party, controlling its organization and directing its action in Congress, represented in the press, forum, and pulpit by such men as [Horace] Greely, [William] Phillips, and [Henry Ward] Beecher, I assert that this preamble is a false pretense, and an attempted imposition upon the people. I deny that it is the purpose of the party in power to either maintain the Constitution or restore the Union. By their acts, not professions, let them be judged.

When the people of the North were aroused to a full sense of the indignity and humiliation the national honor had sustained in the assault upon and reduction of Fort Sumter, there was but one sentiment among the people, without regard to party, as to their duty to sustain the Executive in upholding and maintaining the Federal authority throughout the country. In response to the President's proclamation and call for seventy-five thousand men to assert that authority, to repossess the forts and other public property taken by the insurgents, there was an uprising and rush to arms on the part of the masses without parallel in the previous history of the country or world. It was enough for them to know that that starry flag, emblem of unity and liberty, representing a great nation, respected upon every sea, protecting the humblest of her citizens in every land, and carried triumphant and in honor through every contest in which the country united had engaged, had been stricken down and trailed in the dust by the fratricidal hands of its sworn supporters. They hesitated not, though the call came from a President who had not been their choice. There was no longer any controversy as to the causes of the impending war[1]; no question as to responsibility for this dread arbitrament of the sword, which four fifths of all the people had desired to avert and firmly believed might have been averted by honorable and just conciliation and compromise, such as had been presented and was embodied in the Crittenden proposition. . . .

With this call for troops came that for the assembling of the representatives of the people and the States in Congress, that convened in special session nearly three months after, to consider and act upon such measures as they might deem necessary to the public safety. Every proposition having in view the suppression of the insurrection and restoration of the Federal authority under the Constitution, by force of arms, met with an almost unanimous support at that session. The Executive asked for four hundred thousand men and $400,000,000—Congress granted him five hundred thousand men and $5,000,000. . . .

I see nothing but an aggravated, hopeless, and interminable revolutionary struggle so long as this policy obtains and holds its unchecked sway, or that anarchy which will bring all its horrors, desolation, and blood to our own doors, in the revolution that its continuance and an attempt to enforce this conscription will almost certainly produce. . . . I would counsel the majority to abandon this bill, or so modify it as to make the requisitions for additional troops through those channels that are contemplated and required by the Constitution and all laws; drafted, if need be, and organized from the enrolled militia of the States, under their own constitutions and regulated by their own laws; offered by men of their own choice, commissioned by and under the direction of their only legitimate heads, the Governors, and for periods of service not exceeding that already extended from three to nine months.

How can you expect the farmer, the mechanic, the poor laboring man, with a family dependent upon the production of his farm, wrought out by the sweat of his brow under the genial showers and smiling suns of a beneficent Providence, or on the skill of the other and the toil of the latter, who will subject to the harsh provisions of this relentless conscription, known only to and enforced under some of the despotic monarchical Governments of the Old World, to be dragged from their homes, their helpless families, by military satraps, for an indefinite service, in a cause and for a purpose they believe utterly wrong, useless, and impracticable? You propose to make an exemption upon the payment of $300. I shall make an effort to amend the section containing this provision, reducing it to a sum within the reach of the poor man—the man with limited resources and large demands upon his purse and hands by a numerous family or other necessities and peculiar circumstances.

Congressional *Globe*, 37th Congress, 3rd Session, February 28, 1863, 161–163.

NOTE

1. In December 1860, Senator John J. Crittenden of Kentucky tried in vain to pass through Congress a bill that would reestablish the 36° 30' line dividing free and slave territories. This measure failed to win support in either House.

ENLISTMENT OF AFRICAN AMERICANS

An interesting issue Lincoln faced during the war was the use of African Americans in combat. After the Confederate attack on Fort Sumter in April

1861, thousands of young men, in both regions, rushed to volunteer for military service. Among those who sought to enlist were young black men, mostly in the North, although there also were attempts on behalf of some free blacks to fight for the Confederacy. For much of the war, Lincoln rejected the notion of enlisting blacks into the military, primarily for political reasons. There was widespread opinion that Northern white troops would oppose the enlistment of African Americans, and the president sought to avoid any policies that would dampen the morale of the military.

Lincoln had good reason to be concerned about the impact of deploying black troops. Most Northern soldiers were opposed to slavery, but the majority did so on behalf of the Union. Moreover, racist attitudes in the North led most to believe that blacks were incapable of soldiering, despite several instances in prior wars in which African American troops distinguished themselves in battle. However, the issue gained increasing attention throughout the war, and by late 1863 Lincoln had to make a decision on the matter.

There were several reasons as to why the question increased in importance. First, African American leaders continued to push for black enlistment. Second, Lincoln's Emancipation Proclamation focused attention on slavery, and those who supported the enlistment of black troops could ask publicly why African Americans would be refused the opportunity to serve in the cause to liberate slaves. Finally, there was a concern over troop levels. Conscription, adopted in 1863, had bolstered the Union armies, but within a year the number of enlisted men had begun to drop again. Advisors offered to Lincoln the enlistment of blacks as one means of restoring troop strength. Incredibly, by 1864, the Confederate government was considering the same idea, with a few officials even suggesting that slaves be offered emancipation for serving the Southern cause.

African American leaders such as the former slave and renowned abolitionist Frederick Douglass were instrumental in bringing the issue to the attention of Lincoln. In the following exchange in his publication *Douglass' Monthly*, a letter to the editor from "Immaterial" raises the issue and proposes that blacks were ready and willing to serve in the war. Douglass's response was a strong affirmation, arguing that blacks should be allowed to participate in a war in which the status of African Americans in the South was the crucial question.

Lincoln's concerns about opposition to enlisting and arming black troops was not without reason. Many Northerners held to the racist view that blacks were incapable of serving in combat roles and resented the idea of fighting alongside them. The following speech by a Democratic congressman from Pennsylvania, in 1863, offers views as to why the policy would be damaging to the Union cause. Much of the argument is based on the notion that the United States is a nation of white citizens, and as such only whites should fight her wars. Also, the point is made that the enlistment of black troops might make residents in the border states more hostile to the United States government. The speech is a reminder that despite the importance of slavery in the war, most Northerners continued to view blacks as inferior and incapable of military service.

In the end, Lincoln concluded that there was little reason why blacks should not be allowed to enlist in the cause. Beginning in 1863, the United States government began to accept black enlistees; by the end of the war almost 200,000 African Americans had enlisted, most of them former slaves who were liberated in the final stages of the war. While black troops were segregated and often were relegated to menial tasks, a considerable number of African Americans distinguished themselves on the battlefield. While individual blacks had served in the military in prior wars, the Civil War was historic in being the first in which black regiments were recruited for service.

FREDERICK DOUGLASS, ON THE ENLISTMENT OF BLACK TROOPS (BOSTON, MA, MAY 1861)

Mr. Editor:

This present war arises out of the indignant protest of the North against the unreasonable and inadmissible demands of the South with regard to slavery extension; in fact, it is liberty making for the first time a decided stand against slavery. In this state of things, it seems to me extremely proper that the descendents of Africans should take a prominent part in a war which will eventually lead to a general emancipation of the race. Africans have fought well in the Revolution. There were two regiments of them, and the record of these times show that they made efficient, zealous, and reliable soldiers. Gen. Jackson spoke highly of colored men who fought at New Orleans. Most of our national vessels have a squad of colored sailors, who mess together, and serve the same gun, which is called the black gun. Officers in the navy say the black gun is always the best served. Every body knows what bravery the blacks displayed in St. Domingo.

I think that at least one fine regiment could be raised from colored men in the North and East. Canada would likely furnish a good number, and I have no doubt these volunteers would give a good account of themselves on the field of battle. Then think of the moral effect such a regiment would have if carried with the rest of the forces in the very heart of slavedom. It would form a nucleus for the organization of slaves emancipated by the proclamation that will surely come from "Old Age," when the army is fairly on its march through the South, and he begins to settle his accounts with the rebels. . . .

My plan would be to advertise for the formation of an African Zouave regiment. I suppose a sufficient number of vigorous and nimble fellows could be enrolled. Abolitionists throughout the country would no doubt favor the idea, and subscribe freely to uniform the regiment, the arms to be furnished by the State. When you are sure of say two hundred men, offer the regiment to the Governor of New York, or Massachusetts. Perhaps it would be better to communicate to the Governor your intentions before taking the trouble to enlist anybody. If he favors the plan, you can go ahead; if he does not, it would be useless to attempt raising a regiment that would not be mustered with the rest, and of course would not pay. I think myself that before we get through with the war, every man, black or white, able and willing to carry a musket, will be wanted, and the Government will accept readily the services of all those who shall offer to bring this infernal confederated rebellion to an end. This will be a frightfully bloody war; but if a race is to be redeemed by it, it will be.

Immaterial

N. B.–France has some regiments of native Africans, who are incarnate devils on a field of battle. The Austrians had a touch of their quality in Italy. Nothing would please me more, and bring the race into favor, than to see Southern chivalry well whipped by an equal number of black men. It would, indeed, be refreshing.

Remarks

The measure recommended by "Immaterial" meets our entire approval. He speaks only what is passing in the minds of all thoughtful colored men of the North. If we are not seen in the present conflict, the fault is not with us, but with our circumstances. For the present, at least, we are between two fires. The slaveholders are willing to take free blacks to fight for slavery, but neither Mr. Lincoln at Washington, nor Mr. Davis at Montgomery, wants us to fight for freedom; and if we fight, we must fight against the North as well as the South, Abraham Lincoln as well as Jefferson Davis. Mr. Lincoln in his war proclamation assured the man stealers and pirates of the Cotton Confederacy that he shall not war upon their *"property."* We all know that means no attempt will be made to destroy slavery. Those of our number who have offered our services to the Government, have been coldly turned away, and in one instance, at Fort Pickens, sent back to slavery in irons to be whipped to death.

Our men are ready and eager to play some honorable part in the great drama of revolution now going forward; but we want to fight for freedom, and to know who we shall have to fight. Until another stage shall be reached in the progress of the war, we should be between two fires. Nevertheless, we do most earnestly urge our people everywhere to drink as deeply into the martial spirit of the times as possible; organize themselves into societies and companies, purchase arms for themselves, and learn how to use them. The present war may, and in all probability will reach a complexion when a few black regiments will be absolutely necessary. Let us not only be ready on call, but be casting about for an opportunity to strike for the freedom of the slave, and for the rights of human nature.

Frederick Douglass Papers, Library of Congress Speech File, Reel 14, 32.

REPRESENTATIVE H.B. WRIGHT (D-PA), OPPOSING THE USE OF BLACK TROOPS (WASHINGTON, DC, JANUARY 30, 1863)

It is proposed in this measure of legislation under consideration that we shall enroll one hundred and fifty thousand negroes to fight our battles. This is a Government, as I have always supposed, of white men; and if our Government is to be preserved and its liberties handed down to our children, our battles must be fought by white men. I will concede, without hesitation, that if an army of one hundred and fifty thousand negroes can but accomplish the object which you have at heart, and save the Union, I should be the last man to interpose such an objection. But I do not conceive that this will effect the great purpose you have in view. I know, as gentlemen on the other side of the Chamber know, that in regard to the negro there is a deadly hostility of opinion between the two parties in this House and in the country, and that the moment that question is introduced, here or elsewhere, it is always the prolific subject of bitter and vindictive debate. I am willing to concede, for argument, all that had been said on the other side of the House with regard to the valor of the negro. I am willing to take the record which you have furnished with regard to the prowess he has exhibited in arms in past times. I am willing take it all for granted. But assuming it all, would you incur the risk of demoralizing the army which you already have in the field? Would you incur the risk of driving eight hundred thousand white men out of the field for the purpose of introducing one hundred and fifty thousand negroes into it? I know the hostility on the part of the northern soldier against fighting side by side with the negro. I cannot do away with that hostility of feeling. It is not in my power. Neither is it in yours. You know that there is this imbittered feeling between the races; and you know, at least you ought to know, that if you bring this large number of black men into the ranks you not only incur the risk of demoralization of the army of white men in the field, but you incur the still greater risk of driving them from it forever.

Mr. Speaker, the fact that we have met with reverses does not furnish me with a reason to abandon the idea of fighting on to the restoration. The end can be attained if our counsels here can be established on a mutual basis—one which shall unite the action of this House. I am not one of those who are willing to believe that we may for any cause abandon our country. It is a great empire which we occupy. It is a great Government under which we live. Its citizens are surrounded with such privileges as are enjoyed nowhere else. Let us cling to it for very life. To us it is everything. Therefore the white race will, in my opinion, fight for the existence of the Union so long as there is at least the chance or opportunity of its preservation. I mean the *loyal* white race.

Mr. Speaker, the bill is one which on the border States will, I fear, work incalculable mischief. We have been told here, by the eloquent gentleman from Kentucky, that this bill, adopted, drives that State out of the Union. The same argument reached Tennessee, Maryland, and New Virginia. With these border states gone, where will we stand? Kentucky had some forty thousand men in arms on the side of the Union. The others I have named have furnished their quota. We cannot, in this emergency, afford to lose the great conservative and patriotic State of Kentucky. We cannot afford to lose Maryland, with Baltimore, its great commercial city. We cannot afford to lose that portion of Virginia which we have incorporated into a new State. We cannot afford to lose any portion of these border States, which have made common cause with us in the preservation of the Union. Why then do you wish to separate them from us by ill-advised legislation? . . .

If you pass your bill putting one hundred and fifty thousand negroes in the field, you will not find me backing from my position in support of the Union. If you put a million negroes into the field as any army, it will not in any degree lessen my attachment for the Union. I am willing to stand my flag while there is a solitary stripe of bunting left. Under no pretext will I abandon it. In prosperity or defeat, I honor and adore it; but while I speak for myself, I cannot speak for others. I have no feeling or prejudices toward the black man. Unfortunately, it was fastened on the Government. I am sorry it was.

But gentlemen must remember that we must deal with it in a spirit of candor; it must not be made the cause of our ruin. There are the feelings and prejudices and passions of loyal men where it exists that must be taken into account, and if it is possible they must be reconciled, reconciled by mutual conciliation and just and well-conceived legislation. No hasty or inconsiderate act should separate the two sides of the Chamber from the adoption of a common line of policy, which, if not agreeable to both in every particular, will at least produce a result which we all, I trust, hope and pray.

Sir, I do not know what is to be the destiny of this bill. Perhaps it may become a law. But, sir, in my intercourse with the soldiers of the Army within the last three or four days, many officers of the Army, northern men, have told me that if you send the black man to fight the battles of the country it is in fact a condemnation of the courage and valor of the present Army, and they will so regard it, and will seek the earliest opportunity to leave the service. How far that feeling may extend in the Army I do not know, but I do know that it exists.

Congressional *Globe*, 37th Congress, 3rd Session, January 30, 1863, 75–76.

AMNESTY AND RECONSTRUCTION

While most of the debates surrounding reconstruction took place during Andrew Johnson's administration, Lincoln faced the question of how to deal with the defeated Southerners as early as 1863. By the end of that year, crucial Union victories had turned the tide. The fall of Vicksburg, a strategic port on the Mississippi River, the Confederate defeat at Gettysburg, and the Union victory at Chattannooga, Tennessee, all contributed to a sense that the rebellion ultimately would be defeated. The question that Lincoln and the Congress faced was how to reconstruct the South if and when an armistice was secured.

Lincoln had refused to recognize the legitimacy of the Confederate government, a view that had important ramifications for how he viewed amnesty. The leaders of the rebellion might be penalized, but most Southerners had agreed to go along with secession in an attempt to maintain their way of life. Always cautious to avoid further alienating Southerners, particularly those in the border states, Lincoln attempted to fashion what he hoped would be a smooth transition to peace. In his address to Congress on December 8, 1863, Lincoln explains his plans for amnesty. His Proclamation for Amnesty and Reconstruction provided that after ten percent of the voting population of a Southern state pledged an oath of loyalty to the United States, a new Union government could be implemented. Lincoln's plan excluded Confederate military officers, political leaders, and judges. There would be no military occupation of the South following the war. Southern states had not lost their identity during the rebellion; the Confederate leadership had been most responsible for the war, and average citizens would be welcomed back into the Union when ready.

Yet Lincoln also was careful to point out that slavery would not return to the South. This was no small point. Northerners who applauded the Emancipation Proclamation were concerned that without military occupation following the war, the Southern states would revert back to their status before the war. While attempting to assure citizens that the Union welcomed Southerners back, he also made clear that the Union no longer would allow slavery to exist anywhere. Such pronouncements, Lincoln hoped, would placate the more militant wing of the Republican party.

Maintaining a moderate course on the sensitive issue was difficult. Some Republicans in Congress took a harder line on the issue of amnesty. Lincoln was content to allow Southerners to develop political and social institutions on their own. The so-called Radical Republicans argued that secession meant that Southerners, in effect, had forfeited their right to rule as sovereign states—a theory referred to as "state suicide." Radicals hoped to bring deeper change to the South, particularly in guaranteeing citizenship to freedmen. Some discussed the prospects of transforming the Southern economy so it resembled that of the North. Senator Charles Sumner of Massachusetts, a leader in the more militant wing of the Republicans, explains in an address to the Senate that any discussions of reconstruction must begin with the assumption that the Southern states had forfeited their right to rule. As such, the United States government had the authority and the responsibility to attempt a more fundamental restructuring of Southern society. With this as a starting point, the Radicals rejected moderate plans for amnesty and argued that a majority of white males in the South would have to take a more detailed and far-reaching oath that repudiated the Confederacy and pledged past loyalty to the Union.

Lincoln's assassination prevented his taking part in the heated debates over reconstruction that marked Andrew Johnson's administration. However, Lincoln's moderate views on amnesty were consistent with his view of the sanctity of the Union and the illegitimacy of secession that guided him throughout the war.

ABRAHAM LINCOLN, ON AMNESTY
AND RECONSTRUCTION
(WASHINGTON, DC, DECEMBER 8, 1863)

Looking now to the present and future, and with reference to a resumption of the national authority within the States wherein that authority has been suspended, I have thought it fit to issue a proclamation, a copy of which is herewith transmitted. On examination of this proclamation it will appear, as is believed, that nothing will be attempted beyond what is amply justified by the Constitution. True, the form of an oath is given, but no man is coerced to take it. The man is only promised a pardon in case he voluntarily takes the oath. The Constitution authorizes the Executive to grant or withhold the pardon at his own absolute discretion, and this includes the power to grant on terms, as is fully established by judicial and other authorities.

It is also proffered that if in any of the States named a State government shall be in the mode prescribed set up, such government shall be recognized and guaranteed by the United States, and that under it the State shall, on the constitutional conditions, be protected against invasion and domestic violence. The constitutional obligation of the United States to guarantee to every State in the Union a republican form of government and to protect that State in the cases stated is explicit and full. But why tender the benefits of this provision only to a State government set up in this particular way? This section of the Constitution contemplates a case wherein the element within a State favorable to republican government in the Union may be too feeble for an opposite and hostile element external to or even within the State, and such are precisely the cases with which we are now dealing.

An attempt to guarantee and protect a revived State government, constructed in whole or in proponderating part from the very element against whose hostility and violence is to be protected, is simply absurd. There must be a test by which to separate the opposing elements, so as to build only from the sound; and that test is a sufficiently liberal one which accepts as sound whoever will make a sworn recantation of his former unsoundness.

But if it be proper to require as a test of admission to the political body an oath of allegiance to the Constitution of the United States and to the Union under it, why also the laws and proclamations in regard to slavery? Those laws and proclamations were enacted and put forth for the purpose of aiding in the suppression of the rebellion. To give them their fullest effect there had to be a pledge for their maintenance. In my judgement, they have aided and will further aid the cause for which they were intended. To now abandon them would be not only to relinquish a lever of power, but would also be a cruel and an astounding breach of faith. I may add at this point that while I remain in my present position I shall not attempt to retract or modify the emancipation proclamation, nor shall I return to slavery any person who is free by the terms of that proclamation or by any of the acts of Congress. For these and other reasons it is thought best that support of these measures shall be included in the oath, and it is believed that the Executive may lawfully claim it in return for pardon and restoration of forfeited rights, which he has clear constitutional power to withhold altogether or grant upon the terms which he shall deem wisest for public interest. It should be observed also that this part of the oath is subject to the modifying and abrogating power of legislation and supreme judicial decision.

The proposed acquiescence of the National Executive in any reasonable temporary State arrangement for the freed people is made with the view of possibly modifying the confusion and destitution which must at best attend all classes by a total revolution of labor throughout the whole States. It is hoped that the already deeply afflicted people in those States may be somewhat more ready to give up the cause of their affliction if to this extent this vital matter be left to themselves, while no power of the National Executive to prevent an abuse is abridged by the proposition.

A Compilation of the Messages and Papers of the Presidents, vol. 7, James D. Richardson, ed. (New York: Bureau of National Literature, Inc., 1897), 3380–3392.

SENATOR CHARLES SUMNER (R-MA), ON AMNESTY AND "STATE SUICIDE" (WASHINGTON, DC, FEBRUARY 11, 1862)

1. Resolved, That any vote of secession or other act by which any State may undertake to put an end to the supremacy of the Constitution within its territory is inoperative and void against the Constitution, and when sustained by force it becomes a practical *abdication* by the State of all rights under the Constitution, while the treason which it involves still further works an instant *forfeiture* of all those functions and powers essential to the contin-

ued existence of the State as a body politic, so that from that time forward the territory falls under the exclusive jurisdiction of Congress as other territory, and the state being according to the language of the law, *felo-de-se*, ceases to exist.

2. Resolved, That any combination of men assuming to act in the place of such States, and attempting to insnare or coerce the inhabitants thereof into a confederation hostile to the Union is rebellious, treasonable, and destitute of all moral authority; and that such combination is a usurpation, incapable of any constitutional existence, and utterly lawless, so that everything dependent upon it is without constitutional or legal support.

3. Resolved, That the termination of a State under the Constitution necessarily causes the termination of those peculiar local institutions which, having no origin in the Constitution or in those natural rights which exist independent of the Constitution are upheld by the sole and exclusive authority of the State.

4. Resolved, That slavery being a peculiar local institution, derived from local laws, without any origin in the Constitution or in natural rights, is upheld by the sole and exclusive authority of the State, and must therefore cease to exist legally or constitutionally when the State on which it depends no longer exists; for the incident cannot survive the principal.

5. Resolved, That in the exercise of its exclusive jurisdiction over the territory once occupied by the States, it is the duty of Congress to see that the supremacy of the Constitution is maintained in its essential principles, so that everywhere in this extensive territory slavery shall cease to exist practically, as it has already ceased to exist constitutionally or legally . . .

9. Resolved, That the duty directly placed upon Congress by the extinction of the States is reinforced by the positive prohibition of the Constitution that "no State shall enter into any confederation," or "without the consent of Congress keep troops or ships-of-war in time of peace or enter in any agreement or compact with another State," or "grant letters of marque or reprisal," or "without the consent of Congress lay any duties on imports or exports," all of which have been done by these pretended governments, and also by the positive injunction of the Constitution, addressed to the nation, that "the United States shall guaranty to every State in this Union a republican form of government"; and that in pursuance of this duty cast upon Congress, and further enjoined by the Constitution, Congress will assume complete jurisdiction of such vacated territory where such unconstitutional and illegal things have been attempted, and will proceed to establish therein republican forms of government under the Constitution; and in the execution of this trust will provide carefully for the protection of all the inhabitants thereof, for the security of families, the organization of labor, the encouragement of industry, and the welfare of society, and will in every way discharge the duties of a just, merciful, and paternal government.

Congressional *Globe*, 37th Congress, 2nd Session, February 11, 1862, 736.

RECOMMENDED READINGS

Baker, Jean H. *Mary Todd Lincoln: A Biography*. New York: W.W. Norton & Co., 1987.

Donald, David. *Lincoln*. New York: Simon & Schuster, 1996.

Foner, Eric. *Free Soil, Free Labor, Free Men*: *The Ideology of the Republican Party Before the Civil War*. New York: Oxford University Press, 1995.

———. *Reconstruction: America's Unfinished Revolution*. New York: Harper & Row, 1988.

Glatthar, Joseph T. *Forged in Battle: The Civil War Alliance of Black Soldiers and White Officers*. New York: The Free Press, 1990.

McPherson, James. *Battle Cry of Freedom: The Civil War Era*. New York: Oxford University Press, 1988.

———. *Abraham Lincoln and the Second American Revolution*. New York: Oxford University Press, 1990.

Oates, Stephen B. *With Malice Toward None: The Life of Abraham Lincoln*. New York: Harper & Row, 1977.

5

ANDREW JOHNSON

(1865–1869)

INTRODUCTION

When Andrew Johnson was sworn in as president on April 15, 1865, he faced perhaps the greatest challenges in the history of the republic, including those of his predecessor. Abraham Lincoln guided the nation through the Civil War with a combination of firmness and finesse that has gained him the admiration of historians. However, even Lincoln found the questions that lay ahead more perplexing than the war itself. For over a year, as Union armies closed in on the Confederacy, Lincoln had come to realize that reorganizing the South would be fraught with difficulty. Much was at stake. Northerners feared their sacrifice might be in vain if a clear course of action were not designed in the months to come.

Although his detractors were numerous, Lincoln had become the accepted leader as the war pressed into its fourth year. There would be difficulties ahead. Lincoln already had encountered opposition to his views of reconstruction and amnesty. Republicans passed a bill that planned a more stringent amnesty policy, which Lincoln promptly rejected. Until the Confederacy surrendered, such discussion was speculative. However, the two weeks prior to Lincoln's death had indicated that the Southern armies were on their last gasp. The Confederate government was driven out of its capital at Richmond, with General Ulysses S. Grant in fast pursuit of Robert E. Lee's collapsing army. On April 9, 1865, Lee surrendered to Grant at Appomattox Court House, Virginia. Only days later Lincoln lay dead.

Public mourning in the wake of Lincoln's death soon turned to trepidation. Few Americans knew much about the vice president, who had served all of six weeks at the time of the assassination. His one time in the national spotlight, during the inauguration in early March, had been disastrous. Having suffered from illness for several days, Johnson had been unable to eat the day before the festivities. Instead, doctors prescribed for him "medications strong in alcohol content. That, combined with a large amount of wine at a gala the night before had rendered him quite weak the morning of the inauguration. Unfortunately, he selected whiskey as his morning remedy. By most accounts, Johnson was practically incoherent during his speech, which followed Lincoln's. Opponents, delighted at the spectacle, spread rumors of excessive drinking that followed Johnson throughout his presidency.

Johnson certainly was no drunkard, as those close to him knew very well. He was, in fact, an ambitious, serious, and dedicated politician whose rise from an impoverished childhood was extraordinary. His parents were poor and illiterate tavern workers who had their second son Andrew in December 1808, in Raleigh, North Carolina. When Andrew was four years old, his father Jacob died attempting to rescue two people from drowning in a stream. His mother Mary then raised the two boys while working as a house servant, remarrying in 1814. As with most boys of his station, education was not a priority. He evidently learned the alphabet and taught himself basic reading skills, but was unable to write until adulthood. At age fourteen, Johnson and his brother William were apprenticed to a tailor in Raleigh. After a minor scrape with the law in Raleigh, he and his brother fled to South Carolina and worked for a tailor. Eventually, Andrew returned to North Carolina but found few opportunities to work. Still legally bound as an apprentice, no one would hire him, and his employer would neither release him from service nor give him work.

Meanwhile, Johnson's parents placed all their possessions in a horse-drawn cart and relocated across the Smokey Mountains, to East Tennessee. Andrew went along, and when the family settled in Rutledge, he found work as a tailor. In 1827 he moved to the small town of Greeneville and opened his own business. He also met and married Eliza McCardle, the daughter of a local businessman. Eliza was far from wealthy, but her father was in good standing with the community and she had an elementary education. Morever, Eliza saw potential in the young man. She taught him to read and helped him to make his way into local society. In time Johnson's business was a success; the two of them had five children and became highly regarded in Greeneville.

Johnson was a working man, but he had other interests that may have sparked Eliza's attraction. He worked diligently to perfect his reading and writing skills, never ashamed at his circumstance, and cherished the chance to talk with others about issues of the day. He joined a debating club at the local college, and was elected alderman in 1828, at age twenty. In 1831 he became mayor of Greeneville. In 1835, Johnson was won a seat in the state legislature, representing two counties of East Tennessee. His first experience in state politics, however, was unsuccessful. He lost a re-election bid in 1837, but learned enough from the experience to win again in 1839. Had this been the extent of Johnson's career he would have been considered a man of considerable achievement, given his background.

Yet Johnson's early years in politics brought out an energy and dedication that propelled him to greater successes. He became a member of the Democratic Party and in 1842 ran successfully for a seat in the United States House of Representatives. He served for five terms. In 1853, he won election as governor of Tennessee and was elected to the United States Senate in 1857, on the heels of a strong Democratic showing in the state legislature. By 1860 Johnson had established himself as a leader within the Democratic Party, even though he was not widely known outside Tennessee.

Johnson's political views were perhaps typical of a border state resident. As a Democrat, he supported the main features of the party's platforms. He campaigned in his early days against the national bank, backed James K. Polk in 1844, and advocated the annexation of Texas. He voted as a Southerner on the slavery question. Johnson believed that Wilmot Proviso, which sought to exclude slavery in all territories acquired as a result of the Mexican War, was an affront to Southern rights and dangerously divisive. He championed the Fugitive Slave Law and supported wholeheartedly the Compromise of 1850. In 1854, he came out in support of the Kansas-Nebraska bill that granted these territories "popular sovereignty" with respect to slavery, which generated outrage in the North. Southern Democrats had reason to believe that Johnson was a man who could be trusted to support slaveholding rights, which was vital to a candidate with national aspirations.

There was another side of Johnson, perhaps linked to his modest background, that made him a more complex political figure. The former apprentice tailor had a natural contempt for the genteel class of Southerners and viewed himself as a representative of the working classes. He often referred to poor farmers, wage workers and the like with pride as "plebeians" and promised to advance their cause. This at times brought him into conflict with the planter class. In the late 1840s, much to the consternation of most Southern Democrats, Johnson supported homesteading legislation that would provide Western lands to farmers at very low prices. The Democratic Party consistently opposed such schemes, and James Buchanan vetoed a homestead bill sponsored by Republicans. Yet Johnson continued to support the concept until such legislation was passed by the Republican-dominated Congress during the Civil War.

Another facet of Johnson's politics was his undying support for the Union, which ultimately forced him to break with most Southern Democrats. He campaigned for the Democratic presidential nomination in 1860 and supported the Southern Democrat John C. Breckenridge in the fall campaign. However, he came out strongly against secession and equated the act with treason. Convinced until hostilities began that a new sectional compromise could be worked out, Johnson supported the efforts of Senator John J. Crittenden to work out a new agreement on slavery in the territories and even developed his own plan. In time, Johnson found himself in the difficult position of supporting the Union in a state that by the end of 1861 had joined the Confederacy.

Johnson, however, was undeterred. He had traveled throughout the state on the eve of the legislature's secession vote seeking to persuade anyone who would listen that the nation should be saved at all cost. After the vote, he attempted to remain in Tennessee but was urged to leave by associates who feared for his life. He left his family behind and went to Kentucky and continued to make speeches against secession. He was vilified in the Confederacy but became popular in the North, winning the adoration of the administration. Johnson was a natural choice for Lincoln to serve as military governor of Tennessee after the Union army secured it in 1862, a position he carried out for three years. During the period of military rule, he worked closely with Lincoln to build a pro-Union legislature in the state.

Johnson became a perfect choice for Lincoln as a running mate in his 1864 election campaign. Lincoln's wing of the Republican Party, sensitive to the dangers of attaching themselves too closely to the Radicals, emphasized conciliation to attract moderates, even changing the name of the party to the Union party. He had done very little in his few weeks of service as vice president before tragedy struck. In the days after he was sworn in, Radical Republicans and Democrats met with Johnson to learn more about the Southerner who had fought so diligently for the Union. Both groups at first did not know what to make of him. Democrats were pleased that one of their own was in the White House but quite concerned about his close relationship with Lincoln. Republicans were pleased that Johnson had opposed, not without bravery, secession but wondered where his true sympathies lay. He was, in a sense, a man without a party.

For a time Johnson was able to strike a delicate balance between these opposing forces. As debate heated up over conditions in the South, he found the middle ground lonely and difficult to maintain. The problems were overwhelming. The Southern economy had all but collapsed. Currency had become worthless; few Southerners had emerged from the upheaval with wealth. The planter class virtually had been wiped out as the cotton market came to a standstill. For average Southerners, conditions were worse. Farm foreclosures left many without property; those who still owned property often lived in areas ravaged by the fighting. In some areas, food shortages threatened starvation.

Compounding these difficulties, of course, was the problem of the freedmen. The millions released from bondage celebrated initially, but in the weeks and months to follow they faced the harsh reality that freedom without opportunity translated into little freedom at all. During the war, large numbers of former slaves left plantations; some moved North while others stayed in the South where rumors circulated that free land would be distributed after the war concluded. In some areas, Northern military commanders began the process of dividing up plantation lands for blacks. However, official policy was quite vague. Meanwhile, the majority of freedmen, landless and without employment or even a rudimentary education, elected to stay on their masters' farms or move into cities, where they encountered hostile whites.

White Southerners were defeated on the battlefield, but the war over hearts and minds was just beginning. While accurate numbers always will prove elusive, many Southerners who had been lukewarm to the idea of secession developed a strong hatred for the North as the war became increasingly brutal. Even after Appomattox, a strong majority had no expectations of seeing their society change in any fundamental way. Most believed that Lincoln's announcement of emancipation would not hold, although a significant percentage of the population had come to terms with the fact that slavery had been rendered obsolete. The greatest fear was the issue of black equality. Southerners were almost unanimous in the view that emancipation was one thing, but that political equality, meaning the franchise, was another issue entirely. The federal government faced the task of addressing the status of blacks at a time when all whites, North and South, disagreed sharply as to the proper course of action.

The dominance of the Republican Party during the war, the natural result of secession, disguised the degree of discord in Congress over the questions of amnesty and reconstruction. Lincoln's policy during the war was clear. Secession had been an illegal and illegitimate act; as such, the process of establishing loyal state governments should be smooth and efficient. Lincoln also had the war itself to confront. As long as there were Southerners who might come to their senses and seek reconciliation, Lincoln wanted to offer them a clear opportunity to do so. In late 1863, he issued a Proclamation of Amnesty and Reconstruction that allowed any Confederate state to form a Union government when 10 percent of eligible voters took an oath of loyalty to the nation and received a presidential pardon. The policy proved to be effective in a few states. In 1864, new governments were formed in Louisiana, Arkansas, and Tennessee. These, of course, were unrecognized by the Confederacy, and Congress refused to seat representatives from them, but their very existence was a powerful political victory for Lincoln.

Lincoln's policy was challenged by the vocal Radical Republicans who believed that fundamental change had to take place in the South before any talk of reunion could be entertained. Led by influential senators such as Thaddeus Stevens, Charles Sumner, and Benjamin Wade, the Radicals rejected Lincoln's claim that the constitutional authority to grant pardons placed responsibility for reconstruction in his hands. Using their strength in Congress, the Radicals in 1864 pushed through the Wade-Davis Bill that required a majority of white males to take an oath to the United States and also denounce the Confederacy. The bill listed other requirements for statehood, most notably the exclusion of Confederate political and military leaders from positions of authority in the new governments. Lincoln refused to sign the bill, arguing that the bill was divisive and would prolong the war. Days before his death, Lincoln reaffirmed his belief that new governments in the South should be established in a spirit of conciliation.

Johnson was in complete agreement with Lincoln. However, several factors worked against Johnson that ultimately led to political failure. Historians have offered several explanations as to why the relationship between Johnson and Congress disintegrated as it did over the following three years. Some focus on Johnson himself. Lincoln had disagreed with the Radicals, but they trusted his abilities, were willing to work with him, and feared attacking him publicly. Others stress that while Johnson agreed with Lincoln on secession, their views on slavery were quite different—a significant difference for the Radicals. Lincoln might have taken a more active approach to the condition of freedmen after the war. Still others point to Congress rather than Johnson, claiming that the Radicals became more powerful after the war. By 1867, neither Lincoln nor Johnson could have overcome their power.

All these views most likely are correct to some degree. Johnson was less sensitive to the circumstances of African Americans than Lincoln. There also is much to the claim that Radicals never trusted nor respected Johnson, as they did Lincoln. When they disagreed with Johnson, they were more confident in both the moral and intellectual superiority of their arguments. Furthermore, the power of the Radicals in Congress increased over time. Much of this, however, also had to do with Johnson's controversial decisions on reconstruction that pushed many moderates to side with the Radicals.

At the outset, most Republicans viewed Johnson with cautious optimism. In some respects, he seemed more promising than Lincoln, who refused to use incendiary language toward secessionists while Johnson had few qualms about invoking the word "treason" to describe Confederates. Underneath this veneer of confrontation, however, lay a president more moderate on reconstruction than his predecessor. A part of the deterioration of Johnson's relationship with Congress had to do with misunderstandings about his views. Johnson never intended to remake Southern society—his goal was to bring the rebel states into the Union immediately. By the end of 1865, most Southern states had assembled conventions and drawn up new constitutions. Johnson had done away with the 10 percent loyalty requirement, and the new constitutions failed to include reforms that most Republicans had expected. Most of them recognized emancipation, although Mississippians even refused to ratify the Thirteenth Amendment.

Southern states also passed the so-called "Black Codes" designed to limit the freedom of blacks under the guise of legal protection. Some laws pertaining to blacks actually were notable advancements. In most states, African Americans were allowed to own property and to sue in courts. However, most of the laws were restrictive. In Mississippi, blacks were not allowed to own farmland; in most states they had to purchase permits to conduct business. In some states blacks were not allowed to own firearms without a license and vagrancy was punishable by fine, imprisonment, or forced labor. Particularly troublesome were labor laws that required blacks to sign year-long contracts for employment that were punishable by imprisonment or enforced labor. Radicals in Congress howled that Southerners were devising legal methods to revive a system of forced labor.

Their assumptions were validated by the results of a special commission set up by Congress to study and report on conditions in the South. Months of testimony from Northern military commanders stationed in the South, along with Unionist civilians, revealed that the plight of the freedmen had become desperate. Congress responded by passing bills that addressed the crisis. One renewed and strengthened the Freedmen's Bureau, a government agency established during the war that provided aid to emancipated slaves. Another was a Civil Rights bill, which guaranteed basic rights of citizenship to blacks in Southern states. Each of these bills was the result of compromise between Radicals and moderates in Congress. As a consequence, advisors to the president advised him to sign them into law as a compromise step that would undercut the complaints of Radicals.

Johnson, however, refused to support either, a decision that set the president on a collision course with Congress as moderates began to side with Radicals. By mid-1866, Congress had overridden Johnson's vetoes of the Freedmen's Bureau Bill and the Civil Rights Bill. With the Radicals in positions of control, the Congress went even further. A constitutional amendment, the Fourteenth, was passed that made permanent the civil rights provisions granted in the earlier bill. Another act, designed to limit the power of the president, prohibited Johnson from removing from office government officials whose appointments initially required Senate approval—without the same approval for dismissal. The fear in Congress was that Johnson was recklessly firing advisors who disagreed with him. The most important new bill, however, took control of Reconstruction out of the hands of the president altogether. The First Military Reconstruction Act gave the United States military political authority in the South and imposed strict requirements for states to enter the Union, including ratification of the Fourteenth Amendment. Johnson denounced Congressional reconstruction policy as unconstitutional, but his complaints mattered little. By the end of 1866 strong majorities in both Houses had broken from the president.

The impeachment of Johnson was an unfortunate coda to an embattled administration. Radicals brought charges against the president for his attempt to remove Secretary of War Edwin Stanton without Senate approval in violation of the recently passed Tenure of Office Act. The impeachment trial, held in the spring of 1868, brought the president within one vote of removal from office. He survived the proceedings, but his presidency lay in shambles. He completed the remainder of his term powerless, as Congress carried out its Reconstruction policies. Johnson left office convinced that the actions of Congress had been a usurpation of federal power. He went home to Tennessee, but in 1875 returned to Washington when elected to the Senate. He died that same year and was buried at Greeneville, Tennessee.

History has not treated Johnson well. His critics, not without reason, have attacked his failure to recognize the severe nature of the social crisis that confronted freedmen. Politically, he was unable or unwilling to compromise on difficult issues that generated passion on all sides. Johnson was a stubborn, principled, at times reckless, and at other times vindictive leader who had little patience for negotiation. His intransigence may be viewed as an admirable quality; in the realm of politics, however, it may also be disastrous.

MILITARY RECONSTRUCTION

The feud between Johnson and congressional Republicans over the course of Reconstruction raged throughout the year 1866. Johnson's veto of several Republican bills, including a Civil Rights Bill for Southern blacks, a law to extend the vote to African Americans in the District of Columbia, and the Freedmen's Bureau Bill, led the Radicals to take control of Reconstruction. To add insult to injury, the Fourteenth Amendment was failing to achieve ratification, not only in the South, but also in the border states of Maryland, Delaware, and Kentucky. By the end of the year, congressional leaders had arrived at the view that attempts to restructure Southern society and institutions were at a pivotal juncture. More extreme measures, they argued, were necessary to ensure that the Southern states did not revert to their prewar status. If the Fourteenth Amendment were not ratified, then how could Congress carry out its Reconstruction plans?

One method used to raise awareness of the continuing problems in the South was the formation of a Joint Committee on Reconstruction, which for months heard testimony from military officials and others who had been in the former Confederacy. Stories of abuse against the freedmen lent credence to the view that Johnson's Reconstruction plan, which emphasized conciliation between the sections, was a failure. In January 1867, Radical Republican Senator Thaddeus Stevens of Pennsylvania proposed that Congress wipe the slate clean, so to speak, by declaring all southern state governments void and establishing new state constitutions. Johnson and congressional Democrats warned that such action would make a mockery of the Constitution.

Yet momentum was with the Radicals. In February, Congress passed the First Military Reconstruction Act, a pivotal law that placed Reconstruction policy in the hands of the legislature. The law divided the former Confederacy into five military districts, each under the authority of a commander who could deploy troops to enforce the laws. Also, new elections were to be held in Southern states that would refashion their respective governments. These new elections would include black voters and whites who qualified. Finally, the law declared that the Southern states would not be granted representation in Congress until they ratified the Fourteenth Amendment. The act, a compromise between moderates and Radicals who sought wide-scale land redistribution in the South, was more far-reaching than previous Reconstruction initiatives.

The testimony of military officers before the Joint Committee on Reconstruction did a great deal to convince moderate Republicans that a new Reconstruction plan was necessary. Colonel Edward Whittlesey, stationed in North Carolina, testified before the Committee in February 1866. Colonel Whittlesey describes the South as a place where freedmen are not protected by the laws and where those who commit crimes against blacks are seldom prosecuted. Whittlesey and scores of other military officials testified that an increased military presence was necessary to guarantee the safety of the former slaves. Such testimony convinced majorities in Congress to support military Reconstruction.

Johnson's reaction to the law was predictable. He vetoed the measure and offered a lengthy explanation for his actions. Military reconstruction, he believed, was blatantly unconstitutional in its replacement of civil authority with military authority during a time of peace. Furthermore, Johnson argues that the policy would create more discord in the South and prolong attempts to bring peace and stability to the region. As he had stated in his veto messages on other Reconstruction bills, Johnson places faith in the existing political and legal institutions in the Southern states. By 1867, most Republicans had come to disagree with the president.

The First Military Reconstruction Act, which was passed over the president's veto, did transform Southern politics, at least for a time. New state conventions resulted in historic levels of participation by African Americans in Southern politics. In the new state governments formed after these conventions ratified the Fourteenth Amendment, hundreds of freedmen served in the Southern state legislatures, fourteen blacks were elected to the United States House of Representatives along with two senators. Over the next decade, however, whites in the South used a combination of intimidation, legal restraints, and Northern apathy to scale back the achievements made by blacks in the political arena. When in 1877 military Reconstruction formally ended, most African Americans who had served in these bodies were no longer there, and black participation in the electoral process had faded considerably.

ANDREW JOHNSON, IN OPPOSITION TO MILITARY
RECONSTRUCTION IN THE SOUTH
(WASHINGTON, DC, MARCH 2, 1867)

I have examined the bill "to provide for the more efficient government of the rebel States" with the care and anxiety which its transcendent importance is calculated to awaken. I am unable to give it my assent, for reasons so grave that I hope a statement of them may have some influence on the minds of the patriotic and enlightened men with whom the decision may ultimately rest.

The bill places all the people of the ten States therein named under the absolute domination of military rulers; and the preamble undertakes to give reason upon which the measure is based and the ground upon which it is justified. It declares that there exists in those States no legal government and no adequate protection for life or property, and asserts the necessity of enforcing peace and good order within their limits. Is this true as a matter of fact?

It is not denied that the States in question have each of them an actual government, with all the powers—executive, judicial, and legislative— which properly belong to a free state. They are organized like the other States of the Union, and, like them, they make, administer, and execute the laws which concern their domestic affairs. An existing *de facto* government, exercising such functions as these, is itself the law of the State upon all matters within its jurisdiction. To pronounce the supreme lawmaking power of an established state illegal is to say that law itself is unlawful.

The provisions which these governments have made for the preservation of order, the suppression of crime, and the redress of private injuries are in substance and principle the same as those which prevail in the Northern States and in other civilized countries. They certainly have not succeeded in preventing the commission of all crime, nor has this been accomplished anywhere in the world. There, as well as elsewhere, offenders sometimes escape for want of vigorous prosecution, and occasionally, perhaps, by the inefficiency of courts or the prejudice of jurors. . . . All the information I have on the subject convinces me that the masses of the Southern people and those who control their public acts, while they entertain diverse opinions on questions of Federal policy, are completely united in the effort to reorganize their society on the basis of peace and to restore their mutual prosperity as rapidly and as completely as their circumstances will permit.

This bill, however, would seem to show upon its face that the establishment of peace and good order is not its real object. . . . The excuse given for the bill in the preamble is admitted by the bill itself not to be real. The military rule which it establishes is plainly to be used, not for any purpose of order or for the prevention of crime, but solely as a means of coercing the people into the adoption of principles and measures to which it is known that they oppose, and upon which they have an undeniable right to exercise their own judgement.

I submit to Congress whether this measure is not in its whole character, scope, and object without precedent and without authority, in palpable conflict with the plainest provisions of the Constitution, and utterly destructive to those great principles of liberty and humanity for which our ancestors on both sides of the Atlantic have shed so much blood and expended so much treasure. . . .

This is a bill passed by Congress in time of peace. There is not in any one of the States brought under its operation either war or insurrection. The laws of the States and of the Federal Government are all in undisturbed and harmonious operation. The courts, State, and Federal, are open and in the full exercise of their proper authority. Over every State comprised in these five military districts, life, liberty, and property are secured by State laws and Federal laws, and the National Constitution is everywhere in force and everywhere obeyed. What, then, is the ground on which this bill proceeds? The title of the bill announces that it is intended "for the more efficient government" of these ten States. It is recited by way of preamble that no legal State governments "nor adequate protection of life or property" exist in those States, and that peace and good order should be thus enforced. The first thing which arrests attention upon these recitals, which prepare the way for martial law, is this, that the only foundation upon which martial law can exist under our form of government is not stated or so much as pretended. Actual war, foreign invasion, domestic insurrection—none of these appear; and none of these, in fact, exist. . . .

While we are legislating upon subjects which are of great importance to the whole people, and which must affect all parts of the country, not only during the life of the present generation, but for ages to come, we should remember that all men are entitled at least to a hearing in the councils which decide upon the destiny of themselves and their children. At present ten States are denied representation, and when the Fortieth Congress assembles on the 4th day of the present month sixteen States will be without a voice in the House of Representatives. This grave fact, with the important questions before us, should induce us to pause in a course of legislation which, looking solely to the attainment of political ends, fails to consider the rights it transgresses, the law which it violates, or the institutions which it imperils.

A Compilation of the Messages and Papers of the Presidents, vol. 8, James D. Richardson, ed. (New York: Bureau of National Literature, Inc., 1897), 3696–3709.

COLONEL EDWARD WHITTLESEY, TESTIMONY IN FAVOR
OF MILITARY RECONSTRUCTION (WASHINGTON, DC, 1866)

Question. What would be the effect of allowing the negro to vote in North Carolina; what effect would it produce on the white people?

Answer. There is no disposition to allow him to vote there. That would be a very obnoxious measure to all the people.

Question. Would it be followed by scenes of violence and riot?

Answer. Yes, sir. I think if the negro should go to the polls and attempt to vote, without the presence of a military guard, there would be trouble and violence. . . .

Question. Do you think of anything else that you wish to speak of on this examination?

Answer. As to the necessity of United States troops there. I do not know that you have asked me any question on that point directly. If the Freedmen's Bureau is to be continued, it will need the presence of a military force to give it any efficiency at all. In many places it would be unsafe for an officer of the bureau to attempt to discharge his duties without a military force somewhere in the State to which he could apply. A small force of three to four thousand men scattered over the State will be sufficient to preserve order, and to give security to the officers of the government acting either under the Freedmen's Bureau or the Treasury Department, or any other department of the government. The colored schools I am sure would not be allowed to go on in certain country districts without some force to appeal to. In the large towns, where there is more intelligence and a better class of people, I think the schools will gain the good will of the community, and be allowed to continue without any assistance. The freedmen themselves would be, I think, in great peril if there was not a United States force kept in the State—not that there would be any general attack upon them, or that the better class of people would countenance any outrages. There are enough of the bitter and worthless people, who positively hate the negroes, to do them great wrong, and the better classes would not interfere. I am satisfied, in a great many instances, to see these persons punished and justice done to the freedmen. I will give you one fact which is the foundation of that remark: In Pitt County, some two months ago, four young men, some of whom had been in the rebel service, riding armed through the county, came across a negro man on his road to Washington—a negro who had been in the service of the father of one of them as a slave. They seized him, beat him cruelly, and left him on the ground in such a state that he died before morning. They went on to the town of Washington, in Beaufort County; rode through the town; fired at a white citizen, with whom they had a falling out, missed him, but hit another citizen; attacked another negro, fired at him, and, in short, took possession of the town. There were no troops there. I had a lieutenant there, and he called upon the police to arrest these men. There has been a kind of semi-military police established in every county of the State under military orders. The police declined to interfere, and the men went back to their own county. . . . The case was reported fully to me. I went to Newbern and applied to General Paine, in command there. He gave me a military escort of mounted men. I went into the county and tried to find these men. The citizens everywhere assured me that they had gone out of the county, and, in their opinion, out of the State. They could not be found, and I had to return without succeeding in arresting them. Within a week from this time they appeared at Greenville, the county seat, and voted at the State election without being challenged. The chief of police was there with his force, and made no attempt to arrest them. . . . I again reported the fact that they were present to the military commanders, and requested that they might be arrested, or that the police be dealt with as they should be failing to discharge their duty. When I came away the matter was still pending. A force was being organized and a plan started for getting hold of these men. I state these facts to show that the citizens will not take any steps to arrest the murderers of negroes, and that you cannot trust even the police organized under military orders to do that work.

United States Congress, *Report of the Joint Committee on Reconstruction* (1866), 181–185.

THE FREEDMEN'S BUREAU BILL

Among the more controversial issues of Reconstruction was the Freedmen's Bureau. In March 1865, Congress established under the auspices of the War Department the Bureau for Refugees, Freedmen, and Abandoned Lands for the purpose of bringing order to the emergent chaos in parts of the South. Since the issuance of the Emancipation Proclamation, hundreds of thousands of freedmen had left plantations and farms in search of new opportunities. However, for these masses of uneducated and largely sheltered people, and in the midst of war, there were few opportunities. Many flocked to cities; others settled in makeshift refugee camps run by the United States military. In Washington, those who had seen the situation in the South claimed that direct action had to be taken to address the growing crisis.

The Freedmen's Bureau was charged with providing freedmen in need with food, clothing, medical aid, and shelter. The Bureau also negotiated labor contracts between whites and blacks and was given jurisdiction in legal disputes involving black labor. In addition, Congress expected the Freedmen's Bureau to address long-range issues relating to former slaves, such as creating schools and distributing lands confiscated or abandoned as a result of the war.

The Freedmen's Bureau was the source of much criticism, North and South. Southerners and Northern Democrats claimed that the agency had been granted broad legal and political authority that rendered it unconstitutional. Accusations of corruption also plagued the Bureau. Among white

Southerners, the Freedmen's Bureau became a symbol of congressional authoritarianism.

President Johnson's views on the Freedmen's Bureau tended to support the claims of its critics, although at times he acknowledged the social crisis confronting the South. By early 1866, however, radical Republicans were convinced that Johnson sought to prevent substantial social and political change from occurring in the former Confederacy. As part of the growing struggle between the president and the Congress, Republicans passed a bill that renewed the Freedmen's Bureau beyond its 1867 expiration date and broadened its powers. The new bill set aside some 3 million acres of specific land for distribution to blacks and loyal whites; it provided funds and land for schools and asylums for freedmen; and it allowed for the use of military tribunals in cases of civil rights violations involving freedmen.

The bill passed Congress in early 1866 along party lines. Support among Republicans was unanimous; opposition by Democrats was nearly unanimous. Johnson vetoed the Freedmen's Bureau Bill, much to the outrage of many Republicans. Carl Schurz, a German immigrant, Union army veteran, and senator from Massachusetts, toured the South in 1865 and wrote about his impressions of life in the recently defeated South. He writes of the status of freedmen and the dire need for the Bureau to address the conditions of freedmen. Johnson's veto address was consistent with his reaction to other Reconstruction initiatives put forth by the Republicans. The bill, he claims, is unconstitutional in granting broad legal and policing powers to a federal agency. The president places faith in the existing legal and political structures of the states to address crimes against freedmen; he also maintains that former slaves do not require special legal protection.

Johnson's veto of the Freedmen's Bureau Bill was but one battle in the broader war between the Executive and the Congress. Months later, having gained support from many moderates as opinions on Reconstruction polarized, Republicans pushed through another, almost identical bill. Again Johnson vetoed it for the same reasons. This time, however, supporters garnered sufficient votes to override the president's rejection. The Freedmen's Bureau became a symbol of Reconstruction—hated by Southerners and hailed by Republicans—even though the agency never had the power or influence that either group assumed.

ANDREW JOHNSON, VETO OF THE FREEDMEN'S BUREAU BILL (WASHINGTON, DC, FEBRUARY 19, 1866)

I share with Congress the strongest desire to secure to the freedmen the full enjoyment of their freedom and property and their entire independence and equality in making contracts for their labor, but the bill before me contains provisions which in my opinion are not warranted by the Constitution and are not well suited to accomplish the end in view.

The bill proposes to establish by authority of Congress military jurisdiction over all parts of the United States containing refugees and freedmen. It would by its very nature apply with most force to those parts of the United States in which the freedmen most abound, and it expressly extends the existing temporary jurisdiction of the Freedmen's Bureau, with greatly enlarged powers, over those States "in which the ordinary course of judicial proceedings have been interrupted by the rebellion." . . . The agents to carry out this military jurisdiction are to be selected either from the Army or from civil life; the country is to be divided into districts and subdistricts, and the number of salaried agents to be employed may be equal to the number of counties or parishes in all the United States where freedmen and refugees are to be found. . . .

I can not reconcile a system of military jurisdiction of this kind with the words of the Constitution which declare that "no person shall be held to answer for a capital or otherwise infamous crime unless on a presentment or indictment of a grand jury, except in cases arising in the land or naval forces, or in the militia when in actual service in time of war or public danger," and that "in all criminal prosecutions the accused shall enjoy the right to a speedy and public trial by an impartial jury of the State and district wherein the crime shall have been committed." The safeguards which the experience and wisdom of ages taught our fathers to establish as securities for the protection of the innocent, the punishment of the guilty, and the equal administration of justice are to be set aside, and for the sake of a more vigorous interposition in behalf of justice we are to take the risks of the many acts of injustice that would necessarily follow from an almost countless number of agents established in every parish or county in nearly a third of the States of the Union, over whose decisions there is to be no supervision or control by the Federal courts. The power that would be thus placed in the hands of the President is such as in time of peace certainly ought never to be intrusted to one man. . . .

Undoubtedly the freedman should be protected, but he should be protected by the civil authorities, especially by the exercise of all constitutional powers of the courts of the United States and of the States. His condition is not so exposed as may at first be imagined. He is in a portion of the country where his labor can not well be spared. Competition for his services from planters, from those who are constructing or repairing railroads, and from capitalists in his vicinage or from other States will enable him to command almost his own terms. He also possesses a perfect right to change his place of abode, and if, therefore, he does not find in one community or State a mode of life suited to his desires or proper remuneration for his labor, he can move to another where labor is more esteemed and better rewarded. In truth, however, each State, induced by its own wants and interests, will do what is necessary and proper to retain within its borders all the labor that is needed for the development of its resources. The laws that regulate supply and demand will maintain their force, and the wages of the laborer will be regulated thereby. There is no danger that the exceedingly great demand for labor will not operate in favor of the laborer.

Neither is sufficient consideration given to the ability of the freedmen to protect and take care of themselves. It is no more than justice to them to believe that as they have received their freedom with moderation and forbearance, so they distinguish themselves by their industry and thrift, and soon show the world that in a condition of freedom they are self-sustaining, capable of selecting their own employment and their own places of abode, of insisting for themselves on a proper remuneration, and of establishing and maintaining their own asylums and schools. It is earnestly hoped that instead of wasting away they will by their own efforts establish for themselves a condition of respectability and prosperity. It is certain that they can attain to that condition only through their own merits and exertions. . . .

The bill under consideration refers to certain of the States as though they had not "been fully restored in all their constitutional relations to the United States." If they have not, let us at once act together to secure that desirable end at the earliest possible moment. It is hardly necessary for me to inform Congress that in my own judgement most of those States, so far, at least, as depends upon their own action, have already been fully restored and are to be deemed as entitled to enjoy their constitutional rights as members of the Union. Reasoning from the Constitution itself and from the actual situation of the country, I feel not only entitled but bound to assume that with the Federal courts restored and those of the several States in the full exercise of their functions the rights and interests of all classes of people will, with the aid of the military in cases of resistance to the laws, be essentially protected against unconstitutional infringement or violation. Should this expectation unhappily fail, which I do not anticipate, then the Executive is already fully armed with the powers conferred by the act of March, 1865, establishing the Freedmen's Bureau, and hereafter, as heretofore, he can employ the land and naval forces of the country to suppress insurrection or to overcome obstructions to the laws.

In accordance with the Constitution, I return the bill to the Senate, in the earnest hope that a measure involving questions and interests so important to the country will not become a law, unless upon deliberate consideration by the people it shall receive the sanction of an enlightened public judgement.

A Compilation of the Messages and Papers of the Presidents, vol. 8, James D. Richardson, ed. (New York: Bureau of National Literature, Inc., 1897), 3596–3603.

SENATOR CARL SCHURZ (R-MA), ON THE NEED
FOR A FREEDMEN'S BUREAU
(WASHINGTON, DC, DECEMBER 18, 1865)

The true nature of the difficulties of the situation is this: The General Government of the republic has, by proclaiming the emancipation of the slaves, commenced a great social revolution in the South, but has, as yet, not completed it. Only the negative part of it is accomplished. The slaves are emancipated in point of form, but free labor has not yet been put in the place of slavery in point of fact. And now, in the midst of this critical period of transition, the power which originated the revolution is expected to turn over its whole future development to another power which from the beginning was hostile to it and has never yet entered into its spirit, leaving the class in whose favor it was made completely without power to protect itself and to take an influential part in that development. The history of the world will be searched in vain for a proceeding similar to this which did not lead either to a rapid and violent reaction, or the most serious trouble and civil disorder. It cannot be said that the conduct of the Southern people since the close of the war has exhibited such extraordinary wisdom and self-abnegation as to make then an exception to the rule.

In my despatches from the South I repeatedly expressed the opinion that the people were not yet in a frame of mind to legislate calmly and understandingly upon the subject of free negro labor. And this I reported to be the opinion of some of our most prominent military commanders and other observing men. It is, indeed, difficult to imagine circumstances more unfavorable for the development of a calm and unprejudiced public opinion that those under which the Southern people are at present laboring. The war has not only defeated their political aspirations, but it has broken up their whole social organization. When the rebellion was put down, they found themselves not only conquered in a political and military sense, but economically ruined. The planters, who represented the wealth of the Southern country, are partly laboring under the severest embarrassments, partly reduced to absolute poverty. Many who are stripped of all available means, and have nothing but their land, cross their arms in gloomy despondency, incapable of rising in a manly resolution. Others, who still possess means, are at a loss how to use them, as their old way of doing things is, by the abolition of slavery, rendered impracticable at least where the military arm of the government has enforced emancipation. Others are still trying to go on in the old way, and that old way is in fact the only one they understand, and in which they have any confidence. Only a minority is trying to adopt the new order of things. . . .

The machinery by which the Government has so far exercised its protection of the negro and of free labor in the South—the Freedmen's Bureau—is very unpopular in that part of country, as every institution placed there as a barrier to reactionary aspirations would be. That abuses were committed with the management of freedmen's affairs; that some of the officers of the bureau were men of more enthusiasm than discretion, and in many cases went beyond their authority: all this is certainly true. But, while the Southern people are always ready to expatiate upon the shortcomings of the Freedmen's Bureau, they are not so ready to recognize the services it has rendered. I feel warranted in saying that not half of the labor that has been done in the South this year, or will be done there next year, would have been or would be done but for the exertions of the Freedmen's Bureau. The confusion and disorder of the transition period would have been infinitely greater had not an agency interfered which possessed the confidence of the emancipated slaves; which could disabuse them of any extravagant notions and expectations and be trusted; which could administer to them good advice and be voluntarily obeyed. No other agency, except one placed there by the National Government, could have wielded that moral power whose interposition was so necessary to prevent Southern society from falling at once into the chaos of a general collision between its different elements. That the success achieved by the Freedmen's Bureau is as yet very incomplete cannot be disputed. A more perfect organization and a more carefully selected personnel may be desirable; but it is doubtful whether a more suitable machinery can be devised to secure to free labor in the South that protection against disturbing influences which the nature of the situation still imperatively demands.

Speeches, Correspondence, and Political Papers of Carl Schurz, vol. 1, Frederic Bancroft, ed., (New York: G.P. Putnam's Sons, 1913), 356–361.

CIVIL RIGHTS FOR FREEDMEN

President Johnson's relationship with congressional Republicans deteriorated during his first year in office. If at first the Radicals of the party were encouraged by the strong words the president used when discussing secessionists, in time they came to the view that he was in league with Southerners and Democrats who sought to block any significant change in the former Confederacy. By December 1865, Republican leaders were ready to take Reconstruction policy into their own hands by forming a Joint Committee on Reconstruction charged with investigating conditions in the South. The fear among the Radicals was that so-called Black Codes, passed in the Southern states, which placed legal, political, and economic restrictions on the freedmen, threatened to resurrect the South's old ways and render the North's wartime sacrifices worthless.

In the early months of 1866, Republicans waged a political war with the president, drawing from the increasing evidence of social injustices taking place in the South. First came a decree that the Southern states, yet to be reconstructed properly, would not be allowed to seat congressmen in the coming session. The decision, interpreted by Democrats as an effort to protect large Republican majorities in both the Senate and House of Representatives, only served to make Johnson more intractable. In February, a bill passed Congress renewing the Freedmen's Bureau, only to meet with a veto by the president. The veto caught the Radicals by surprise, as they had been led to believe that Johnson would sign the bill. To make matters worse, the Republicans could not gather the votes necessary to override the veto. Johnson's move only made the Radicals more determined to change the course of Reconstruction policy.

The next step in the showdown between Congress and the president was the introduction of a Civil Rights Bill that guaranteed basic rights for the freedmen. The bill declared that all people born in the United States, save for "Indians not taxed," would be granted citizenship. Furthermore, the bill extended to all citizens equal legal and contractual rights and maintained that all individuals would receive due process and equal protection under the law. Moreover, the bill guaranteed these rights by federal authority.

The Civil Rights Bill of 1866 received strong Republican support, even from the moderates who previously had refused to side with the more radical voices in Congress. Senator John Broomal of Pennsylvania argues that the legislation was consistent with constitutional principles of equality and liberty. He focuses on the issue of citizenship for former slaves. All human beings are citizens of a country, he explains, and it would be absurd to deny citizenship to freedmen since they were born in the United States. Broomal also rejects the notion that citizenship cannot be granted by federal authority, but only by states.

State authority was the central argument in Johnson's veto address. Republicans were stunned by the president's decision to reject a bill they considered to be fair and reasonable. Johnson points out that it was untenable for Congress to make decisions on citizenship in the South when the Southern states themselves had been excluded from Congress. Reflecting his consistently Unionist position, Johnson believed that the exclusively Northern Congress could not speak for all Americans and that legislation such as the Civil Rights Bill would make reconciliation more difficult. Johnson also argues that the legislation would make the already sensitive relationship between Southern whites and freedmen more hostile.

Johnson's veto of the Civil Rights Bill was a pivotal act in his presidency. A significant number of moderate Republicans shifted allegiances to the Radicals in response to the president's decision, placing him on the defensive for the remainder of his term. Furthermore, the bill had sufficient support in Congress to override the veto and become law.

Perhaps most important, the Civil Rights Bill served as the basis for the Fourteenth Amendment. In the months following the passage of the bill, Republicans sought to make the law permanent by amending the Constitution to guarantee due process and equal protection under the law, as well as federally protected rights of citizenship for individual citizens in all states.

The ratification of the Fourteenth Amendment had far-reaching effects on the political landscape of the nation. States could no longer abridge the rights of individuals under the guise of state sovereignty, and the rights of individuals now fell under the jurisdiction of the federal government. In a sense, the Fourteenth Amendment was the culmination of the debates over states' rights that had consumed the nation for decades.

ANDREW JOHNSON'S VETO OF A CIVIL RIGHTS BILL
(WASHINGTON, DC, MARCH 27, 1866)

I regret that the bill, which has passed both Houses of Congress, entitled "An act to protect all persons in the United States in their civil rights and furnish the means of their vindication," contains provisions which I can not approve consistently with my sense of duty to the whole people and my obligations to the Constitution of the United States. I am therefore constrained to return it to the Senate, the House in which it originated, with my objections to its becoming a law.

By the first section of the bill all persons born in the United States and not subject to any foreign power, excluding Indians not taxed, are declared to be citizens of the United States. . . . It does not purport to declare or confer any other right of citizenship than Federal citizenship. It does not purport to give these classes of persons any status as citizens of the States, except that which may result from their status as citizens of the United States. The power to confer the right of State citizenship is just as exclusively with the several States as the power to confer the right of Federal citizenship is with Congress.

. . . If, as is claimed by many, all persons who are native born already are, by virtue of the Constitution, citizens of the United States, the passage of the pending bill can not be necessary to make them such. If, on the other hand, such persons are not citizens, as may be assumed from the proposed legislation to make them such, the grave question presents itself whether, when eleven of the thirty-six States are underrepresented in Congress at the present time, it is sound policy to make our entire colored population and all other excepted classes citizens of the United States. Four millions of them have just emerged from slavery into freedom. Can it be reasonably supposed that they possess the requisite qualifications to entitle them to all the privileges and immunities of citizens of the United States? Have the people of the several States expressed such a conviction? It may also be asked whether it is necessary that they should be declared citizens in order that they may be secured in the enjoyment of the civil rights proposed to be conferred by the bill. Those rights are, by Federal as well as State laws, secured to all domiciled aliens and foreigners, even before the completion of the process of naturalization; and it may safely be assumed that the same enactments are sufficient to give like protection and benefits to those for whom this bill provided special legislation. Besides, the policy of the Government from its origin to the present time seems to have been that persons who are strangers to and unfamiliar with our institutions and our laws should pass through a certain probation, at the end of which, before attaining the coveted prize, they must give evidence of their fitness to receive and exercise the rights of citizens as contemplated by the Constitution of the United States. The bill in effect proposed a discrimination against large numbers of intelligent, worthy, and patriotic foreigners, and in favor of the negro, to whom, after long years of bondage, the avenues to freedom and intelligence have just now suddenly opened. . . . Yet it is now proposed, by a single legislative enactment, to confer the rights of citizens upon all persons of African descent born within the extended limits of the United States, while persons of foreign birth who make our land their home must undergo a probation of five years, and can only then become citizens upon proof that they are "of good moral character, attached to the principles of the Constitution of the United States, and well disposed to the good order and happiness of the same."

It is clear that in States which deny to persons whose rights are secured by the first section of the bill any one of those rights all criminal and civil cases affecting them will, by provisions of the third section, come under the exclusive cognizance of the Federal tribunals. It follows that if, in any State which denies to a colored person any one of all those rights, that person should commit a crime against the laws of a State—murder, arson, rape, or any other crime—all protection and punishment through the courts of the State are taken away, and he can only be tried and punished in the Federal courts. How is the criminal to be tried? If the offense is provided for and punished by Federal law, that law, and not the State law, is to govern. It is only when the offense does not happen within the purview of Federal law that the Federal courts are to try and punish him under any other law. Then resort is to be had to "the common law, as modified and changed" by State legislation, "so far as the same is not inconsistent with the Constitution and the laws of the United States." So that over this vast domain of criminal jurisprudence provided by each State for the protection of its own citizens and for the punishment of all persons who violate its criminal laws, Federal law, whenever it can be made to apply, displaces State law. . . .

I do not propose to consider the policy of this bill. To me the details of the bill seem fraught with evil. The white race and the black race of the South have hitherto lived together under the relation of master and slave—capital owning labor. Now, suddenly, that relation is changed, and as to ownership capital and labor are divorced. They stand now each master to itself. In this new relation, one being necessary to the other, there will be a new adjustment, which both are deeply interested in making harmonious. . . .

This bill frustrates this adjustment. It intervenes between capital and labor and attempts to settle questions of political economy through the agency of numerous officials whose interest it will be to foment discord between the two races, for as the breach widens their employment will continue, and when it is closed their occupation will terminate. . . .

Entertaining these sentiments, it only remains for me to say that I will cheerfully cooperate with Congress in any measure that may be necessary for the protection of the civil rights of the freedmen, as well as those of all other classes of persons throughout the United States, by judicial process, under equal and impartial laws, in conformity with the provisions of the Federal Constitution.

A Compilation of the Messages and Papers of the Presidents, vol. 8, James D. Richardson, ed. (New York: Bureau of National Literature, Inc., 1897), 3603–3611.

SENATOR JOHN BROOMAL (R-PA), IN FAVOR OF A CIVIL RIGHTS BILL (WASHINGTON, DC, MARCH 8, 1866)

The object of the bill is twofold—to declare who are citizens of the United States, and to secure them the protection which every Government owes to its citizens. It will hardly be said that these are not proper subjects of legislation, and especially the latter one. If the same thing has not been attempted before, it was partly because there never before was the same necessity, and partly because of the long continued and remarkable forbearance of those for whom what necessity there was existed.

The first provision of the bill declares that all persons born in the United States and not subject to any foreign Power are citizens of the United States. As a positive enactment this would hardly seem necessary. Even as a declaration of existing law, a proposition that at most can only be said to embrace the true meaning of the word "citizen" would seem to find a more appropriate place in the elementary treatises upon law rather than on the statute-books. What is a citizen but a human being who by reason of his being born within the jurisdiction of a Government owes allegiance to that Government? . . .

The objection to this part of the bill is that it calls the negro a citizen. And why should it not? Civilized man must of necessity be a citizen somewhere. He must owe allegiance to some Government. There is some spot upon the earth's surface upon which it is possible for him to commit treason. Now, the negro in America is civilized. Ask the minister of religion where he finds the most sincere devotion, the school-teacher where he finds the greatest desire to learn. Ask the very southern rebel, whose representatives are most earnest against the bill, where he found the most implicit and unquestioning obedience to law and order under circumstances hardly justifying the hope of obedience to law and order.

The American negro is civilized, and of necessity must owe allegiance somewhere. And until the opponents of this measure can point to the foreign Power to which he is subject, the African potentate to whom after five generations of absence he still owes allegiance, I will assume him to be, what the bill calls him, a citizen of the country in which he was born.

Let those who say with the air of such omnipotent authority that this is the country of the white man, explain how it happened that the Ruler of the universe suffered it to be occupied by the red man for countless ages of the past. And then let them say, if they know, whether it may not be His purpose to suffer some small portion of it to be occupied by the black man for countless ages of the future. No, our country is the country of its inhabitants. Our Government is the Government of the governed. . . .

But it is said by the minority in this body that we have no right under the Constitution to pass the law; that the General Government was never intended to be intrusted with the power to protect individual persons; that that was to be left to the States. What, then, does the preamble mean? . . . This certainly has the appearance of being designed to protect the rights of individuals within as well as beyond the jurisdiction of the Government. Yet, strange as it may seem, while the Government has been always held competent to protect its meanest citizen within the domain of any European potentate, it has been considered powerless to guard the citizen of Pennsylvania against the illegal arrest, under cover of State law, of the most subordinate officer of the most obscure municipality in Virginia. . . .

If the Government has not the power, by appropriate legislation, to protect its citizens within as well as without its jurisdiction, I would like to know what the eighth section of the first article of the Constitution means when it empowers Congress to provide for the general welfare of the United States, and when it empowers Congress to pass all laws necessary for that purpose. Does it not pertain to the "general welfare" that "the citizens of each State," in the language of the second section of the fourth article of that instrument, "shall be entitled to all privileges and immunities of citizens in the several States?" . . .

The Government now stands guard over the lives and fortunes of these people. They are imploring us not to yield them up without condition to those into whose hands recent events have committed the destinies of the unfortunate South. A nation which could thus withdraw its protection from such allies, at such a time, without their full and free consent, could neither hope for the approval of mankind nor the blessing of Heaven.

Congressional *Globe*, 39th Congress, 1st Session, March 8, 1866, 1262–1266.

THE ACQUISITION OF ALASKA

President Johnson's administration was dominated by domestic concerns, particularly those relating to Reconstruction. One important event in the realm of foreign affairs was the purchase of Alaska from Russia, completed in March 1867. Johnson's secretary of state was the ardent expansionist William H. Seward, who once declared that the United States eventually might acquire the entire Western Hemisphere. Thus when Seward saw the chance to acquire the enormous territory of Alaska, he seized the moment.

That chance came rather unexpectedly. The Russian government, experiencing financial difficulties, had decided that selling the region to the United States would improve its economic condition. Moreover, the Russians had little desire to keep the area and expected Americans to begin settling there in larger numbers in the future. The Russian minister to the United States, Baron Edouard de Stoeckl, was given orders to offer Alaska for purchase.

Seward and Stoeckl completed negotiations in only a few days, primarily because Seward wanted the transaction completed before Congress ended its current session. Seward offered the Russians $7 million, significantly more than they were prepared to take. The higher price, however, prevented delays in negotiation. Seward, in fact, was so enthusiastic about the deal that he convinced Stoeckl to sign a treaty at 4 A.M. on March 30, after an evening of discussion. The next day, Johnson approved the treaty and sent it directly to the Senate.

There was overwhelming public and political support for the purchase of Alaska. A few criticized the idea. The Republican New York *Tribune* derided the deal as "Seward's Folly." In Congress, individuals spoke out against the treaty. Representative Hiram Price of Iowa complains that the United States, still recovering from the war, was not in a position financially to make such a purchase. Price compares the action to an individual who makes a large purchase while already in debt. Furthermore, he questions the need for Alaska. If Americans want space for settlement, he maintains, large portions of the country lay relatively uninhabited—some in the South.

Few agreed with Price. Even leading Radical Republicans, such as Thaddeus Stevens, supported the purchase. The arguments for the administration were advanced in Congress by the distinguished war veteran Nathaniel P. Banks. Representative Banks offers a litany of reasons as to why the purchase would benefit the country—strategically, politically, and economically. Most notable is Banks's assertion that Alaska would give the United States a way to take a more active role in Pacific trade sought by presidents since the Jefferson administration. Far from worthless, Alaska, in Banks's view, would enhance the nation's economic opportunities.

The Alaska treaty easily passed through Congress; only two senators voted against the purchase. In a matter of years, the purchase proved to be a beneficial one for the United States. At the turn of the century, large deposits of silver were discovered in the region. In time, oil was discovered and provided the nation with another important resource. Alaska remained a territory until 1959, when it became the nation's forty-ninth state.

REPRESENTATIVE NATHANIEL P. BANKS (R-MA), IN SUPPORT OF THE ALASKA PURCHASE (WASHINGTON, DC, JULY 1, 1868)

It is said that this territory is worthless, that we do not want it, that the Government had no right to buy it. These are the objections that have been urged at every step in the progress of the country from the day when the forefathers from England landed in Virginia or in Massachusetts up to this hour. Whenever and wherever we have extended our possessions we have encountered these identical objections—the country is worthless, we do not want it—the Government has no right to buy it . . .

Now, sir, I propose for a few moments to consider what advantages Alaska possesses for the United States. Is it worthless? Do we need it? Has the Government the right to buy it? I have no desire to affect the judgement of the House. I do not care how gentlemen vote. I have no interest in the question. I discuss it because it is my duty. And first, I speak of its geographical, commercial, and political importance. No man who looks upon the political condition of Europe can fail to see that it is quite possible it may be thrown at a day not distant into the vortex of a terrible war. There are to be great changes in the future; and it is certain that Russia will be among the first and greatest of the Powers of that future, whatever it may be. Whoever is engaged against her will strike for the conquest of this territory on the Pacific which did belong to her, and which will still belong to her if we refuse to execute the treaty for its purchase. This is not mere supposition. In 1790, when Russia declared war against Spain, one of the first enterprises of Spain was to organize a naval expedition in Mexico to take possession of the Russian territory on this continent. The events of the war prevented the success of this enterprise and left Russia in possession. . . .

Here, sir, are events of three quarters of a century, showing the tendency and purposes of the European Governments, unmistakable indications that it is the destiny of this territory to be involved in the great contests of the future, and to be thrown by the chances of war into the possession of some Power or Powers less friendly to us than the Russian government. When, therefore, the opportunity was offered to us upon reasonable and just terms to acquire this territory, we being the nation to whom in the nature of things it should and must ultimately belong, it was, in my judgement, neither expedient nor right to let the opportunity pass unimproved. However reluctant we might have been to advise it, it does not appear to us that a treaty negotiated by a full Senate, with only two dissenting votes, and those representing a small and distant part of the country, with somewhat of rival interests, can be held to be such a departure from duty and right as to justify the House in resorting to the extreme measure of attempting to defeat the treaty by refusing to pass measures necessary for its execution. . . .

Now, sir, the possession of Alaska is the key of this ocean. It is to the North what the ocean is to the South, the controller of the destiny of nations and the progress of mankind. It brings this continent within seventy or eighty miles of the Asiatic coast on the north. It gives us control of the Arctic, whatever it may be, and of that Arctic ocean we yet know nothing. This Arctic ocean, too, has a future, it may be a boundless and glorious future, and it is for us. The possession of Alaska makes Behring sea substantially an American sea. It throws out from its peninsula the mysterious chain of Aleutian Islands almost to the Asiatic coast. Our watermen can communicate with an open boat by this strange chain of islands between America and Asia, between the continents of the New and the Old World, and with the aid of the chain of Kurile Islands, reach by the same boat China, Japan, or India, never being more than two or three days at sea, rarely or never out of sight of land, and exposed to as slight perils of the sea as mariners can ever expect to encounter. . . .

This territory is not worthless; it is necessary to us; the Government had not only a right, but it is bound by a solemn duty to itself, to the people, at a proper time and by proper means to obtain it if they can do it justly and upon just terms.

Congressional *Globe*, 40th Congress, 2nd Session, July 1, 1868, 384–389.

REPRESENTATIVE HIRAM PRICE (D-IA), IN OPPOSITION TO THE PURCHASE OF ALASKA (WASHINGTON, DC, JULY 1, 1868)

The proposition now under consideration, stripped of all verbiage and removed from all ambiguity, is simply this: whether we, the Representatives of the people, the men whose duty it is specially to levy taxes upon the people, and as specially to see that an honest and economical disbursement is made of the money thus raised, whether we, thus situated and thus charged with important duties, are prepared in the present financial condition of the country to purchase any more territory or any other property not absolutely necessary to the life of the nation. I understand this to be the question with which we are brought face to face by the bill reported by the Committee on Foreign Affairs for the purchase of Alaska. . . .

First, sir, we do not want this territory, because as every one knows we have millions of acres of land now, more than we can properly care for or develop. Yes, sir; in the valley of the Mississippi alone there is land enough for an empire, uninhabited, unimproved, and its resources undeveloped because we have not the money to improve the channels and prevent the overflow of the rivers upon the banks of which those lands are situated. In the second place, Mr. Chairman, we have no money with which to make this purchase. I presume I need not inform this House and the country, that as a nation we are in debt, and in debt, too, to such an extent, as to cause considerable anxiety as to how we are to meet our honest obligations. These two facts, sir, it seems to me, ought to settle the question at once and finally, for if an individual who was pecuniarily involved to such an extent that he was compelled to renew his notes from time to time, and beg time from his creditors, should take money which he borrowed at an exorbitant rate of interest to purchase a piece of property which he had no kind of use for, he would be called by all honest and prudent men either a very weak or a very wicked man, and I hold, sir, that the same rule that applies to individuals is equally applicable to nations. We have not one dollar, sir, in the Treasury of the United States to-day that does not belong to our creditors. . . .

But we are told by gentlemen who advocate the passage of this bill that there are several reasons why this purchase should be made. One of these reasons is that it is a splendid country, producing the most luxuriant corn and the finest fur. Now, sir, if this be true it is the only country heard of, since the ark rested upon Ararat, where good corn and fine fur are raised on the same acre. I fear, Mr. Chairman, that the gentlemen who thus paint the picture dip the brush in rather too strong colors.

Another and stronger reason which gentlemen give for the passage of this bill and the purchase of Alaska is that a refusal to do so may offend Russia. I trust, sir, I do not underestimate the friendship of Russia. I have not forgotten, and never shall forget, that she alone of all the important Powers of Europe stood by us amid the darkness of the trial hour through which we have just passed. I remember how gladly I hailed the appearance of her vessels of war in our waters when the English and French ports were open to our enemies to furnish their piratical crafts outfits and reinforcements. . . . All these things I remember, and for all these things I honor her. But, sir, for all this I cannot consent to take the money which is needed for the comfort of the widows and orphans and wounded soldiers of my own land and give it to Russia, noble, generous, and brave as she is. . . .

Mr. Chairman, if this that is called a treaty, but which I deny is one, makes it obligatory on us to vote this money, then I ask gentlemen who are advocating this measure what is to prevent the same parties who made this bargain from buying the balance of the world and compelling us to pay for it. If this doctrine be true, the nation is financially at the mercy of the President and the Senate, and we, the immediate Representatives, are nothing more than so many clerks, whose duty it is to obey their commands and record their edicts. . . .

Let us, sir, not seek to stretch our arms like seas to take in all the shores, but let us rather protect and preserve what we have, develop the agricultural, mineral, and commercial possibilities which we already possess, and thus make this nation the home of hundreds of millions of happy and prosperous people.

Congressional *Globe*, 40th Congress, 2nd Session, July 1, 1868, 382–384.

IMPEACHMENT AND THE TENURE OF OFFICE ACT

As part of its attempt to control Reconstruction, congressional leaders in 1867 passed the Tenure of Office Act, which required Senate approval for the removal of any presidential appointee that initially had required Senate confirmation. President Johnson, upon entering the White House, already had removed some of Lincoln's staff and had threatened to remove others who sided with Republicans in Congress. The law, Republicans believed, would prevent Johnson from dismantling Lincoln's cabinet and creating a new, and perhaps more conservative team. Johnson not only viewed the bill as unconstitutional but had no intention of adhering to the policy. A showdown was inevitable, which resulted in impeachment proceedings against the president.

There was some confusion as to the extent to which this new legislation, passed over Johnson's veto, limited the president's authority. The law stated that individuals appointed by a president and confirmed by Congress would remain in office for the duration of the president's term, plus one month, unless the Senate approved of the removal. Johnson, as did his supporters and even some Republicans, assumed that the president could therefore remove appointments made by Lincoln. Others in Congress disagreed. Few were surprised when Johnson forced the issue by relieving from duty Edwin M. Stanton, the Lincoln-appointed secretary of war whose views on Reconstruction diverged sharply from those of Johnson. Unexpectedly, Stanton refused to step down, a decision reached after consulting with Republicans in Congress. Johnson had hoped to deflect public criticism by naming General Ulysses S. Grant, hero of the war, as his replacement.

Events then led to another showdown between Congress and the president. The Senate refused to approve Johnson's dismissal of Stanton. General Grant, to the president's chagrin, wanted to avoid being caught in the crossfire and refused to accept the appointment. Undeterred, Johnson then appointed General Lorenzo Thomas to the position and ordered Stanton to vacate his office. Days after this, on February 24, 1868, Republicans in the House of Representatives voted to impeach the president. As outlined in the Constitution, a trial would be held in the Senate and Johnson would be removed from office if a two-thirds majority voted for his conviction.

The trial, the first of its kind in the nation's history, began on March 5 and lasted three weeks. The chief justice of the Supreme Court, Salmon P. Chase, presided over the proceedings. The main charge against the president was his violation of the Tenure of Office Act. Opening arguments for the prosecution, Representative Benjamin Butler, a highly regarded war veteran and fiercely partisan legislator, summarizes the charges against Johnson. While most pertain to the removal of Stanton, other articles of impeachment accuse the president of harsh and damaging public condemnation of Congress and efforts to derail Reconstruction policies implemented by the legislature.

Johnson's legal team included Benjamin Curtis, a former Supreme Court justice and noted Boston attorney, who made opening remarks on behalf of the president. The defense maintains that the impeachment case comes down solely to the issue of Stanton; other charges against the president were politically motivated and without legal standing. In the case of the secretary of war, Curtis argues that Johnson had every right to remove a cabinet member appointed by another president under the terms of the Tenure of Office Act. Furthermore, the president's team claims that the act itself was a violation of the separation of powers and that the Constitution does not require Senate approval of cabinet dismissals. Johnson himself issued a lengthy response to each of the impeachment charges but did not testify personally at the trial.

The president's opponents fell only one vote short of the number required for removal from office. In the end, Johnson's ability to work behind the scenes to convince enough moderate Republicans to vote against his removal was a significant political success. Yet the beleaguered president would still face a hostile Congress with strong majorities against him for the remainder of his term. Johnson's impeachment trial was a historical rarity; the next such trial occurred over a century later when the House of Representatives issued charges against William Jefferson Clinton. Placed in the context of the post–Civil War era, the impeachment trial was but one, albeit the most dramatic, of the battles between the president and Congress over the course of Reconstruction.

BENJAMIN CURTIS, IN DEFENSE OF
PRESIDENT JOHNSON IN IMPEACHMENT PROCEEDINGS
(WASHINGTON, DC, MARCH 30, 1868)

Mr. Chief Justice, I am here to speak to the Senate of the United States sitting in its judicial capacity as a court of impeachment, presided over by the Chief Justice of the United States, for the trial of the President of the United States. This statement sufficiently characterizes what I have to say. Here party spirit, political schemes, forgone conclusions, outrageous biases can have no fit operation. The Constitution requires that here should be a "trial," and as in that trial the oath which each one of you has taken is to administer "impartial justice according to the Constitution and the laws," the only appeal which I can make in behalf of the President is an appeal to the conscience and the reason of each judge who sits before me. Upon the law and the facts, upon the judicial merits of the case, upon the duties incumbent on that high officer by virtue of his office, his honest endeavor to discharge those duties, the President rests his defence. . . .

What, then, is that substance of this first article? What, as the lawyers say, are the *gravamenina* contained in it? There is a great deal of verbiage—I do not mean unnecessary verbiage—in the description of the substantive matters set down in this article. Stripped of that verbiage it amounts exactly to these things: first, that the order set out in the article for the removal of Mr. Stanton, if executed, would be a violation of the tenure-of-office acts; second, that it was a violation of the tenure-of-office act; third, that it was an intentional violation of the tenure-of-office act; fourth, that it was a violation of the Constitution of the United States; and fifth, was by the President intended to be so. Or, to draw all this into one sentence which yet be intelligible and clear enough, I suppose the substance of this first article is that the order for the removal of Mr. Stanton was, and was intended to be, a violation of the tenure-of-office act, and was intended to be a violation of the Constitution of the United States. These are the allegations which it is necessary for the honorable managers to make out in proof to support that article. . . .

This first inquiry which arises on this language is as to meaning of the words "for and during the term of the President." Mr. Stanton, as appears by the commission which has been put into the case by the honorable managers, was appointed in January, 1862, during the first term of President Lincoln. Are these words "during the term of the President," applicable to Mr. Stanton's case? That depends upon whether an expounder of this law judicially, who finds set down in it as a part of the descriptive words "during the term of the President," has any right to add "and any other term for which he may afterward be elected." By what authority short of legislative power can those words be put into the statute so that "during the term of the President" shall be held to mean "and any other term or terms for this the President may be elected?" I respectfully submit no such judicial interpretation can be put on the words.

Then, if you please, take the next step. "During the term of the President by whom he was appointed." At the time when this order was issued for the removal of Mr. Stanton was he holding office "during the term of the President by whom he was appointed"? The honorable managers say yes, because, as they say, Mr. Johnson is merely serving out the residue of Mr. Lincoln's term. But is that so under the provisions of the Constitution of the United States? . . .

The Constitution undoubtedly contemplated that there should be executive departments created, the heads of which were to assist the President in the administration of the laws as well as by their advice. They were to be the hands and voice of the President; and accordingly that has been so practiced from the beginning, and the legislation of Congress has been framed on this assumption in the organization of the departments, and emphatically in the act which constituted the Department of War. That provides, as senators well remember, in so many words, that the Secretary of War is to discharge such duties of a general description there given as shall be assigned to him by the President, and that he is to perform them under the President's instructions and directions.

Let me repeat, that the Secretary of War and the other Secretaries, the Postmaster General, and the Attorney General, are deemed to be the assistants of the President in the performance of his great duty to take care that the laws are faithfully executed; that they speak for and act for him. Now, do not these two views furnish the reasons why this class of officers was excepted out of the law? They were to be the advisors of the President, for whom he was to be responsible, but in whom he was expected to repose a great amount of trust and confidence; and therefore it was that this act has connected to the tenure of office to these Secretaries to which it applies with the President by whom they were appointed. . . .

Do not let me be misunderstood on this subject. I am not intending to advance upon or occupy any extreme ground, because no such extreme ground has been advanced upon or occupied by the President of the United States. He is to take care that the laws are faithfully executed. When a law has been passed through the forms of legislation, either with his assent or without his assent, it is his duty to see that that law is faithfully executed. . . . He is not to erect himself into a judicial court and decide that the law is unconstitutional, and that therefore he will not execute it; for, if that were done, manifestly there never could be a judicial decision. . . .

But when, senators, a question arises whether a particular law had cut off a power confided to him by the people, through the Constitution, and he alone can raise that question, and he alone can cause a judicial decision to come between the two branches of the government to say which of them is right, and after due deliberation, with the advice of those who are his proper advisors, he settles down firmly upon that opinion that such is the character of the law, it remains to be decided by you whether there is any violation of his duty when he takes the needful steps to raise that question and have it peacefully decided. . . .

It must be unnecessary for me to say anything concerning the importance of this case, not only now, but in the future. It must be apparent to every one, in any way connected with or concerned with this trial, that this is and will be the most conspicuous instance which has ever been or can ever be expected to be found of American justice or American injustice, of that justice which Mr. Burke says is the great standing policy of all civilized states, or of that injustice which is sure to be discovered and which makes even the wise man mad, and which, in the fixed and immutable order of God's providence, is certain to return to plague its inventors.

United States Congress, *The Impeachment and Trial of Andrew Johnson* (New York: Dover reprint, 1974), 377–415.

REPRESENTATIVE BENJAMIN BUTLER (R-MA), OPENING ARGUMENTS AGAINST ANDREW JOHNSON IN IMPEACHMENT HEARINGS (WASHINGTON, DC, MARCH 30, 1868)

The onerous duty has fallen to my fortune to present to you, imperfectly as I must, the several propositions of fact and law upon which the House of Representatives will endeavor to sustain the cause of the people against the President of the United States, now pending at your bar. . . .

Article first, stripped of legal verbiage, alleges that, having suspended Mr. Stanton and reported the same to the Senate, which refused to concur in the suspension, and Stanton having rightfully resumed the duties of its office, the respondent, with knowledge of the facts, issued an order which is recited for Stanton's removal, with intent to violate the act of March 2, 1867, to regulate the tenure of certain civil offices, and with the further intent to remove Stanton from the office of Secretary of War, then in the lawful discharge of its duties, in contravention of said act without the advice and consent of the Senate, and against the Constitution of the United States. . . . The only question that remains is, does the respondent justify himself by the Constitution and laws?

On this he avers, that by the Constitution, there is "conferred on the President, as a part of the executive power, the power at any and all times of removing from office all executive officers for cause, to be judged of by the President alone, and that he verily believes that the executive power of removal from office, confided to him by the Constitution, as aforesaid, includes the power of suspension from office indefinitely." . . .

This, then, is the plain and inevitable issue before the Senate and the American people:

Has the president, under the Constitution, the more than kingly prerogative at will to remove from office and suspend from office indefinitely, all executive offices of the United States, either civil, military, or naval, at any and all times, and fill the vacancies with creatures of his own appointment, for his own purposes, without any restraint whatever, or possibility of restraint by the Senate or by Congress through laws duly enacted?

The House of Representatives, in behalf of the people, join this issue by affirming that the exercise of such powers is a high misdemeanor in office. . . .

Therefore, by these articles and the answers thereto, the momentous question, here and now, is raised whether the presidential office itself (if it has the prerogatives and power claimed for it) ought, in fact, to exist as a part of the constitutional government of a free people, while by the last three articles the simpler and less important inquiry is to be determined, whether Andrew Johnson has so conducted himself that he ought longer to hold any constitutional office whatever. The latter sinks to merited insignificance compared with the grandeur of the former.

For this most stupendous and unlimited prerogative the respondent cites no line and adduces no word of constitutional enactment—indeed he could not, for the only mention of removal from office in the Constitution is as a part of the judgement in case of impeachment, and the only power of appointment is by nomination to the Senate of officers to be appointed by the President when the Senate is not in session. Whence then does the respondent by his answer claim to have derived this power? . . .

Thus it appears that with full intent to resist the power of the Senate, to hold the tenure of office act void, and to exercise this illimitable power claimed by him, he did suspend Mr. Stanton, apparently in accordance with the provisions of the act; he did give his reasons for the suspension to the Senate, and argued them at length, accompanied by what he claimed to be the evidence of the official misconduct of Mr. Stanton, and thus invoked the action of the Senate to assist him in displacing a high officer of the government under the provisions of an act which he at that very moment believed to be unconstitutional, inoperative and void, thereby showing that he was willing to make use of a void act and the Senate of the United States as his tools, to do that which he believed neither had any constitutional power to do. Did not every member of the Senate, when that message came in announcing the suspension of Mr. Stanton, understand and believe that the President was acting in this case as he had done in every other case under the provisions of this act? Did not both sides discuss the question under its provisions? Would any Senator upon this floor, on either side, so demean himself as to consider the question one moment if he had known it was then within the intent and purpose of the President of the United States to treat the deliberations and action of the Senate as void and of non-effect, if its decision did not comport with his views and purposes; and yet, while acknowledging the intent was in his mind to hold as naught the judgement of the Senate if it did not concur with his own, and remove Mr. Stanton at all hazards, and as I charge it upon him here, as a fact no man can doubt, with the full knowledge also that the Senate understood that he was acting under the provision of the tenure-of-office act, still thus deceiving them, when called to answer for a violation of that act in his solemn answer he makes a shameless avowal that he did transmit to the Senate of the United States a "message wherein he made known the orders aforesaid and the reasons which induced the same, so far as the respondent then considered it material and necessary that the same should be set forth." . . .

Now, is it not well known to all good and grave men ("*bonos et graves*") that Andrew Johnson entered the office of President of the United States at the close of the armed rebellion, making loud denunciation, frequently and everywhere, that traitors ought to be punished, and treason should be made odious; that the loyal and true men on the South should be fostered and encouraged; and, if there were but few of them, to such only should be given in charge the reconstruction of the disorganized States?

So not all men know that soon afterwards he changed his course, and only made treason odious, so far as he was concerned, by appointing traitors to office and by an indiscriminate pardon of all who "came in unto him?" Who does not know that Andrew Johnson initiated, at its own will, a course of reconstruction of the rebel States, which at the time he claimed was provisional only, and until the meeting of Congress and its action thereon? ... Who does not know that when Congress, assuming its rightful power to propose amendments to the Constitution, had passed such an amendment, and had submitted it to the States as a measure of pacification, Andrew Johnson advised and counseled the legislatures of the States lately in rebellion, as well as others, to reject the amendment ...

The responsibility is with you; the safeguards of the Constitution against usurpation are in your hands; the interests and hopes of free institutions wait upon your verdict. The House of Representatives has done its duty.... Never again, if Andrew Johnson go quiet and free this day, can the people of this or any other country by constitutional checks or guards stay the usurpation of executive power.

United States Congress, *The Impeachment and Trial of Andrew Johnson* (New York: Dover reprint, 1974), 89–123.

RECOMMENDED READINGS

Benedict, Michael Les. *The Impeachment and Trial of Andrew Johnson.* New York: W.W. Norton & Co., 1973.

Castel, Albert. *The Presidency of Andrew Johnson.* Lawrence: University of Kansas Press, 1979.

Foner, Eric. *Reconstruction: America's Unfinished Revolution.* New York: Harper & Row, 1988.

McKitrick, Eric. *Andrew Johnson and Reconstruction.* Chicago: University of Chicago Press, 1960.

Stampp, Kenneth M. *The Era of Reconstruction, 1865–1877.* New York: Alfred A. Knopf, 1965.

6

ULYSSES S. GRANT

(1869–1877)

INTRODUCTION

General Ulysses S. Grant had to be exhausted. He had boarded a train at a makeshift depot near Appomattox Court House in Virginia to begin a two-day trip to Washington. The day before, April 9, 1865, General Robert E. Lee had surrendered the Army of Northern Virginia to Grant, thereby ending the bloodiest war in the nation's history. As Grant's train sped toward City Point, where his wife Julia would be waiting, he had to wonder what would come next. Over the past year, since being named supreme commander of the Union Armies by President Lincoln in March 1864, he had become the most popular man in the nation, eclipsing even the president himself. He would soon meet with Lincoln to discuss the future of the South. Grant, as much as anyone, knew that although the fighting had subsided, the arduous task of dealing with the Confederacy was only beginning.

Was Grant considering a future in politics at that moment? Certainly there were strategists who recognized the immense popularity of the man credited with saving the Union. Even if he did not think then of the presidency, Grant had to be aware that his life would never be the same. He had overseen the end of the war. He had accepted the surrender of Lee. The war had become his war; he would have a stake and a responsibility in determining the South's, and by implication the entire nation's, future. In the wake of Lincoln's death, and as the troubled Andrew Johnson administration limped toward impeachment, all signs indicated that Grant would become the next president of the United States.

The story of Grant's life—from a tanner's son to war hero to president—continues to capture the imagination. He was born on April 27, 1822, in

Point Pleasant, Ohio, a settlement on the Ohio River between Ohio and Pennsylvania. The Grant family had come to America in 1630, settling in the Massachusetts Bay colony. Ulysses's grandfather Noah had moved the family from New England to Ohio in the 1790s seeking new opportunities. Noah's son Jesse Root Grant, born into a poor but stable family, was apprenticed to a tanner. Over time, Jesse Grant achieved a modest but sustainable business in Georgetown, Ohio, in Brown County. Here, he and his wife Hannah Simpson Grant had their first son, whom they named Hiram Ulysses, electing to use the middle name as his common appellation. The Grants would have five more children: three girls and two boys.

As the first son, Ulysses received a great deal of attention from his father, who had high expectations for him. Jesse Grant was an energetic, combative, at times difficult man who enjoyed local politics. He served as mayor of Georgetown in the 1830s and fully expected his son to do more with his life than leatherwork. Lacking funds for an elaborate education, Ulysses attended schools in and around Georgetown where he mastered basic skills. In 1839, his father informed him that he would be attending the United States Military Academy at West Point, New York. Jesse, who sided with the Whig Party, had developed acquaintances with local politicians, including United States Representative Thomas Hamer. At Jesse's urging, Congressman Hamer agreed to sponsor young Ulysses, who was less than enthusiastic about attending but gave in to his father's wishes. Thomas Hamer's recommendation was pivotal for more than one reason. In his letter of reference, he mistakenly wrote the name "Ulysses S. Grant," not realizing that his first name was Hiram. The middle initial came from Grant's mother's maiden name. When Ulysses arrived at West Point and found the name "U. S. Grant" on the registry, he claimed it as his own and never changed it.

Interestingly, military life, at least that of West Point, never appealed to Grant. He arrived there at the age of seventeen, standing all of five feet one inch tall and weighing less than 120 pounds. His small size, while excluding him from success at some physical activities, made him a perfect candidate for horsemanship. He developed a lifelong love of horses and broke records in riding and jumping as a student. Grant was an above-average student, scoring particularly well in mathematics. He graduated in 1843 in the middle of his class, along with numerous cadets who would also serve in the Civil War, on both sides. He was commissioned as a Second Brevet Lieutenant in the Fourth Infantry, despite his desire to enter the cavalry.

The disappointment of his commission did not bother him because Ulysses S. Grant had no intention of pursuing a military career. He was required to serve a single tour of duty and he expected to re-enter civilian life afterwards. Whatever his future held, he knew that it would include Julia Dent, the sister of West Point cadet Frederick Dent, Grant's roommate. Grant became acquainted with Julia while stationed near St. Louis after graduation. The Dent home was at White Haven, an estate also near St.

Louis. Julia was short, stout, and by most accounts not attractive, but she had a great deal of energy and enthusiasm for life. Grant undoubtedly was also attracted to her love of horses, an interest the two shared for the remainder of their lives. They were engaged in 1844, while Grant was stationed in Louisiana and then later in Texas. They would have been married sooner had it not been for the onset of war with Mexico, which kept Grant away from St. Louis for two more years. The couple wed in August 1848.

Grant saw a great deal of action in the Mexican War. He fought in every major battle of the conflict except Buena Vista, and was promoted to the rank of Brevet Captain by war's end. Grant never had a positive attitude about the war. Whiggish in his political views, he saw the war as an attempt by Southerners to increase the size of the slavocracy. During the war he believed it to be unjust, as the more powerful United States ran roughshod over its weaker neighbor. Nevertheless, Grant benefited from the war. The question was what to do after a peace was secured.

Most men in Grant's position entered civilian life. The problem was that Grant, now newly married, had little in the way of business prospects. The tanning business held little attraction and Grant had few business contacts. He therefore decided to remain in the military. These were difficult years. After brief assignments in New York and Detroit, Grant ended up on the Pacific Coast, far from Julia and his son Frederick, who was born in 1850. For two years, he held out at the remote Fort Humbolt. His health became poor; rumors circulated that he had become a drunk. In fact, the question of Grant's alcoholism dogged him for the remainder of his days and well after his death. He did drink as a young man, occasionally to excess, particularly when he was away from his family. In later years, however, he refused to drink at all. His sobriety was never an issue during the Civil War or his presidency.

In 1854, Grant resigned his appointment and entered civilian life. For several years he struggled to make a living. The family settled near the Dents outside St. Louis. Grant built a home there for the two of them and their three children, soon to be four, and appropriately named the residence "Hardscrabble." He attempted farming but abandoned it for the real estate business in 1858. By 1860, the family was in dire straits. Grant sold Hardscrabble and moved the family to Galena, Illinois, where his father now had a prospering leather goods store. Ulysses S. Grant had been a failure in the business world. He was thirty-eight years old.

Secession changed Grant's fortunes. He had never taken an active interest in politics, although he was aware of the turmoil over slavery in the West that gripped the nation. He voted for James Buchanan in 1856, but never had strong ties to the Democratic Party. In 1860 he probably sided with the Republicans. However, Grant was clear in his support for the Union and enlisted after the firing on Fort Sumter. After working to enlist volunteers in and around Galena, Grant was commissioned as Colonel of the 21st Illi-

nois Regiment of Volunteers in June 1861. Grant did not enlist with the enthusiasm of so many young men; he had seen war and understood its
realities. Yet he felt a sense of duty to country, and certainly little in Galena
gave him reason to stay home. He traveled to Cairo, Illinois, and soon
found himself in command of the District of Southern Illinois and South-
eastern Missouri.

Grant's meteoric rise through the ranks of the military began in Mis-
souri. While Lincoln was working his way through generals, Grant was
scoring successes in the West, and news of those successes gradually fil-
tered back to Washington. On September 6, 1861, Grant's troops occupied
Paducah, Kentucky, without resistance; over the next two and a half years,
Grant led Union armies on a systematic rout of Confederate forces in the
West. In February 1862, now Brigadier General Grant led an invasion of
Fort Henry, at the Tennessee-Kentucky border, the first invasion into the
Confederacy in the western theater. Ten days later, Grant's troops had
moved up the Tennessee River and taken Fort Donelson. During the assault
on Fort Donelson, he sent word to Confederate General Simon Bolivar
Buckner that he would accept no terms, only an unconditional surrender.
The Northern public, eager for moral victories, celebrated the brash Gen-
eral in the West whose initials now stood for "Unconditional Surrender."
By the spring of 1862, Lincoln had come to view Grant as vital in securing
the West.

Grant's greatest days remained ahead of him. He led forces southward
with plans of joining with General Don Carlos Buell's army, which had
taken Memphis, to begin a massive invasion of the Deep South. His troops
were attacked at Shiloh, Mississippi, in April 1862 by Confederates under
the command of Albert Sidney Johnston. Grant recovered and led a coun-
teroffensive the following day. Two days of fighting left 25,000 dead, more
than had died in the American Revolution, the War of 1812, and the Mexican War combined. Grant's reputation suffered a setback, as some suggested that he had been drinking during the campaign and some called on
Lincoln to remove him from command. Lincoln, recognizing the need for
aggressive leadership, refused. After a brief leave of absence, Grant was restored as General of the Army of Tennessee. Beginning in November 1862,
he headed the Vicksburg campaign, which consisted of leading troops
down the Mississippi River to take the strategic Mississippi port city. Grant
displayed brilliant leadership by crossing over to Louisiana, dropping
south of the city, and then doubling back, thereby cutting off Vicksburg
from the Confederacy. On May 18, 1863, he began a siege of the city that
lasted until July 4, when the supposedly invincible fortress fell. With that
blow, the Confederacy had been divided in half. Grant, reputation restored,
was named commander of the Grand Division of the Mississippi, which
placed him in charge of the West theater.

If Grant's career had ended there he would have been remembered as a great general. However, on March 9, 1864, Lincoln promoted Grant to the rank of Lieutenant General and he became supreme commander of the Union Armies. The president had grown weary of generals who seemed to lack the will to take the fight to the enemy. Here was a man, Lincoln believed, who understood war. In fact, most students of Grant maintain that his view of war was quite simple. Never one to appreciate the classics of military history and science, Grant believed that war was reducible to human will. Some men were willing to kill; others were not. It was a cold calculus, but Grant's philosophy of war gained results. Lincoln, facing criticism from all fronts, wanted results. Grant traveled to Washington and planned with the president a large-scale assault in the East that might bring the war to an end.

With the Union military effort now under Grant's command, he developed military policy at the highest level alongside the president. In May 1864, the Army of the Potomac, 115,000 strong and under the command of George Meade, began to move southward. Grant had assured Lincoln that he would take the fight to the Confederacy. The results often were catastrophic. At Cold Harbor, Virginia, in June, 7,000 Union soldiers were killed in twenty minutes during a frontal assault. Yet Grant only dug in. He continued his attacks on Confederate positions in Virginia, destroying towns and homesteads along the way. He also sent William T. Sherman and 90,000 troops toward Atlanta. That key Southern city fell in September; Sherman then embarked on his "March to the Sea," wreaking havoc all along the way. By February 1865, Sherman was in control of Columbia, South Carolina.

Grant then pushed his Army of the Potomac forward, taking Richmond in April and halting the exhausted Confederates at Appomattox Court House. He received credit for turning the tide in the war and returned to Washington to a hero's welcome. In the aftermath of Lincoln's assassination, Grant was promoted to the rank of full general, the first in the nation's history. For a time, he and the new president worked well together. Johnson sent Grant on a tour of the South in order to better understand how to proceed with Reconstruction. Grant increasingly was forced into making comments on policy, despite his general distaste for politics. Considering the fortunes of Johnson, his reluctance to speak out on policy matters served him well. Instead, he attempted to appear above the political fray. When Congress passed a Military Reconstruction Act that divided the South into military zones, Grant oversaw the deployment of troops. Yet he never criticized Johnson, even as the president's popularity waned. When Johnson attempted to appoint him secretary of war after removing Edwin M. Stanton, the act that resulted in impeachment proceedings, Grant displayed political acumen in agreeing only to serve in a temporary capacity, until Congress addressed the situation. Grant was his own man, and when the political tide turned against Johnson, Grant did not go down with a sinking ship.

As the 1868 election season neared, both parties sought out Grant as a potential candidate. For his part, Grant appeared little interested in the position—a requirement for any presidential hopeful at that time. The Republican Party made the most sense. Grant had served Lincoln loyally and the majority of Northern voters sympathized with the "Grand Old Party," as it came to be called. Currents of popular opinion literally swept Grant into office. Throughout the year, clubs sprung up across the North with the purpose of promoting his candidacy. He responded to the groundswell of support in typical fashion—he said as little as possible. By summer it seemed quite evident that Grant would be the next president of the United States. The only obstacle was the Republican primary, although no one seemed to have a chance to defeat the larger-than-life "Lion of Vicksburg." The general election almost was a forgone conclusion, as the only Southern states participating would be those with Republican-dominated Reconstructed governments.

Grant seemed to care little about issues, although by the autumn of 1868 he had grown comfortable with the idea of being president. The Republican Party platform, forged at their Chicago convention, sought to strike a middle ground to appease its Radical and Moderate wings. Congressional control of Reconstruction was a major plank, as was a demand for the necessity for voting rights for African Americans in the South. The party also recognized the backlash that could result from alienating conservative voters in the North and followed up with a statement that black suffrage there should be left to the individual states. The Republicans also included a plank on monetary reform, calling for all debts to be paid with gold. Speaker of the House Schuyler Colfax was chosen as his running mate.

The Democrats met in New York in July and held a less than enthusiastic convention. With Southern Democrats not yet in the electorate, and with Grant as their opponent, few expected a victory. Former governor of New York Horatio Seymour won the nomination. The Democrats included a plank questioning the extreme nature of congressional Reconstruction. Most importantly, the party took the opposite position on the question of public debt, arguing that bondholders should be paid in the paper currency printed during the war with which they were purchased—the so-called greenbacks. The election results were somewhat startling. Seymour carried eight states, and while Grant's electoral college victory was 214–80, the popular vote was very close. Issues of economics were beginning to take precedence over Reconstruction and matters related to the war, a fact that neither party had yet to recognize fully.

Nevertheless, Grant, who remained at home in Galena throughout the election season, traveled to Washington in triumphant celebration. The proven war hero had shown the ability to win an election; it remained to be seen whether he could succeed in the political arena. He faced extraordinary problems that would have challenged the most seasoned of politicians. There was the lingering problem of Reconstruction. Attempts by Congress to bring about wholesale change in the South constantly were derailed. In some states, the Ku Klux Klan and other secret societies had since 1866 intimidated blacks into staying away from the polls. Southern Democrats gradually regained their power by mobilizing the white vote, and Republicans lost control of the upper South beginning in 1868. In the Deep South, where blacks were in larger numbers, Republicans remained in control for a few more years, but in time white Democrats wrested control of these states. Northern Republicans vacillated between moods of frustration and apathy over conditions in the South. Grant, for his part, did little to mollify those who feared that the South would return to its former ways.

Significantly, issues pertaining to the economy moved to the forefront during the Grant administration, particularly following the financial panic of 1873. The problems were complex—more complex than Grant was equipped to handle. One issue was the greenbacks—paper money printed during the war without the backing of specie, or precious metal. Investors who bought government bonds during the war wanted these redeemed in gold; opponents claimed that such a plan would result in profiteering. Additionally, those who advocated "hard money" called for the elimination of greenbacks altogether, a plan that met with opposition from debtors, particularly farmers and laborers. Grant was cautious in his economic policy, but also consistent, promoting a tightened money supply and redemption of debts in specie—policies that the Republican Party generally supported.

Foreign affairs, perhaps Grant's greatest interest, were of little importance throughout the 1870s. There were a few exceptions. Grant managed to oversee the conclusion of claims against Great Britain dating back to the Civil War for the sale of warships to the Confederacy. Grant also faced the continual problem of uprisings against the Spanish colonial government in Cuba and calls for annexation of the island. For his part, Grant was much more interested in the acquisition of Santo Domingo (now the Dominican Republic). His inability to convince Congress of the need to annex the Caribbean country stood as his greatest disappointment.

As president, Grant most often has been remembered for the myriad scandals that erupted during his two terms in office that have cast a long shadow over his political career. Much of this has been linked to Grant's cabinet appointments, which were made based on ties of friendship rather than talent. There is some truth to these charges. His Secretary of State, Hamilton Fish, was a successful public servant; most, however were disappointments. Friends made during the war and even family members often found themselves in positions of responsibility. During his first year in office, Grant's brother-in-law was part of an effort by wildcat entrepreneurs Jay Gould and Jim Fisk to corner the gold market.

Yet this scheme was only the beginning of the corruption that ran rampant during the Grant years. There also was the Credit Mobilier scandal, in which congressmen and even the vice president were implicated in a scheme that involved selling shares of stock in a railroad construction company to legislators and other government officials at devalued rates in exchange for political favors. Finally, the most embarrassing was the "Whiskey Ring," in which tax collectors skimmed funds and offered kickbacks to officials who looked the other way. Even Grant's longtime friend and personal secretary Orville E. Babcock was implicated. Reformers responded by calling for more honesty in government and sought ways to eliminate corruption, or as critics of the president called it, "Grantism." Efforts to reform the civil service by creating requirements of competence for certain positions gained steam throughout the 1870s, challenging the notion of a "spoils system" that protected the right of a president to make independent appointments, often based on financial contributions to his party.

Equating Grant with scandal is somewhat unfair. The Credit Mobilier incident had begun before the 1868 election, while the Whiskey Ring certainly was not the first instance of revenue extortion in the history of the nation. Furthermore, Grant was never linked directly to any of these scandals. At the same time, Grant does deserve criticism for building a team of advisors of such shortsightedness, and at times, outright greed and dishonesty. Grant had neither the skills nor the desire to confront the massive challenges of a growing nation still recovering from a brutal war. He was indecisive, often contradictory in his policy, and usually withdrawn from the public view. Yet the nation was content with Grant, grateful for his service during the nation's hour of peril, and exhausted from upheaval. These were not years for great statesmen. Grant, the war hero, provided Americans with the symbol of national strength for which they yearned, not the skilled leader they required.

THE FIFTEENTH AMENDMENT

When Grant entered office, Radical Republicans had already controlled Reconstruction for two years. By 1870, much change had taken place in Southern state governments, although little in Southern society had followed suit. All states of the former Confederacy had met the congressional requirements for readmission. Most had been brought back into the Union in 1868, when conventions, elected by universal male suffrage, ratified the Fourteenth Amendment, guaranteed voting rights to blacks, and had elected acceptable officials to government positions. Only three states—Virginia, Mississippi, and Texas—were not readmitted that year.

On the surface, much change had occurred. However, even as these states were creating governments under the watchful eye of Congress, Southerners were attempting to reverse the work completed by the Radicals. At the heart of the matter was black suffrage. The widely held view that African Americans were unworthy of voting rights and that their participation in elections would be the downfall of Southern society prompted large numbers of whites to take action. Most notable among the attempts to remove blacks from the political process was the formation of secret societies such as the Ku Klux Klan, founded in Tennessee in 1866. The movement developed into an organized effort to intimidate blacks and keep them from going to the polls.

For years, reports reached Washington of outrages occurring in the South at the hands of such groups. Indeed, blacks were being removed systematically from the political process in Southern states through a combination of violence and fraud. In some areas, virtually all white adult males had joined the Klan; their numbers included people from all ranks of society. Radicals in Congress rightly feared that as blacks were stripped of the franchise, all Reconstruction plans would be derailed.

Hence in 1869 Radicals pushed through Congress a constitutional amendment that guaranteed the right to vote for all adult male citizens. Congress required the remaining unreconstructed states to ratify the Fifteenth Amendment as a requirement for statehood. Moreover, in May 1870 Congress passed an Enforcement Act providing penalties for those who attempted to abridge a citizen's right to vote. Another Enforcement Act placed congressional elections under the authority of federal election supervisors.

President Grant considered the Fifteenth Amendment to be among the more crucial accomplishments of Reconstruction. His decision to issue a proclamation to Congress in celebration of the legislation illustrates the importance the president placed on guaranteeing the right of freedmen to vote in the South.

While the Fifteenth Amendment and its Enforcement Acts met with opposition in the South, a number of Northern Democrats also criticized the policy. Democrats often claimed that Republicans were doing more than ensuring the franchise; they were attempting to use federal power to guarantee Republican victories in elections. Representative Samuel Cox of New York attacks the measure harshly as a partisan attempt to place federal agents, friendly to the Republican Party, at local precincts in an effort to influence electoral outcomes. Cox also complains that the principle of separation of powers required that states be in charge of their own elections. Placing local elections under federal authority, Cox maintains, is an example of usurpation of power.

The Enforcement Acts became law but did little to turn the tide in the South. Instead, local officials in Southern states simply ignored the law and refused to prosecute cases in which whites were accused of violations. Throughout the early 1870s, the number of black voters in Southern states plummeted. The result was the return of the Democratic Party to power in the South and the gradual erosion of Reconstruction policy. By the end of Grant's presidency, the political makeup of the South had reverted to Democrat-dominated legislatures.

ULYSSES S. GRANT, PROCLAMATION REGARDING
THE FIFTEENTH AMENDMENT
(WASHINGTON, DC, MARCH 30, 1870)

It is unusual to notify the two Houses of Congress by message of the pro-mulgation, by proclamation of the Secretary of State, of the ratification of a constitutional amendment. In view, however, of the vast importance of the fifteenth amendment to the Constitution, this day declared a part of that re-vered instrument, I deem a departure from the usual custom justifiable. A measure which makes at once 4,000,000 people voters who were heretofore declared by the highest tribunal in the land not citizens of the United States, nor eligible to become so (with the assertion that "at the time of the Declara-tion of Independence the opinion was fixed and universal in the civilized portion of the white race, regarded as an axiom in morals as well as in poli-tics, that black men had no rights which the white man was bound the re-spect"), is indeed a measure of grander importance than any other one act of the kind from the foundation of our free Government to the present day.

Institutions like ours, in which all power is derived directly from the people, must depend mainly upon their intelligence, patriotism, and in-dustry. I call the attention, therefore, of the newly enfranchised race to the importance of their striving in every honorable manner to make them-selves worthy of their new privilege. To the race more favored heretofore by our laws I would say, Withhold no legal privilege of advancement to the new citizen. The framers of our Constitution firmly believed that a republi-can government could not endure without intelligence and education gen-erally diffused among the people. The Father of his Country, in his Farewell Address, uses this language:

Promote, then, as an object of primary importance, institutions for the general diffusion of knowledge. In proportion as the structure of a government gives force to public opinion, it is essential that public opinion should be enlightened.

In his first annual message to Congress the same views are forcibly pre-sented, and are again urged in his eighth message.

I repeat that the adoption of the fifteenth amendment to the Constitution completes the greatest civil change and constitutes the most important event that has occurred since the nation came into life. The change will be beneficial in proportion to the heed that is given to the urgent recommen-dations of Washington. If these recommendations were important then, with a population of but a few millions, how much more important now, with a population of 40,000,000, and increasing in a rapid ratio. I would therefore call upon Congress to take all the means within their constitu-tional powers to promote and encourage popular education throughout the country, and upon the people everywhere to see to it that all who possess and exercise political rights shall have the opportunity to acquire the knowledge which will make their share in the Government a blessing and not a danger. By such means only can the benefits contemplated by this amendment to the Constitution be secured.

A Compilation of the Messages and Papers of the Presidents, vol. 8, James D. Richardson, ed. (New York: Bureau of National Literature, Inc., 1897), 4009–4010.

REPRESENTATIVE SAMUEL S. COX (D-NY), IN OPPOSITION TO ENFORCEMENT OF THE FIFTEENTH AMENDMENT (WASHINGTON, DC, FEBRUARY 15, 1871)

If the Democratic party of the city and State of New York were less patriotic than partisan they would be glad to have this measure of forcing elections continue and become intensified by the proposed amendments. The effect would be still to increase their majorities. But I would not favor party success at the peril or mutilation of the form, structure, and genius of our Government.

This bill is substantially the bill of the last session, with "improvements." It makes more officials, deputy marshals, and supervisors. It gives them more capricious power, and shields them from responsibility for their acts. It worms them into the old body of our election laws until the matter will become an inquisitorial nuisance. It allows these officials to arrest without warrant and evidence, and this breaks the oldest constitutional guarantee of liberty. It is an unwarranted, *ex parte* use of power, without fairness, and for the worst purposes, the perpetuation of a fallen and dishonored party....

Mr. Speaker, if this bill becomes a law, as amended, if it be the intention of the majority, in defiance of the will of the people of the city and State of New York, and in defiance of the present Democratic majority in the United States, as developed by the elections of 1870, if you intend to force through this legislation with a view to secure success at the Federal elections by martial means, then I, for one, would advise the Executive and Legislature of New York, and all who inquire, to change the time of holding our State election, so that we may have an election of our own; in which the Federal Government can have no pretext, and no business to interfere. Be sure, sir, that will be the result of this measure. You may go on with your separate elections as to Congressmen; we will election our Congressmen in New York anyhow. Go on with your election in New York for presidential electors; we will carry the State for the Democracy in 1872 anyhow. These pretentious, forceful enactments, however thundering in the index, in the conclusion will roar as gently as a sucking dove. They will result in the free expression of the people, and against the authority now seeking to perpetuate itself by them.

Mr. Speaker, the Republican party if it would save itself in the future from defeat and disgrace might be in better business than passing enactments of this kind. Why does it not do something for the country? Why does it not do something for the currency? Why not relieve the onerous taxes now oppressing the people? Why not take off the duty on salt, coal, leather, lumber, and what not, which has been so urgently demanded? Why not heed the cry which is now coming up from New England even, and abolish your oppressive tariffs on raw materials? . . .

If this bill does become a law, and its enforcement is sought, I give notice to gentlemen that the Legislature of New York, the power there wielding that great empire State, will either carry out its own election laws, without collision, by having a day for the State elections different from that fixed by the Federal law for Federal elections, or it will meet you fairly and squarely with all the power of the great State against your invasions and usurpation. Thus will the great State, whose elements are imperial and whose power is undiminished, best vindicate its early history and present position; and the city of New York, the composite city of refuge and hope—not less for the men that the ideas of all nations, the city of liberal thoughts and charitable action—assert its metropolitan, commercial, and independent character as one of the truly "free cities" of the earth!

Congressional *Globe*, 41st Congress, 3rd Session, February 15, 1871, 127–130.

THE KU KLUX KLAN ACT

During the early years of Grant's administration Radical Republicans feared that the Civil War had become a lost cause. In 1866, Congress had seized Reconstruction policy from Andrew Johnson and passed a wave of new laws to ensure significant political, and in time, social change in the South. The election of Grant generated even more.

Yet by 1870 this optimism was fading, along with the power of the Radicals. A new generation of Republicans seemed less concerned with the plight of freedmen and more focused on the economy. More problematic was the resurgence of the Democratic Party in the South. The number of Southern white Republicans, known as "scalawags," was diminishing, leaving only freedmen. If the party's strength in the South were to last, it would be primarily through their support. This strategy was somewhat promising. In some areas African Americans were the majority; in most places they potentially were a powerful bloc of voters.

Some Southern whites recognized this potential and responded with brutality. Northern writers who traveled to the former Confederacy wrote of organized terror toward freedmen and lack of enforcement of Reconstruction laws. While there were a number of groups—some secret and some not so secret—that worked to limit the political participation of African Americans, the most infamous was the Ku Klux Klan. Founded in Pulaski, Tennessee, in 1866, the secret society that invoked bizarre ritual and costume carried out a systematic campaign to disenfranchise freed-men and strip away their political rights.

Northern leaders warned that if the Ku Klux Klan prevailed, conservative white Democrats would then begin their own reconstruction—the reconstruction of the antebellum slaveholding South. In 1871 Congress passed, and President Grant signed into law, the Ku Klux Klan Act, which allowed for the deployment of more troops into the South and harsher penalties for those who sought to limit the civil rights of others. The law also gave the president the power to suspend the writ of *habeas corpus* in areas where violence seemed imminent. The issue of the president's ability to suspend the rights of accused people had been debated during the war, when Abraham Lincoln suspended the writ in the border states. Grant and the Republicans drew on Lincoln's precedent to justify the provision.

Southerners responded with outrage. Democratic senator John W. Stevenson of Kentucky offers an impassioned plea to deny the president the powers of a "dictator." In what was a typical argument for Southerners throughout the Reconstruction era, Stevenson paints the portrait of a peace-loving South under the thumb of an oppressive federal government. Stevenson also doubts the accuracy of the allegations against the Klan and asks for proof that such violence was occurring. He concludes with an emotional appeal of peace and conciliation rather than an increased military presence.

Many Northerners agreed with Grant that the stakes were too high to allow abuses to continue unanswered. Representative James N. Tyner of Indiana speaks on behalf of the president. Tyner claims that violence led by the Klan represented an insurrection that called for direct military action. He argues that the North had for years been lenient toward the South and that the result was wholesale rejection of the law. He warns Southerners that Northern military might, which prevailed in the war, would return if necessary. Tyner also places faith in President Grant, based on his experiences in the South during the war, to make decisions regarding the use of troops and the suspension of the writ of *habeas corpus*.

The Ku Klux Klan Act became law in April 1871, but the results were negligible. While troops were deployed at times when violence threatened a specific area, few Northern political leaders were willing to support a sustained military occupation of the South. Despite laws intended to reinforce Reconstruction, the Northern presence south of the Mason-Dixon line faded throughout the 1870s. The election of 1877, which included the well-known "compromise" that named Republican Rutherford B. Hayes president, brought remaining troops out of the South and ended Reconstruction.

REPRESENTATIVE JAMES N. TYNER (R-IN), IN
SUPPORT OF THE KU KLUX KLAN ACT
(WASHINGTON, DC, APRIL 5, 1871)

The necessity of legislation to protect the life, liberty, property, and immunities of citizens of the States lately in rebellion ought not astonish any one. It was to have been expected from the upheaving of the foundations on which society there rested. One third of the entire population, in the full enjoyment of all their rights as citizens, with all their privileges undisturbed, and with a representation in the national councils based, not only on their own numbers, but on a part of their property also, for reasons unsatisfactory to the balance of the world, rashly determined to submit their destiny to the arbitrament of the sword. They were defeated, as all armed enemies of a just Government deserve to be. Humiliated by defeat, inflamed by passion, bankrupted in property, and reduced from the enviable position of leaders in national affairs to the humble one of accepting such terms of reconstruction as were prescribed by the United States, it was but natural that they would embrace the situation with ill-conceived disgust.

No matter, sir, how generous and magnanimous the terms on which they were restored to citizenship, they are rebellious still in spirit only because they are compelled to become the political equals of those who were formerly their slaves. It is not in denying to certain of the leaders of the late rebellion the right to hold office, but in the extension of political privileges to colored men, whereby power has departed from its former possessors, that we find an intelligent explanation of their conduct now. Rescind the last three great amendments to the Constitution, and thus revive slavery and the domination of the slave power, and no voice of complaint will come to us by the men whose lawless acts require suppression by the power of the General Government.

I will not pause now to compare notes with gentlemen on the other side of the House who deny the occurrence of outrages in the South and the consequent necessity of legislation to prevent their continuance. Whosoever shuts his eyes to the facts that come to us in such shapes as to convince the most skeptical is willfully blind and will not see. Through all the avenues of information, through the columns of the public press, the medium of private correspondence, and the sworn testimony before an investigating committee of the other branch of this Congress, the story comes fully authenticated and uncontradicted by such evidence as reasoning men deem satisfactory that assassinations, murders, whippings, and mutilations are almost nightly committed on helpless and unoffending citizens of the South, only because they will not bow down before and worship the god of Democracy! That, sir, is the whole story. Democrats of white complexion are not disenfranchised, but colored Republicans are enfranchised, and therefore Democrats wreak their vengeance on whites and blacks alike; and their friends in the North, yea, sir, in this Hall, either deny the fact or seek to palliate the crime. . . .

In a large portion of the States lately in rebellion there is a condition of practical and positive insurrection. The courts are closed, juries intimidated or in complicity with the enemies of the Government, the laws are silent, officers of justice overawed, and the very genius of lawlessness and misrule triumphant. Those who have been dealt with so leniently beyond the claims of either justice or magnanimity now seem determined to drive out or annihilate all who will not follow them in their malignant hostility to the Republican party. It is purely a political proscription. It is the relic and remnant of secession, and must be dealt with by the same strong arm of the military power that crushed the rebellion itself. . . .

The brigand and the robber only plunder or capture for money, and may accept a ransom; but, the Ku Klux in their crimes are inspired by political zeal, hatred of a race, and the bitter memories of a lost cause. All the claims of gratitude to that race for their submission and protection in the days of their struggle and prostration, all the forbearance of this Government in the hour of its triumph, avail nothing to induce this deluded people to return to their allegiance and loyalty. They must again be made to feel the power, as they have disregarded the clemency of the Government. . . .

I have no hesitation in conferring these great powers on the present Executive. His forbearance and magnanimity have been proved to be equal to his power of will and great force of character, and his sense of justice equal to his great military genius and ability. He knows well the condition of affairs at the South and the temper of that people. And they well know him, and upon the passage of this bill they will understand that submission to the laws and constituted authority is all that is left them. Then again will the Government magnify itself, and still stronger intrench itself in the affections of all the people, and we shall have a lasting and benignant peace with all the blessings that follow in its train.

Congressional *Globe*, 42nd Congress, 2nd Session, Appendix, April 5, 1871, 486–488.

SENATOR JOHN W. STEVENSON (D-KY), OPPOSING THE KU KLUX KLAN ACT (WASHINGTON, DC, MAY 21, 1872)

What do you propose? To continue to invest the President of the United States with the absolute power of a dictator by empowering him to suspend the privileges of the writ of *habeas corpus* when in his judgement the public safety demands it. Has Congress the power under the Constitution to enact this law? I utterly deny it. Neither the letter or spirit of that instrument anywhere empowers Congress to invest any department of this Government with arbitrary power over the liberty of the citizen.

The fathers of the Constitution assumed that the *habeas corpus*, with other inviolable guarantees, would intrench and protect their liberties; hence they made it perpetual by an express prohibition of its suspension, "except when in cases of invasion and rebellion the public safety shall require it." Mark well these words; they are full of the wisdom of the patriots who used them. . . .

You still persevere in your unhallowed warfare upon this down-trodden people. With all your courts open, with hundreds of indictments pending for the punishment of these secret, illegal combinations, with a people denied all participation in the Government, broken in fortune, beggared by their reverses, with persons once their slaves now their lawgivers and official superiors, backed by the Army and supported by the Government of the United States, you propose still to clothe the President of the United States, and every military satrap or subordinate belonging to the Army and stationed in the South, in a period of peace, and during a presidential election, with the dictatorial power at his discretion to suspend the writ of *habeas corpus*, and to imprison these unfortunate people at pleasure. . . .

Can these oppressions continue, can the guarantees of constitutional liberty be ruthlessly disregarded and the apprehension of freemen not be aroused? Can our Republican friends be so blinded by party as not themselves to become aroused to the dangerous precedent for the ultimate overthrow of the Constitution which the enactment of this measure must inaugurate? There is, there can be no exigency that demands it not or will demand it hereafter. Why, Mr. President, I have seen and known from my boyhood something of the South. I have talked with eminent men and women unsurpassed in all that adorns the highest type of manhood or womanhood, and that heart must be as cold and callous as stone that would not be touched by the merciless inhumanity and atrocities under which through Federal agencies this generous people are now being crushed. And yet we are told that the perils to public safety demand it. How? Where? What Senator—I care not who—will point out in this mass of testimony the proof of any overt act of the Ku Klux organizations in the South threatening the subversion of Federal or State Governments? Has an iota of proof been introduced going to show any such intent? To say that a rebellion or insurrection exists in any part of our country is a sham, a mockery. It is not true in law; it is not true in fact. Secret combinations, illegal combinations have existed. . . . They have committed acts of violence that call for suppression. I am not the apologist for force or violence anywhere. The majesty of the Constitution and the laws constitute our safety. But it is untrue, as I believe, that their organizations are political. It is equally untrue that they cannot be suppressed and put down by the laws and through the courts. These disorders exist everywhere. Can you point me to a State north or south of the Ohio river where outbreaks and secret combinations or mobs do not occasionally commit violence? . . . If you desire in good faith to get rid of these outbreaks, remove the exciting cause from which they spring. Make them feel safe in their households and their firesides. Strike off the manacles with which arbitrary power, instigated by malice, would fetter them. Whatever their errors in the past, Senators, these brave, oppressed people are the peers of any of us. Treat them with fraternal kindness. Wipe away the remembrance of their errors by a generous and a general amnesty. Interest them in the administration of the Government from which they bravely sought, but in vain, to withdraw themselves. Win them back to love the Constitution and obey the laws. They are our brethren; let us honor them as such. Take my word, Senators, love will accomplish more than the sword.

Congressional *Globe*, 42nd Congress, 2nd Session, Appendix, May 21, 1872, 507–551.

ACQUISITION OF SANTO DOMINGO

The Grant administration faced few challenges in the arena of foreign affairs. Domestic concerns dominated the president's attention. One major foreign policy initiative was Grant's repeated attempts to acquire Santo Domingo (now the Dominican Republic) and ultimately annex the country, a goal from the beginning of his presidency.

The issue was not new. Abraham Lincoln's expansionist secretary of state, William H. Seward, had negotiated with the leaders of Santo Domingo regarding possible annexation. In his first year of office, Grant dispatched Orville E. Babcock, his personal secretary, to the Caribbean to continue these efforts. Meanwhile, Grant made the acquisition of Santo Domingo his primary foreign policy concern. In his annual address of January 1870, the president explains with enthusiasm his reasoning. There were strategic concerns at issue. Grant warns that if the United States fails to annex Santo Domingo, European nations would move into the region. Invoking the Monroe Doctrine, Grant asserts that the United States has a responsibility to acquire the country.

More important were the economic concerns. Grant points out the rich resources of Santo Domingo that would benefit the nation, along with the acquisiton of new markets for American goods. While he does not discuss the matter here, Grant also saw Santo Domingo as a place for freedmen to migrate in an effort to address racial strife—the revival of the decades-old concept of "colonization" of African Americans in an effort to placate Southerners.

Grant enjoyed some support for his plan to annex Santo Domingo, but the majority in Congress, particularly within his own party, questioned the viability of the plan. A treaty of annexation reached the floor of Congress in the summer of 1870 but was defeated. Grant never gave up on the idea, continuing to seek converts for the duration of his presidency.

Carl Schurz, a Republican Senator from Missouri, offers his reasons for rejecting annexation of Santo Domingo. Schurz offers a racial argument that Dominicans, like all peoples of the Caribbean, were predisposed to la-

ziness and that tropical societies were ill-equipped for democratic government. Schurz implies that Santo Domingo would be a burden on the United
States, rather than an asset. Most importantly, he believes that the plan was
but the first step of an attempt to take over the entire Caribbean world. Interestingly, Schurz was an expansionist, but of a different sort. In his speech
he advocates instead a move to annex Canada, an acquisition that would
orient the United States northward.

The United States did not annex the Dominican Republic, although the
country lay within the American political and economic sphere from that
time forward. Grant, in his later years, considered the failure to acquire
Santo Domingo the greatest disappointment of his presidency.

PRESIDENT GRANT, ON THE ACQUISITION OF SANTO DOMINGO (WASHINGTON, DC, DECEMBER 2, 1870)

During the last session of Congress a treaty for the annexation of the Republic of San Domingo to the United States failed to receive the requisite
two-thirds vote of the Senate. I was thoroughly convinced then that the best
interests of this country, commercially and materially, demanded its ratification. Time has only confirmed me in this view. I now firmly believe that
the moment it is known that the United States have entirely abandoned the
project of accepting as a part of its territory the island of San Domingo a free
port will be negotiated for by European nations in the Bay of Samana. A
large commercial city will spring up, to which we will be tributary without
receiving corresponding benefits, and then will be seen the folly of our rejecting so great a prize. The Government of San Domingo had voluntarily
sought this annexation. It is a weak power, numbering probably less than
120,000 souls, and yet possessing one of the richest territories under the
sun, capable of supporting a population of 10,000,000 people in luxury. The
people of San Domingo are not capable of maintaining themselves in their
present condition, and must look for outside support. They yearn for the
protection of our free institutions and laws, our progress and civilization.
Shall we refuse them?

The acquisition of San Domingo is desirable because of its geographical
position. It commands the entrance to the Caribbean Sea and Isthmus transit of commerce. It possesses the richest soil, best and most capacious harbors, most salubrious climate, and the most valuable products of the
forests, mine, and soil of any of the West India Islands. Its possession by us
will in a few years build up a coastwide commerce of immense magnitude,
which will go far toward restoring to us our lost merchant marine. It will
give to us those articles which we consume so largely and do not produce,
thus equalizing our exports and imports. In case of foreign war it will give
us command of all the islands referred to, and thus prevent an enemy from

ever again possessing himself of rendezvous upon our very coast. At present our coast trade between the States bordering on the Atlantic and those bordering on the Gulf of Mexico is cut into by the Bahamas and the Antilles. Twice we must, as it were, pass through foreign countries to get by sea from Georgia to the west coast of Florida.

San Domingo, with a stable government, under which her immense resources can be developed, will give remunerative wages to tens of thousands of laborers not now upon the island. This labor will take advantage of every available means of transportation to abandon the adjacent islands and seek the blessings of freedom and its sequence—each inhabitant receiving the reward of his own labor. Porto Rico and Cuba will have to abolish slavery, as a measure of self-preservation, to retain their laborers.

San Domingo will become a large consumer of the products of Northern farms and manufactories. The cheap rate at which her citizens can be furnished with food, tools, and machinery will make it necessary that contiguous islands should have the same advantages in order to compete in the production of sugar, coffee, tobacco, tropical fruits, etc. This will open to us a still wider market for our products. The production of our own supply of these articles will cut off more than one hundred millions of our annual imports, besides largely increasing our exports. With such a picture it is easy to see how our large debt abroad is ultimately to be extinguished. . . .

The acquisition of San Domingo is an adherence to the "Monroe Doctrine"; it is a measure of national protection; it is asserting our just claim to a controlling influence over the great commercial traffic soon to flow from west to east by way of the Isthmus of Darien; it is to build up our merchant marine; it is to furnish new markets for the products of our farms, shops, and manufactories; it is to make slavery insupportable in Cuba and Porto Rico at once, and ultimately so in Brazil; it is to settle the unhappy condition of Cuba and end an exterminating conflict; it is to provide honest means of paying our honest debts without overtaxing the people; it is to furnish our citizens with the necessaries of everyday life at cheaper rates than ever before; and it is, in fine, a rapid stride toward that greatness which the intelligence, industry, and enterprise of the citizens of the United States entitle this country to assume among nations.

In view of the importance of this question, I earnestly urge upon Congress early action expressive of its views as to the best means of acquiring San Domingo. My suggestion is that by joint resolution of the two Houses of Congress the Executive be authorized to appoint a commission to negotiate a treaty with the authorities of San Domingo for the acquisition of that island, and that an appropriation be made to defray the expenses of such a commission. The question may then be determined, either by the action of the Senate upon the treaty or the joint action of the two Houses of Congress upon a resolution of annexation, as in the case of the acquisition of Texas. So convinced am I of the advantages to flow from the acquisition of San

Domingo, and of the great disadvantages—I might almost say calamities— to flow from nonacquisition, that I believe the subject has only to be investigated to be approved.

A Compilation of the Messages and Papers of the Presidents, vol. 9, James D. Richardson, ed. (New York: Bureau of National Literature, Inc., 1897), 4053–4055.

SENATOR CARL SCHURZ (R-MO), OPPOSED TO THE ANNEXATION OF SANTO DOMINGO (WASHINGTON, DC, JANUARY 11, 1871)

Suppose we annex the Dominican republic; will there be an end to our acquisitions? . . . Is there a man on the floor of the Senate who thinks that when we have the one half of that island we shall stop before we have the other? . . . It is an absolutely preposterous idea that we should content ourselves while part of that island is in the hands of another Power. . . .

But there we cannot stop. Look at the map and you will find that the island of Cuba lies between San Domingo and the coast of Florida; thus there will be foreign territory inclosed between one possession of ours and another. Must we not have Cuba? Of course we must, for the purpose of securing the continuity of our possessions. This is not in conjecture; it is not even denied, for the Senator from Indiana openly avowed on this floor that of course we must and shall have Cuba; that, too, is a foregone conclusion. With Cuba, Porto Rico will come, and the Senator from Indiana has already included it in his programme, which he openly laid before us.

But there you will not stop. The Anglo-Saxon race is somewhat notorious for its late hunger, and such appetites are always morbidly stimulated by eating. Having San Domingo, Cuba, and Porto Rico, you will not rest until you possess, also, the other West Indies islands; and what then? Then your possessions will fill the Caribbean Sea and closer encircle the Gulf of Mexico; and, possessing the islands and the sea, how long will it be before you are driven by the spirit of adventure or by the apparent necessities of your situation to move for the annexation of the continent bordering that sea on the other side? Once started in that course you will not be able to control yourselves; you will want more and more and more; and it is my sincere conviction that you will not stop until we have everything down to the Isthmus of Darien. Does it not occur to Senators that here is a question presenting itself far greater than the mere acquisition of the Dominican Republic?

We may be asked, why should we not have all this? Are not those countries rich, fertile, and beautiful? Do they not offer all the magnificence of tropical production? Are not their mountains full of precious ore? Yes, they are rich; I do not deny it; they are fertile; they may be considered as possessing magnificent resources; and yet I would ask every Senator before me, before he lays his hand upon that seductive portion of the globe for incorporating it in this Republic, and fusing it with our political system, is there not a voice speaking within him telling him to consider it well, to pause, to ponder, and to beware? Consider: if you incorporate those tropical countries with the Republic of the United States, you will have to accept them as a component and cooperative element in that system of government, the blessings of which we now enjoy. This is an imperative necessity which you cannot escape; the logical consequence of your beginning; and before this one consideration all others, that of money, of the Dominican debt, of Baez and Cabral, of sugar, coffee, cotton, salt, gold, and precious stones, dwindle down into utter nothingness.

The grave question arises: is the incorporation of that part of the globe and the people inhabiting it quite compatible with the integrity, safety, perpetuity, and progressive development of our institutions which we value so highly? If it is not, is the price which we are to pay worth the bargain? Let us look at the history of these islands; and that history, I would respectfully suggest, we know without the report of this commission, and I do not think the gentlemen to be sent to San Domingo will be able to give us much new light upon it. Read that history, read that of all other tropical countries, and then show me a single instance of the successful establishment and peaceable maintenance for a respectable period of republican institutions, based upon popular self-government, under a tropical sun. To show me one, do not confine your search to the West Indies; look for it anywhere else on the face of the globe in tropical latitudes. I challenge Senators to point their fingers to a single one. There is none, sir. But, more than that, show me a single instance in any tropical country where labor when it was left free did not exhibit a strong tendency to run into shiftlessness, and where practical attempts to organize labor did not run in the direction of slavery. Show me a single one, not only in the West India Islands, but anywhere in any tropical country under the sun. You find none. . . .

What, then, is the true American policy? It seems to me clear. Let the American people devote their great energies to the vast domain we possess, to that magnificent field of labor and of enterprise where the genius of our race, as I said before, is fed the very atmosphere. Do we feel cramped in our domain? Let us expand, then, where were are healthy and strong. Is not there a magnificent field left for our ambition of aggrandizement? Yes, and it fills my soul with delight when I see events preparing themselves which will lead the whole continent north of us into our arms. That will indeed be a natural, congenial, and happy association. And the day when that consummation takes place this Republic will be stronger than ever before; stronger, for the very seat of her empire, the center of gravity, will then be more firmly fixed than ever under the healthful influences of the northern sky. But beware of every addition in that quarter where the very sun hatches out the serpent's eggs of danger to our republican institutions; beware until by further development and accretion the preponderance of northern civilization become so firmly fixed that nothing in the world can shake it.

Congressional *Globe*, 41st Congress, 3rd Session, Appendix, January 11, 1871, 25–33.

THE SPOILS SYSTEM AND CIVIL SERVICE REFORM

The Grant administration oversaw Reconstruction, forged a postwar policy on currency and economic development, and implemented a new foreign policy strategy, but the legacy of the administration were the scandals that plagued Grant's presidency. The "Whiskey Ring" that implicated government officials, including Grant's personal secretary, along with the Credit Mobilier affair that exposed widespread fraud and embezzlement in Congress and the administration, left many Americans concerned about the legitimacy of their government. While Grant himself was never linked to these scandals (although even Mrs. Grant had been involved in one affair), the fact that much of this activity occurred in and around him raised the issue of his integrity, or perhaps his competency.

For years reformers had questioned the basic assumptions of the "spoils system" of patronage that dated back to the Andrew Jackson administration. The Civil War had brought about an expansion of the civil service, which meant more political maneuvering for appointments. While the president was responsible for the majority of patronage, the political parties, particularly within Congress, had become powerful agents in the assigning of government jobs. Party leaders often made recommendations to the president on the basis of donations made by candidates to the party's treasury. Once appointed to a position, the recipient of patronage was expected to continue to work for the party and make annual donations. Under this method, appointments to government jobs had fallen under the control of congressional leaders.

The scandals of the Grant administration renewed efforts to overhaul the methods by which civil service employees were hired. Among the more popular proposals was the introduction of an examination system for appointments, an effort to recruit government employees based on talent and merit. President Grant approved of efforts to reform the civil service as a means of deflecting criticism. In 1871 he created a civil service commission charged with examining the patronage processes and developing alternatives that might eliminate corruption. The commission lasted only three years, however, and brought about little change in the system.

A few congressional leaders had proposed new methods to make the appointment process less political. Senator Lyman Trumbull of Indiana, for example, proposed a bill that would have prohibited Congress from making recommendations to the president for the hiring of government employees. Trumbull and others, including John Sherman of Ohio, believed that eliminating Congress from the process might allow the president to make political appointments without the immense pressure of his party. Others disagreed. Senator Oliver P. Morton of Indiana declared the bill unconstitutional. Any citizen, Morton claimed, should have the right to advise the president on such matters, if requested. Morton also argued that party leaders in Congress are in the best position to offer advice to the president on candidates for positions from their respective states. To place on the president the burden of evaluating all candidates for all positions, which for each administration could number in the hundreds, was unrealistic.

The civil service bill was only one attempt to address the problem of corruption with respect to patronage and did little to change the system. The first significant legislation regarding the civil service was implemented in 1883, in the wake of the assassination of President James Garfield by a disgruntled patronage seeker. The Pendleton Act established an examination system for some government positions in the postal service and customs houses; gradually the examination system was expanded to many more sectors of the civil service. Despite Grant's efforts to champion civil service reform, the stigma of corruption and scandal stain his presidency to this day.

SENATOR JOHN SHERMAN (R-OH), IN SUPPORT OF CIVIL SERVICE REFORM (WASHINGTON, DC, JANUARY 4, 1871)

I have thought a good deal of this bill since it was under discussion at the last session of Congress. At first my impressions were against it, on the simple ground that it changed the established customs of the country since the foundation of the Government; but the more I have reflected upon it the more I see that it is necessary, not only to relieve ourselves, but to relieve the President from the embarrassment of his position. The position in which the President is now placed with regard to Congress is a constant source of irritation. Members of Congress, especially of the House of Representatives, claim the right to dictate local appointments, and if their wishes are not yielded to in every case it creates at once a cause of quarrel, which finds its outlet in some legislation or other. In the Senate, perhaps, that is not so much so; but even here we cannot deny that the power claimed by Senators and members to interfere in appointments does create a constant state of irritation between the legislative and executive departments of the Government. These two departments should be as distinct and marked as if they were separated by a broad river. The only connection between the executive and legislative departments, so far as appointments are concerned, should be between the President and the Senate. The legislative power ought to be strongly marked and defined, and separated from the executive branch of the Government.

The objection which at first occurred to me to this bill was this: how can the President in our great country, spreading over so vast an extent, gain the requisite information as to the various local appointments to be made? There is a great deal of force in that objection, and there I would not vote for this bill unless the President had the right, at his option, to call upon a member or a Delegate in Congress for local information. It seems to me that without such a provision the bill would be wrong.

These appointments ought, in the first place, to come from the President, unbiased either by the judicial or the legislative branches of the Government; but the President ought to have the right to seek information everywhere, not only from members of Congress, but from Governors of States, from his Cabinet officers, and from all his surroundings; but in the selection of officers he ought not to be embarrassed by the demands of persons upon whose votes he is daily subject, in the course of ordinary legislation, and over whom he might by patronage establish a control.

I have regarded this measure for the last year as being not a complete civil service reform in itself, but as being an entering wedge indispensably necessary to bring about a civil service reform. You will never be able to pass through Congress a bill for civil service reform separating the civil service in the Executive Departments entirely from the legislative until the unconstitutional habit that has sprung up in this country of allowing members of Congress to control appointments is broken up. Unless we ourselves abdicate, surrender, give up that power of control over the executive appointments, we cannot expect to agree upon a civil service reform. I am, for one, entirely prepared to surrender the little power I may be thought to have in recommending appointments, and to leave the President unembarrassed, uncontrolled by me in appointments to office. If he desires any information from me he can get it. In that way the intercourse between the legislative and executive departments of the Government can be put upon its constitutional footing of absolute and entire independence, and then neither the President can interfere with the duty of a member of Congress, nor can a member of Congress interfere with the duty of the President, and the Senate can exercise its proper check and control over appointments when submitted to it in the constitutional way.

Congressional *Globe*, 41st Congress, 3rd Session, January 4, 1871, 293–294.

SENATOR OLIVER P. MORTON (R-IN), ON CONGRESS AND THE SPOILS SYSTEM (WASHINGTON, DC, JANUARY 4, 1871)

. . . The bill, in my opinion, is unconstitutional from beginning to end, and proceeds upon false principles. I undertake to say that this Government could not be readily nor safely administered upon this bill.

Why, sir, what does the bill propose to do? It makes a penal offense for me to exercise a right that belongs to every citizen of the United States. Every person in these galleries, every postmaster has the right to recommend to the President for appointments to office; but this bill proposes to make it a criminal offense for a Senator to do so. Why, sir, the proposition needs but to be stated to be understood. The chosen representatives of the States, and chosen Representatives of the people in the other House, are the only persons in the United States who are to have no rights in making recommendations for office, and are criminals if they do. And then the President is a criminal if he dares make an appointment that has been advised by a Senator, if it is done with the knowledge of the person whose appointment is advised. Have we a right to make the President a criminal for doing that?

Why, sir, what is the effect of it? If a Senator recommends a man with his knowledge he becomes ineligible. Have we a right to establish a qualification for office of that kind? It would be a clear violation of the Constitution of the United States. It has been decided by the Senate, that where a State constitution provided that a man holding a State office, for example that of a Governor of a State, was not eligible during his term of office to be elected to the Senate of the United States, such provision was a nullity, and no State constitution had the power to fix an additional qualification for office; that if a man possessed the qualifications prescribed by the Constitution of the United States no State could make him ineligible for any other ground. And yet here we propose to make a man ineligible, in other words, to make the President a criminal for his appointments, if he shall have been recommended by the chosen representative of a State, or chosen Representative of the people in the other House.

Mr. President, this is the most extraordinary proposition that I ever heard of in the Senate. The President has the right to appoint whom he pleases to office if the man is eligible under the Constitution of the United States, and we cannot make him a criminal for so doing, no matter who has recommended him, or whether he has been recommended by anybody or not.

But, sir, how do we degrade ourselves! The proposition, upon its very face, is one degrading to the Senate. We propose to say that we are the only men in this country who cannot be trusted to recommend a man for office. I know that there are some people in this country who believe that everybody in Congress is corrupt, and if we pass this bill they will have a right to believe that we think so; that we ourselves are willing to legislate on the idea that we cannot safely be trusted to recommend men for appointments....

Mr. President, I have been betrayed into this little speech. It seems to me most wonderful that we should propose to legislate ourselves as the only class of men in this country who cannot be trusted with the power of making recommendations to the President for appointments. Why, sir, the election of a man as a Senator from a State implies at least that he has got some character, and that there is a portion of the people of that State who believe that he is a respectable and good man. He has that indorsement and he comes here with it. The election of a Representative in the other House brings with it the indorsement that at least a part of the people of that district believe him to be a worthy and responsible man. It is not for me to say whether these presumptions are good or not; but I say these presumptions do exist. And yet by this bill we are not permitted to give our opinion on the subject of appointments to office, but the President is required to fall back upon others who have no official or political or public responsibility whatever, who may recommend for the most venal or mercenary purposes, and yet the public will never know that they were instrumental in procuring the appointment of a bad man.

Congressional *Globe*, 41st Congress, 3rd Session, January 4, 1871, 294–295.

CURRENCY AND PAPER MONEY

As Reconstruction lost momentum in the 1870s, economic issues took center stage during a time of rapid expansion. Among these were questions of tariffs and trade, taxation, and federal support of industrial development. Perhaps the most hotly debated issue was related to currency. The composition of the money supply became a central problem that remained at the forefront of politics for the remainder of the century.

There were two basic positions regarding the money supply—those who advocated "hard" currency versus the supporters of "soft" currency. In essence it was a debate over the amount of currency in circulation. Soft currency proponents called for an increase; their opponents demanded a contraction of the money supply. During the Civil War, the inflationists had their way; the government responded to a money shortage by issuing large amounts of paper money, not backed by precious metal, or specie. The so-called "greenbacks" served their purpose during the war, but the question then emerged as to what to do with this paper currency.

Debtors usually called for the retention of the greenbacks and even an expansion of paper money. More dollars in circulation meant a decline in the value of money, hence loans would be worth less in the future than in the present day. Naturally, creditors promoted a decrease in or elimination of the greenbacks. Deflationists understood that less money in circulation meant an increasing value of the money that remained in the economy; therefore, loans would appreciate over time. While there were exceptions, the currency issue was drawn on party lines. Republicans tended to support a hard money position, calling for the retirement of greenbacks and the return to a monetary system based on gold. Democrats tended to support an expansion of the currency.

Grant, no expert on matters of economics and finance, followed the suggestions of his advisors in developing a hard money policy. In 1873, in response to a nationwide financial panic, Congress passed a bill that increased the number of greenbacks in circulation, which Grant promptly vetoed. In 1875, Grant signed into law the Resumption Act, a bill backed by Republicans that provided for the government to pay its debts in specie, thereby placing the nation on a gold-backed currency. In his annual address of December 1874, the president makes clear that the American economy should be based on a "sound money" policy.

Not everyone agreed. Inflationist Democrats claimed that hard money policy served the interests of bankers and financiers at the expense for laborers and farmers. Representative John W. Killinger of Pennsylvania criticizes the Grant administration's currency policies. Killinger argues that the problem facing the American economy was a lack of currency. He compares the amount of currency in circulation per individual citizen in France, England, and the United States and points out that the United States is far below the others in the size of its money supply. With increasing amounts of currency, Killinger implies, those in debt would have access to more money. Grant rejects the notion that the financial shortfalls of individuals would be improved by the creation of more dollars as "absurd."

While Republicans won the debates over currency during Grant's term, the issue remained an important one for decades. The controversy culminated in the 1896 presidential election, the "Battle of the Standards" that focused almost exclusively on the currency.

ULYSSES S. GRANT, ON PAPER CURRENCY AND THE ECONOMY (WASHINGTON, DC, DECEMBER 7, 1874)

Since the convening of Congress one year ago the nation has undergone a prostration in business and industries such as has not been witnessed with us for many years. Speculation as to the causes for this prostration might be indulged in without profit, because as many theorists would be advanced as their would be independent writers—those who expressed their own views without borrowing—on the subject. Without indulging in theories as to the cause of the prostration, therefore, I will call your attention only to the fact, and to some plain questions as to which it would seem there should be no disagreement. . . .

A great conflict for national existence made necessary, for temporary purposes, the raising of large sums of money from whatever sources attainable. It made it necessary, in the wisdom of Congress—and I do not doubt their wisdom in the premises, regarding the necessity of the times—to devise a system of national currency which it proved to be impossible to keep on part with the recognized currency of the civilized world. This begot a spirit of speculation involving extravagance and luxury not required for the happiness or prosperity of a people, and involving, both directly and indirectly, foreign indebtedness. The currency, being of fluctuating value, and therefore unsafe to hold for legitimate transactions requiring money, became a subject of speculation within itself. These two causes, however, have involved us in a foreign indebtedness, contracted in good faith by borrower and lender, which should be paid in coin, and according to the bond agreed upon when the debt was contracted—gold or its equivalent. The good faith of the government can not be violated toward creditors without national disgrace. But our commerce should be encouraged; American shipbuilding and carrying capacity increased; foreign markets sought for products of the soil and manufactories, to the end that we may be able to pay these debts. Where a new market can be created for the sale of our products, either of the soil, the mine, or the manufactory, a new means is discovered of utilizing our idle capital and labor to the advantage of the whole people. But, in my judgement, the first step toward accomplishing this object is to secure a currency of fixed, stable value; a currency good wherever civilization reigns; one which, if it become superabundant with one people, will find a market with some other; a currency which has as its basis the labor necessary to produce it, which will give to it its value. Gold and silver are now the recognized medium of exchange the civilized world over, and to this we should return with the least practicable delay. In view of the pledges of the American Congress when our present legal-tender system was adopted, and debt contracted, there should be no delay—certainly no unnecessary delay—in fixing by legislation a method by which we will return to specie. . . . It is easy to conceive that the debtor and speculative classes may think it of value to them to make so-called money abundant until they can throw a portion of their burdens upon others. But even these, I believe, would be disappointed in the result if a course should be pursued which will keep in doubt the value of the legal-tender medium of exchange. A revival of productive industry is needed by all classes; by none more than the holders of property, of whatever sort, with debts to liquidate from realization upon its sale. But admitting that these two classes of citizens are to be benefited by expansion, would it be honest to give it? Would not the general loss be too great to justify such relief? Would it not be just as honest and prudent to authorize each debtor to issue his own legal-tenders to the extent of his liabilities? . . . These propositions are too absurd to be entertained for a moment by thinking or honest people. . . .

It is the duty of Congress to devise the method of correcting the evils which are acknowledged to exist, and not mine. But I will venture to suggest two or three things that seem to me as absolutely necessary to return to specie payments, the first great requisite in a return to prosperity. The legal-tender clause to the law authorizing the issue of currency by the National Government should be repealed, to take effect as to all contacts entered into after a day fixed in the repealing act—not to apply, however, to payments of salaries by Government, or for other expenditures now provided by law to be paid in currency, in the interval pending between repeal and financial resumption. Provision should be made by which the Secretary of the Treasury can obtain gold as it may become necessary from time to time from the date when specie redemption commences. To this might and should be added a revenue sufficiently in excess of expenses to insure an accumulation of gold in the Treasury to sustain permanent redemption.

I commend this subject to your careful consideration, believing that a favorable solution is attainable, and if reached by this Congress that the present and future generations will ever gratefully remember it as their deliverer from a thraldom of evil and disgrace.

A Compilation of the Messages and Papers of the Presidents, vol. 9, James D. Richardson, ed. (New York: Bureau of National Literature, Inc., 1897), 4238–4241.

REPRESENTATIVE JOHN W. KILLINGER (D-PA), ON PAPER CURRENCY AND THE ECONOMY (WASHINGTON, DC, FEBRUARY 19, 1874)

The inaction, if not indifference, of Congress has hung through the winter like a dark cloud over the whole country, threatening disaster to business enterprises, and involving many families in actual ruin. It has appeared to me that we have failed to appreciate the prostrate condition of many of our manufacturing and mechanical interests. Thousands of able-bodied men have been subjected to enforced idleness during all the time that this Congress has been in session. The managers of those beneficent establishments have been unable to procure the currency to meet their monthly payments without serious sacrifice and inconvenience. I rejoice to believe, however, that the cloud is lifting and that the skies are brightening. With the recuperative energy which is essentially a feature in the American character our people are struggling against adverse fate, and are overcoming, in good degree, the obstacles which have been in their path. . . .

When currency is scarce, its possession gives the lender great power and advantage over the borrower, and oppression and extortion are too often the result. It seems indisputable that with the increase of population and the multiplication of business, larger facilities would be required. The census reports of 1850 showed the gross amount of property in the United States to be $7,135,780,000. In 1870 it was reported to be $30,000,000,000. Common sense would indicate that the circulating medium should increase with resources, population, and trade. If, instead thereof, the policy of the Government is continual contraction of the currency, common sense likewise teaches that we must retrograde in business, decay in enterprise, and lose prestige among the commercial nations of the world.

Estimating our own population at forty millions, we have a circulation of about fourteen dollars per capita. According to the last report of the Comptroller of the Currency, England has a circulation per capita of nineteen dollars, and France of twenty-five dollars. That is to say, while our currency averages fourteen dollars to every man, woman, and child of our population, that of England averages nineteen dollars, and that of France twenty-five dollars. So far from needing less currency, all the circumstances surrounding us require more. With an area of the country nearly equal to the whole of Europe, developed under higher prices paid for labor, and greater transportation distances, involving more time and money relatively to effect our exchanges; with railways spanning the continent from ocean to ocean as parts of a vast system compared to which those of Europe dwindle into insignificance; with an ever-increasing population, stimulated by emigration, and with an immense crop of cereals and cotton blocking our commercial capacities in their efforts to reach a market—can there be a doubt that we have outgrown our circulation? Twenty-five dollars per capita would give us a currency of one thousand millions; and, in my judgement, the interests of the country, the wants of legitimate business, require that amount. But no human intelligence can fix unalterably the limit of currency required, for it varies with the seasons, and is constantly changing with the lapse of time. As well try to fix the number of yard-sticks or half-bushel measures needed in the country as to make the allowance fixed and unchangeable. Let us have currency free as water, to adjust itself to the level which business supplies. This is what our people want, and sooner or later will have. If this Congress fails to respond to the public demands, the next may be more mindful of the popular will. . . .

Like our greenback system, the Bank of England owes its existence to the necessities of war. It was organized in 1694, in the reign of William and Mary. It has scarcely ever redeemed its circulation in specie, and in 1797 was actually restrained from doing so by an order from the privy council. England cannot pay one-tenth of her debt in gold, without borrowing. The basis of her commercial prosperity, therefore, is not the bullion of her vaults, but her paper-money system, surrounded by checks and balances, and sustained by the confidence of her people in the stability of their bank and government.

Standing as we do, Mr. Speaker, on the eve of our centennial celebration, with a history and an experience peculiar and significant, it is not becoming in us to bend in humble adoration before the brazen god of gold! This colossal idol, like the golden calf of old, must be shattered before we reach our Canaan. A gold currency, or a resumption of specie payments, so called, is a delusion and a snare. It is no more essential to our financial prosperity that the fly on the driving-wheel is essential to the speed of the train. Our people want a Government currency, bearing the impress of solvency and security, and plenty of it, to enable them to solve the problem of their manifest destiny.

Congressional *Globe*, 43rd Congress, 1st Session, Appendix, February 19, 1874, 52–53.

RECOMMENDED READINGS

Foner, Eric. *Reconstruction: America's Unfinished Revolution*. New York: Harper & Row, 1988.
McFeely, William S. *Grant: A Biography*. New York: W.W. Norton, 1981.

Perret, Geoffrey. *Ulysses S. Grant: Soldier and Statesman*. New York: Random House, 1997.

Scaturro, Frank J. *President Grant Reconsidered*. Lanham, MD: University Press of America, 1998.

Simpson, Brooks D. *Ulysses S. Grant: Triumph Over Adversity, 1822–1865*. Boston: Houghton Mifflin, 2000.

Smith, Jean Edward. *Grant*. New York: Simon & Schuster, 2001.

BIBLIOGRAPHY

Bauer, Jack P. *Zachary Taylor: Soldier, Planter, Statesman of the Old Southwest.* Baton Rouge: Louisiana State University Press, 1985.

Bauer, K. Jack. *The Mexican War, 1846–1848.* New York: Macmillan, 1974.

Benedict, Michael Les. *The Impeachment and Trial of Andrew Johnson.* New York: W.W. Norton & Co., 1973.

Commager, Henry Steele. *Fifty Basic Civil War Documents.* Malabar, FL: R.E. Krieger Pub. Co., 1982.

De Voto, Bernard. *The Year of Decision, 1846.* Boston: Little, Brown & Company, 1843.

Donald, David. *Lincoln.* New York: Simon & Schuster, 1996.

Ferenbacher, Don E. *The Dred Scott Case: Its Significance in American Law and Politics.* New York: Oxford University Press, 1978.

Fleming, Walter L. *Documentary History of Reconstruction: Political, Military, Social, Religious, Educational and Industrial, 1865–1906.* 2 vols. New York: McGraw-Hill, 1966.

Foner, Eric. *Free Soil, Free Labor, Free Men: The Ideology of the Republican Party Before the Civil War.* New York: Oxford University Press, 1995.

———. *Reconstruction: America's Unfinished Revolution.* New York: Harper & Row, 1988.

Foote, Shelby. *The Civil War: A Narrative.* 3 vols. New York: Random House, 1958–1974.

Franklin, John Hope. *The Emancipation Proclamation.* Garden City, NY: Doubleday, 1963.

Gara, Larry. *The Presidency of Franklin Pierce.* Lawrence: University of Kansas Press, 1991.

Grayson, Benson Lee. *The Unknown President: The Administration of President Millard Fillmore.* Lanham, MD: University Press of America, 1981.

HarpWeek L.L.C. Harper's Weekly Online. http://www.harpweek.com/.

Holt, Michael F. *The Political Crisis of the 1850s.* New York: Wiley Publishers, 1978.

Johannsen, Robert W. *Stephen A. Douglas.* New York: Oxford University Press, 1973.

Johnson, Michael P., ed. *Abraham Lincoln, Slavery, and the Civil War: Selected Writings and Speeches.* Boston: Bedford/St. Martin's, 2001.

Levine, Bruce. *Half-Slave and Half-Free: The Roots of the Civil War.* New York: Hill & Wang, 1992.

Library of Congress Online. *A Century of Lawmaking for a New Nation: U.S. Congressional Documents and Debates, 1774–1783.* http://lcweb2.loc.gov/ammem/amlaw/lawhome.html.

———. *The Abraham Lincoln Papers Online.* http://memory.loc.gov/ammem/alhtml/malhome.html.

McKitrick, Eric. *Andrew Johnson and Reconstruction.* Chicago: University of Chicago Press, 1960.

McPherson, James. *Battle Cry of Freedom: The Civil War Era.* New York: Oxford University Press, 1988.

———. *Abraham Lincoln and the Second American Revolution.* New York: Oxford University Press, 1990.

Oates, Stephen B. *To Purge This Land with Blood: A Biography of John Brown.* Amherst: University of Massachusetts Press, 1984.

———. *With Malice Toward None: The Life of Abraham Lincoln.* New York: Harper & Row, 1977.

Oates, Stephen B., and Buz Wyeth. *The Approaching Fury: Voices of the Storm, 1820–1861.* New York: HarperCollins, 1997.

Perman, Michael, ed. *Major Problems in the Civil War and Reconstruction: Documents and Essays.* Lexington, MA: D.C. Heath, 1991.

Potter, David M. *The Impending Crisis, 1848–1961.* New York: Harper & Row, 1976.

Richardson, James D., ed. *A Compilation of the Messages and Papers of the Presidents.* 20 vols. New York: Bureau of National Literature, Inc., 1897.

Simpson, Brooks D. *Ulysses S. Grant: Triumph Over Adversity, 1822–1865.* Boston: Houghton Mifflin, 2000.

Smith, Elbert B. *The Presidencies of Zachary Taylor and Millard Fillmore.* Lawrence: University of Kansas Press, 1988.

Smith, John David. *Black Voices from Reconstruction, 1865–1877.* Brookfield, CT: Millbrook Press, 1996.

Stampp, Kenneth M. *America in 1857: A Nation on the Brink.* New York: Oxford University Press, 1990.

———. *The Era of Reconstruction, 1865–1877.* New York: Alfred A. Knopf, 1965.

INDEX

About the Author

JEFFREY W. COKER is Assistant Professor of History at Belmont University in Nashville, Tennessee, where he teaches courses in United States history with an emphasis on biography. He holds a Ph.D. from Ohio University and the Contemporary History Institute.